Praise for West End Girls

'A truly fascinating, entertaining and heart-warming glimpse ... ne of So o's mos ... ut g charact ... *nday xpress*

'H we ng ve this affectiona te memoir of th rackety Soho of 6 years ago is e sharp awareness that Barbara could easily have ended up like the lost girls she describes . . . her book acknowledges with humility and grace, as well as wit, how close she came to living the tough, funny and colourful but ultimately tragic life she describes' *Daily Mail*

'Readers of a shockable disposition should avoid this book – everyone else should rush out and buy a first edition. It is a jawdropping account of Soho prostitutes in the late forties . . . [Tate] always said she wanted to paint one perfect picture before she died: she has certainly written one perfect book' *Sunday Times*

'This frank memoir of a lost bohemian culture and under-world [is] told with warmth and sympathy' *Saga*

'A winning mixture of art and prostitution . . . One of the great strengths of this unexpectedly charming memoir is that it abounds with . . . detail about the working life of a prostitute in the Forties . . . a splendidly evocative memoir' *Mail on Sunday*

'Not only is this memoir told with candour and compassion but it also affords a fascinating glimpse into a lurid byway of London's social history . . . Tate's memoir fizzes with anecdotes and the quality of her writing is superb' *Daily Express*

Barbara Tate was born in Uxbridge in 1927. After she left her Soho life, Barbara went on to marry, raise a family and become a successful painter.

A fellow of the Royal Society of Artists and the Society of Botanical Artists, Barbara was a long-time president of the Society of Women Artists and a lifetime honorary president. Accolades for her paintings include gold and silver medals from the Paris Salon, the Grand Prix de la Cote d'Azur and an honorary professorship from Thames University. Barbara died in 2009.

West End Girls

The real lives, loves and friendships
of 1940s Soho and its working girls

~

BARBARA TATE

An Orion paperback

First published in Great Britain in 2010
by Orion
This paperback edition published in 2011
by Orion Books Ltd,
Orion House, 5 Upper Saint Martin's Lane,
London WC2H 9EA

An Hachette UK company

1 3 5 7 9 10 8 6 4 2

ISBN 978-1-4091-2023-0

Typeset by Input Data Services Ltd,
Bridgwater, Somerset

Printed and bound in Great Britain by
CPI Mackays, Chatham, Kent

www.orionbooks.co.uk

To my dear friend

There is a devil ever bending,
To whisper in my ear
Things I do not want to know
But try so hard to hear.

I think he talks of huge delights,
And says my days are few.
He tells me that my summer suns
Could have more shimmering hue.

He seems to say there is no Hell,
And Heaven's a man made dream;
That he himself is but a myth.
I feel this is his theme.

But if he is a myth, then who
Is whispering in my ear
These things I do not want to know
Yet try so hard to hear?

B.T.

Author's Note

In this narrative, I have sought to convey in authentic detail the public and private lives of Soho's prostitutes and the people and atmosphere surrounding them. I have adhered strictly to the truth – for otherwise the whole exercise would be pointless – though in the endeavour I have found that nothing could be more apt than Oscar Wilde's observation that 'Truth is rarely pure, and never simple.' The only deviation I have made from accuracy is that, for obvious reasons, I have had to alter the names of most of the people described, and be vague about some of the locations.

One

~

My affair with Soho started at seven thirty one winter's morning, just as I was about to have breakfast: an odd time for a romance to begin, but that is how it was. I was seventeen years old.

My youngest uncle – then about twenty-five and trying hard to be a man-about-town – had recently bought his first made-to-measure suit. This seemed to have automatically invested him with the knowledge of which wine should be drunk with what and a desire for foreign travel, all of which I found very impressive. He came down to breakfast on that particular morning and announced with an air of self-conscious nonchalance that on the previous evening he had dined 'at a rather interesting little restaurant in Soho'.

My grandmother, who was frying eggs at the time, swung round in horror – fish slice poised and dripping fat all over the quarry-tiled floor. Her face was a picture of outraged shock.

'Henry!' she bellowed.

I gazed from one to the other, fascinated. My first thought was a selfish one: perhaps the interruption might result in a well-cooked egg instead of the usual 'healthily' raw one my grandmother always insisted on dishing up. My overriding amazement, though, was caused by the fact that Henry – her favourite child, who usually managed to get away with all sorts of minor wrongdoings – was about to be scolded.

'Henry!' she bellowed again.

She fixed him with the gaze that all of us – including my grandfather – dreaded. Storm clouds first, and now the thunder.

'How dare you go to such a place! Soho indeed. I haven't brought you up to be a gentleman for you to start leading that sort of life. Anything could happen to you in a place like that. Don't let me hear that you've gone there again, and don't ever mention it again—especially in front of her!'

She jerked her head and flapped the fish slice in my direction. Then she hurled an egg on to each of our plates and marched out of the kitchen, slamming the door behind her. An inveterate door-slammer at such times, my grandmother always liked the whole household and half the street to know when she was angry. My uncle, now humbled and looking sheepish, ate his egg in silence. So did I, speculating all the time about Soho.

I should perhaps explain why it was that it had been left to my grandmother to defend me from wickedness. I was born in Uxbridge, west London. My father was a lorry-driver and a carpenter. I remember once lying curled up on the floor of his workshop, falling asleep among the golden wood-curls and the smell of pine. I remember too a journey in the cab of his lorry, with him saying delightedly, 'Sheep hearts for supper tonight, Babs. Imagine!' Most of my early memories, however, are not so happy. My father was a violent man, apt to vent his rages on whoever walked into his path, including on occasion me.

I recall one incident, when I must have done something to enrage him. He carried me up to an upstairs window, strung a little noose of wire round my neck, and attached the other end to the top of the casement. I had to stand on tiptoe, because if I did not, the wire tightened round my throat and began to choke me. I don't know exactly how long I was there, but it must have been some hours, because I recall the muffin man walking up and down the street with a basket of bread on his head, clanging his bell as he went. Then, much later, the street traders gave way to the lamplighter, making his way up the street, lighting the gas lamps as he went. Night had properly fallen before my mother found me and rescued me. I was three years old at the time.

The rescue didn't last for long. One day when I was about three and a half, my father announced to my mother and me that if we were still in the house when he arrived back from work, he would kill us both. We had reason to believe him, since he owned a gun and had once fired it into a bedroom door during one of his outbursts. We packed hurriedly and left the same day to stay with friends. Not long afterwards, my mother announced that I would have to stay with my grandmother for a day, because she needed to go off to Bristol for some reason.

Even as a little girl, I did not like my grandmother. Florence was a forbidding woman who ruled her household with steely determination and rarely a smile. Her family were all terrified of her and for a toddler, having to spend the day with her was not an attractive prospect. My mother, Doris, handed me over and left, promising to be back to collect me before nightfall.

Later that evening, my grandmother made up a bed for me out of two chairs pulled together.

'But I can't go to bed,' I protested. 'Mummy's coming back for me.'

'Oh, she can collect you in the morning,' Grandmother

told me, and I climbed obediently into the makeshift bed.

It was in fact more than five years later that I next saw – or rather, almost saw – my mother. I was eight or nine years old. I was in disgrace for some reason and had been sent to the corner. I was sitting alone, facing the wall, feeling sorry for myself, when there was a knock at the door. My grandmother went to answer it, and I heard her say, 'Why, Doris, fancy seeing you here.' As she walked back in she added, 'But don't speak to Babs; she's been naughty.' Sure enough, my mother ignored me and left again soon after without a word.

My grandmother's was a household ruled by the iron phrase 'What would people think?' – that, and an over-riding fear of vulgarity. On 8 May 1945, VE day, the day when six long years of war in Europe finally ended and families up and down the country tumbled out on to the streets to cheer, and flirt, and eat, my grandmother refused to alter her routine a single iota. We weren't allowed outside, and in our house at least, Hitler's fall went completely uncelebrated.

My mother's distance towards me might perhaps be explained by her own experience of childhood, but I had also been born out of wedlock, and it had been her unwanted pregnancy that had forced her into what was seen as an inferior marriage to a violent and unstable man. She would remarry again in due course and have two further daughters. When they got married in a double ceremony years later, my mother turned to me and complained how hard it was 'to lose both my daughters on the same day'.

This, however, is to lose my thread. In my grandmother's house, I was a sucker for anything that suggested a spirit of love, beauty or community – in fact, almost anything that seemed to promise a life different from the one I knew. The conversation I had just heard over breakfast seemed to offer a clue to where such a life might be found.

I had read about exotic places like Marseille and the Casbah and gathered from my grandmother's reaction that Soho belonged to the same, notorious group. But whereas Marseille and the Casbah seemed to be on another planet entirely, in relation to the small suburb of Southall where we lived, Soho was apparently within easy reach – at least for my uncle Henry. I longed to ask him about it, but my grandmother's word was law and she had said it must not be mentioned. I was never allowed to speak unless spoken to first, but I was determined to find out what this Soho was all about.

In spite of my lack of any real communication with anyone in the house, Uncle Henry – although taciturn almost to the point of neurosis – was my idol. He was completely different from the rest of the family. I would note the books he brought home from the library and, as soon as possible, read them myself. They were mostly philosophy and the classics, and at seventeen, I struggled hopelessly with Nietzsche and Jung. His other interests were equally challenging to my young self: symphony concerts, opera and the arts. I tried to understand all these things, at first to gain his approval but then, gradually, for the joy I found in them for their own sake. Of all these, it was painting that really captivated me, and I even seemed to have some aptitude for it. A couple of years earlier, encouraged by an art teacher at my school, I'd managed to win a scholarship to Ealing Art School, a few miles away on the west London fringe. Financially, it would have been impossible for me to take the offer up were it not for all sorts of grants made available to me to cover everything – right down to clothing and school meals.

On the morning of Uncle Henry's revelation, I had about another year of my scholarship to run. All day Soho was uppermost in my mind, and between lessons I managed to find out more from my more worldly fellow pupils. Yes, Soho was in London, and no, nice people didn't go there. Someone even showed me its location on a map. Satisfied at last, I filed away all this knowledge for further reference and applied myself to schoolwork once more.

When I was nearly eighteen, the headmaster sent for me and asked what my plans were. I told him I must somehow find a job. He seemed upset: he felt I should stay on long enough to get a teaching diploma. He even suggested it might help if he had a talk with my grandmother.

'I would be able to explain to her,' he said, 'that there are various further grants available to students who I feel are sufficiently promising – private grants, you under-stand,' he added confidentially.

If there has been one burning, all-pervading ambition in my life that has never varied, never flagged, it is that before I die, I will paint the perfect picture. I was tempted by his offer, but I had the pride and longing for independence of those who have very little else. It was a difficult decision for me to make, but that pride won in the end.

'You have been very kind,' I said. 'I'm more than grate-ful, but the thought of accepting any more charity makes me feel quite ill. I can't do it.'

He was an understanding man; he realised how I felt and that was that.

And so, during my nineteenth year, I left art school. It had taught me so much. I knew the shape and disposition of every bone, muscle and vein of *Homo sapiens* and most other animals; I knew perspective in all its forms; I knew historic architecture; I was conversant with the lives and works of the great artists and their techniques. But the war had just ended and I realised that, with continuing austerity, the last thing England needed at that moment was an aspiring artist with no knowledge of the world.

So, predictably, my first job had little to do with art. It was in the darkroom of a photographic firm, and I found the work repetitive and lonely. I tried again: this time at the National Film Library, which was, again, not for me. Then – about a year after the war had ended – people began to want pretty things around them once more. I took the opportunity to improve my lot, and found a job in a studio that had just started painting flowers, birds and such things on lampshades and other articles. They had begun in a very small way and I think I was only their second employee. It was still certainly a very far cry from my dreams of becoming a great painter, but using a brush for eight hours every day made it become almost a part of my body and taught me a dexterity and fluidity whose value I have since come to recognise.

So far, nothing had diminished the fascination Soho held for me. I had even contrived for all my jobs to be nearby, and I snatched every chance to get closer. Most of my wages went to my grandmother, so as a necessary economy, I always took sandwiches for lunch. This proved to be a happy arrangement, for it gave me plenty of time during my lunch hour to explore Soho's perimeter. This delighted me, and the temptation to delve into Soho itself grew. Still, I did not dare to actually do so, as my grandmother seemed to have an uncanny ability to know everything I did – a sort of third eye that hovered over me wherever I went.

I knew Soho's border formed a rectangle and that walking right round it, you covered about two miles. On the northern edge was Oxford Street, on the west, Regent Street; the southern side consisted of Piccadilly Circus,

Coventry Street, Leicester Square and Cranbourn Street and the eastern boundary was formed by the Charing Cross Road.

For me, the wonders of this two-mile circuit never palled. Oxford Street, with its glamorous department stores on one side, and on the other, the small but still glamorous shops that backed on to Soho itself. These were mainly ground-floor shops with the upper floors occupied by a miscellany of small firms, and the entranceways were dotted with a profusion of interesting name boards. As well as the usual solicitors, architects and import agents, there were enter-tainment and detective agencies, and more bizarre pro-fessions like 'Madam Zaz – Palmist', and a few doors further along, 'Mustapha ben Ali – Astrologer' or 'Offenbach – Trance Medium'. These were usually high up in the build-ings, where rents were cheaper.

Along the grandly curving Regent Street, the shops became more expensive and precious, and I found it hard to believe that anyone was rich enough to buy things there. On reaching Piccadilly Circus, I'd pause at the statue of Eros, newly freed from its wartime wrappings, surrounded by people sitting gazing at the milling life around them. It is said that if you sit near Eros long enough, everyone you've ever known will eventually pass by.

Not keen to be reunited with anyone from my past, I'd head on to Coventry Street, which in those days held the most amazing Lyons Corner House. It consisted of floor upon floor of different restaurants, and I feel sad for people who are too young to have known it. Despite its magnificent interior and service, it was not at all expensive to eat there. On the ground floor was a huge patisserie-cum-delicatessen-cum-everything. There was a vast array of edible things to buy and take away in boxes tied with coloured braid. Opening off this were the many tearooms

8

and snack bars, each with their own distinctive decor. On the floors above were all sorts of restaurants catering for different pockets and tastes. The Salad Bowl on the top floor was my particular joy when I could afford it. Here, it was self-service, with counters filled with rows and rows and rows of containers brimming with every kind of salad the mind could dream up. There were great baskets full of crispy rolls, piles of butter, and tables groaning with enormous shivering jellies, trifles, blancmanges and tremendous squashy gateaux. For the sum of two-and-sixpence you could eat your fill. Oh, a truly wonderful place! But Mr Lyons, in his wisdom, had foreseen that certain people might have limitless time to do this. So at intervals during the day, this department was emptied of customers and closed.

Slightly further along, and opening out from Coventry Street, was the fabulous Leicester Square, surrounded by all the great cinemas – the Ritz, Empire, Warner, Odeon and Leicester Square theatres, where premieres were regularly held. The great stars arrived in limousines while the excited, surging crowds were restrained by lines of policemen. In those days, television sets were still incredibly rare, and so the cinema was the land of dreams and its stars were held in near-godlike regard.

Outside these cinemas on ordinary days there were always long queues of people waiting to go in, and it was, I should think, about the most lucrative place in London for buskers. Musicians, escapologists and all sorts of novelty acts performed in the middle of the busy road, and the traffic had to skirt them carefully. In the midst of all this was the central square, like an oasis, full of trees. When dusk fell, starlings from all over London came to roost.

At the junction with Charing Cross Road, opposite Wyndham's Theatre, Soho's final boundary was reached, and this road was a real delight to me. There were book-shops on either side, nearly all of them with trestle tables outside stacked with second-hand books, and you had to almost fight for a place to look at them. In those days, the greatest of these were Zwemmer's and Foyles. The latter also had the most enormous second-hand department inside – almost a whole floor. It was here that I most loved to browse whilst surreptitiously eating my sandwiches.

Shaftesbury Avenue cut this stretch of the road at Cambridge Circus, which was alive with its flotilla of fruit and shellfish stalls and hot chestnut braziers. Further along were the Tatler News Theatre, the Phoenix Theatre and the Astoria Cinema and Ballroom — always emblazoned with colourful hand-painted posters. The busy St Giles' Circus at the top of Charing Cross Road marked my reunion with Oxford Street and my wandering would be over for another day.

Those lunch hours were the happiest part of my day, but I worked hard at my painting job, getting little pay rises here and there, though these left me no better off, as they always went straight to my grandmother. Not that that mattered to me very much, as I'd never had the opportunity to develop a desire for clothes or cosmetics (I was not allowed to wear make-up of any kind – even face powder – and my face had that permanent shine that I'm sure only Sunlight soap can give), though I would have liked to have bought some paints.

The next two years passed slowly. I was given more and more responsibility at work and gained a slight degree of self-assurance. My life at home, though, had become increasingly impossible and my grandmother more and more demanding. She had reached the conclusion that the only way in which I could repay all her charity was by becoming her support in her old age. Had she been a kind, loving person, I would have naturally and willingly fallen into that role; but as it was, I felt nervous and caged. I was only allowed out one evening a week – Friday – on the express understanding that I went to the pictures and nowhere else.

So it was that the day after I reached the longed-for age of twenty-one – the day I legally became an adult – I made all my possessions up into two parcels and, with my grandmother's curses following me, left her house, completely alone in the world.

Two

~

I made my way up stairs covered with cracked and brittle linoleum to the room I had rented several days earlier in west London and let myself in with the key that had been hanging like a talisman around my neck. It was June, and I'd worn my thick winter coat to save packing it, so I felt hot and sick. I dumped everything on the narrow iron bed and gazed around me with pleasure.

Anyone who could have gazed with pleasure at that particular room must have been in a pretty parlous state. It was filthy and barely functional. Apart from the bed, it contained an ancient chest of drawers, a mirror hanging from a nail above it, a small battered table and two wooden chairs. A wardrobe had been achieved by curtaining off a corner of the room in the same fabric that covered the windows – blackout material that was grey with dust. There was also an enormous, ancient gas fire, a single ring for cooking and an ominous-looking meter. That was all, except for what stood on the table: a thick china cup and saucer, two plates, a battered kettle, a large ewer of chipped white enamel and a few assorted items of cheap metal cutlery.

I was overjoyed. For the first time in my life I had a home that I had a right to be in. I had paid the rent; I had the key. For me, those four drab, dun-coloured walls spelt peace and independence. I had had to ask for an advance on my wages to pay the two weeks' rent. This left me with exactly three pounds in my purse to last me for the next ten days. Even this fact was not allowed to dampen my spirits.

I tried the top drawer of the chest. One of its white china knobs fell off, but the drawer opened in a lopsided sort of way. It contained a slice of toasted cheese, resting bleakly in the centre. That might come in handy, I thought, if I was living on bread and water until the next payday. The other drawers revealed nothing but crumbs and, in the bottom one, a mousetrap.

I thought about freshening up but there was no running water, hence the enamel jug. To get water, I had to go downstairs and out into the back yard, then in through another door and into a small scullery, where there was a tap. The toilet was thereabouts too. No time for all that now, I thought. It was eight thirty a.m. and I was due at work by nine. I ran a comb through my hair in front of the filthy mirror, then ripped open one of my parcels and found a cardigan. I grabbed my handbag and, carefully locking the door behind me, shot off to work.

The firm had expanded a lot, and now, instead of the original two, there were twenty-eight girl painters, of whom I was head. Meantime, the original owners had sold out to a man who did nothing but wander around tapping his teeth with a pencil and asking silly questions. He called me his 'kingpin' – and it was no exaggeration. I supervised all the other girls, sorted out the orders and kept an eye on the packers; I mixed the paints and worked out the wages; I did my share of the painting; I created new designs and I did a hundred and one other things. For this I was paid five pounds – a pound a week more than the other girls – and I had the doubtful privilege of hiring and firing.

During that first day of freedom, although to all appearances I was my usual composed self, inside I was dancing with joy. I had never in my life been so happy, and was making all sorts of plans for that crummy little room. At lunchtime, daringly, I spent some of my three pounds on soap, disinfectant, a scrubbing brush and a bowl.

In the afternoon, I asked my boss if I could have a few of the plentiful supply of rags we kept for cleaning our brushes. He told me to help myself and, with a twinkle in his eye that I was too naïve to interpret, said that he would have to come up sometime to take a look at this famous room of mine.

The following week, my boss decided that an evening's stocktaking should take place. While we were engaged in this, the merry twinkle in his eye turned verbal, and he intimated that a little more than coffee and a chat wouldn't come amiss at the end of the evening. To explain, perhaps I should say that in those days, 1948-ish, it was very unusual for a girl to leave home before marriage. To do so for any other reason, I found, meant that people assumed you were fast, and out for a bit of fun. Anyway, that's the way my boss chose to see it, and though I naturally took up the time-honoured stag-at-bay stance, he was undaunted and even turned up at my bed-sitter the following Saturday to ask if I'd thought it over.

I got rid of him as pleasantly as possible, but inside I was raging. There I was, practically running his business for him, and on top of that, he wanted me as his ... the word 'doxy' sprang to my mind (I was reading Georgian literature at the time). On the heels of my anger came the fear that I might lose my job if I kept saying no to him, and then where would I be? After not too much thought, I realised I needed an evening job. I had already worked out that on my wages I was going to be able to do little more than scrape by, and that to save up to prettify the room or to buy my own paints would take years. If I could get a second job, I would be able to buy things for the flat as well as the art materials I wanted, and best of all, it would be a backup if I got sacked.

A few days later, during my lunch break, I saw a news-agent pinning new advertisement cards in his glass-fronted display case. Almost instantly, my eye lighted on one that read:

Bright girl needed for evening work in small club.
No previous experience necessary.

This was followed by a phone number. It seemed the very thing: I reckoned I was fairly bright, and I certainly had no previous experience. I copied the telephone number and rushed to the nearest underground station, where there was a phone box. I dialled and a man's voice answered. I explained what I had rung about.

'When can you come and see me?' the voice asked.

'Well, I finish work at five.' I told him where I worked.

'If you took a taxi, you could be here in five minutes,' he said. He gave me the name and address of the club, which I jotted down. 'When you get here, ask for Jim. See you!' and he put the phone down.

I was in a fever of nerves all afternoon. At five o'clock, I tentatively applied the powder and pale lipstick that so far I'd only had the nerve to experiment with in the privacy of my little room.

It was the first taxi I had ever been in, and once I'd given the address, I sat perched uneasily on the edge of the seat, hoping very much that something would come of the interview. We were travelling along Oxford Street when the cab suddenly turned. I hadn't had a chance to find out exactly where the club was, but I realised I was actually being driven into Soho. I was paralysed. The taxi made a few tortuous turns through those mysterious streets and finally stopped. When I got out and paid the driver, I found that my knees were shaking.

I'm what you would call a 'brave coward', so when the cab had driven away, I firmly told my knees to behave and reread the bit of paper with the address and name of the club on it. Sure enough, painted on a small board just where I was standing were the words The Mousehole. Beyond stretched a long, narrow passage, lit by one heavily shaded bulb. At the end, I found a staircase leading down, above which was another board – also reading The Mouse-hole – this time with an arrow pointing downwards. I giggled nervously: there was nowhere else you could go but down.

I went through a bamboo curtain at the bottom and was immediately in a pleasant, very dimly lit room. There was a bar at one end and a man in a white jacket moving around behind it against a glitter of glasses and bottles. Except for this, and two men who were sitting at a table near the middle, the room was empty. The men's conversation was interrupted by the clicking noise the curtain made as I pushed it aside, and the barman gave me an enquiring look.

'I was told to ask for Jim,' I said.

'That's him, over there,' he answered laconically, nodding in the direction of the two men.

I thanked him and went towards them. I got a similar enquiring look from one, so I guessed he must be Jim. I said that I had phoned about the job at lunchtime.

'Wages fifteen bob a night and your cab fare home – that's if you don't live too far off.'

'No, not far,' I assured him.

'What's your name?'

'Barbara.'

'That's a nice name. You ready to start?'

'What, now?' I gasped.

'As good a time as any!'

I turned, feeling slightly dazed by the speed of it all. He broke into a grin.

'Ronnie there' – he motioned towards the barman – 'will fix you up with an apron. Oh, and by the way,' he added, 'no need to come till six after tonight.'

Never again would I have such a quick interview. I murmured my thanks and went to the bar. Without seeming to be bothered whether I heard or not, the man sitting with Jim remarked, 'Bit different from your usual type, isn't she?'

I heard Jim reply, 'Might be a change to have a bit of class.'

That surprised me too; I'd never thought of myself as having what could be termed 'class'. I began to feel a bit more confident.

Ronnie gave me a friendly smile and handed me an apron. He was a dapper little man with a thin, bird-like face and could have been any age between forty and sixty.

'Ever done this work before?' he asked.

'No,' I replied nervously. I didn't dare tell him that I'd never even been inside a pub before, and that my grandmother considered anything stronger than cider shandy to be devil's brew.

'Not to worry, ducks,' he said kindly, as I tied on the apron. 'It's mostly just collecting glasses and ashtrays and things like that, and washing them – and being friendly with people. You'll be all right. When I get a minute here and there, I'll show you what to do about drinks.' He paused and studied my face as I watched him gravely. 'Cheer up, love, it may never happen!'

I laughed and, all at once, felt much more at ease.

'S'better,' he said approvingly. 'Now cop hold of this cloth and get cracking with them glasses.'

Later on, the club became crowded and noisy, and we were all kept busy. I could quite see why they needed someone to deal with the glasses. I passed the evening in a sort of dream, now and again recalling with amazement that at last I was actually in Soho. It seemed incredible. After everything I'd been told, I was surprised to find that everyone here seemed warm and friendly and I didn't feel wicked at all: just happy.

Jim had asked a cab driver who'd been in for a drink to come and pick me up at the end of the evening. He arrived soon after the final customer had left. I hurriedly washed a few last things and took off my apron.

Jim complimented me with what appeared to be genuine satisfaction.

'You've done very well, love. See you tomorrow then?'

'Thanks,' I replied, and calling good night to Ronnie, I followed the driver up the stairs.

At the front doorway, with the security of the club left behind me, I took a quick glance up and down the dark street. There was no doubt Soho could be a frightening place – although for no reason I could actually specify. There was a slight breeze that carried pieces of litter before it. Here and there I saw solitary, aimless figures in the dim lamplight. It was very quiet – not the quietness of peace, but rather that of waiting and listening. I would never have had the courage to find my way out of here on foot, and was more than glad that only a few paces away was the faintly glowing refuge of the taxi.

'All aboard the Skylark!' came the cheery voice of the cabby, and I hurried across to get in.

Soho is not a large place, and it wasn't long before we

reached the brightly lit streets I was familiar with. All the same, I couldn't dispel my impression that the place we'd left behind was brooding and sinister, and that anything could happen there at any time. And what were those human-looking bundles huddled in some of the doorways we'd flashed past?

Now that we were covering ground that I recognised, I discovered just how weary I really was, and settled back on to the comfortable seat. At the same time, I realised I was absolutely ravenous and I couldn't wait to get home.

Suddenly I recalled the memory of Uncle Henry's dining in Soho and smiled to myself. Dining indeed! I was working there!

Three

~

At the end of a month at The Mousehole, I had benefited in several ways. My money worries were over, my room was much more comfortable and I'd lost about a stone in weight from all the running around.

My fears about losing my position at the studio had not materialised, but my boss had become curt and sometimes downright unpleasant. I longed to find a way of leaving. Ronnie suggested I should chuck the daytime job, go on the dole and take things a bit easier. But having been brought up to regard receiving dole as tantamount to 'going on the parish', I refused his advice. My early reluctance to accept charity had not lessened with the passing years.

Life was exhausting. My alarm would rouse me from my few hours of sleep at seven thirty, when I had to get ready to rush to work. We painted without pause, even during our tea break. I would only have time for a sandwich at the end of the day before dashing off to the club. I was never home before midnight, by which time I barely had the energy to wind the alarm. By midnight on Fridays, my energy was beginning to flag somewhat. Fortunately the studio was closed at weekends, giving me the chance to keep my little room spick and span, but the club stayed open, so work still beckoned in the evening.

I often wished I liked alcohol, as it certainly seemed to

have an invigorating effect on the customers at the club. I was often treated to a drink, and changed my choice each time in my hunt for one that did not taste like medicine. I ran the gamut without success, and eventually reverted to lemonade, but in a small glass, trusting that to an onlooker it would pass for gin and tonic.

I was soon quite enjoying my evening work. As more faces became familiar, I could join in with the quips and jokes. The women were brilliantly blonde, wore ankle-strapped shoes, loose bracelets and pretended to be dumb, which was very much the in thing at the time. Their men were the pencil-moustachioed, two-tone-shoed, chalk-stripe-suited sort, with cheap rings and cufflinks. These 'wide boys' or 'spivs' comprised most of our membership. Their conversation was always about racing, betting systems and where scarce commodities could be obtained on the black market. They were all showy, noisy and self-assured – but they were kind.

One Saturday night, my shift had just begun and I was keeping my fingers crossed that the evening would be free of the scuffles that invariably happened at weekends. I was not to know that this particular evening was going to mark a change in my life I would never forget.

In the lull before the rush, Jim and Ronnie had gone over to Benito's for a meal. From there they could keep an eye on who went into the club and judge when I would begin to need help. They'd worked all through the after-noon trade and had left a pile of glassware for me to wash, fresh ice to break for the lager bucket and four already settled customers to look after.

A burly, smiling man entered, wearing the look of slight desperation that I had come to recognise on all our male customers. He needed urgently to get within ordering dis-tance of a bar. Whilst waiting, his anxious expression remained firmly in place, as though he feared everything might be sold out at any moment. Only when I had taken his order could he relax and burst into bloom, acknowledging me with a 'How's tricks?' This was Syd: a staunch regular, along with all his pals, fellow meat porters at Smithfield Market.

I turned back to the washing-up; I could see that, as usual, Syd was settling down for a chat, but I wanted to get the work done first or I'd never catch up. I'd been caught like that by him once before.

The jukebox was on automatic, as it always was when there were too few people in to feed it with coins. I surveyed the room while I polished glasses. It was strange to see how nice it could look with the lights dim, knowing how tatty it really was when the bright overhead lighting was switched on for cleaning.

The other four customers consisted of a young couple huddled over a table in a far corner of the room – who, under cover of the music, were engaged in deep and private conversation – and two women who were sitting together on stools at the end of the bar furthest from Syd. One of them was a young and spectacular blonde, while her companion was a stout, frowsy woman in her fifties. Neither spoke to the other, and although the blonde occasionally ordered gin and bitters for the other woman, she had barely touched her own. The stout woman grimaced whenever she caught my eye, communicating her silent dislike of her partner.

My chores done, I noticed Syd waving his glass again. As I refilled it, he gave a mock scowl.

'Talk about a bluebottle!' he complained, 'You never stand still, do you?'

'I'm standing still now,' I said, plonking my elbows on the counter.

He started talking about work. Meat was still on ration after the war, and his work as a porter meant he was full of stories.

'What an interesting job you've got,' I remarked.

'Not half as interesting as hers, I shouldn't think,' he said, lowering his voice and giving a sort of jerk of his head in the direction of the two women.

'Which one, the young one?'

'Naturally.'

'Why, what does she do?' I asked, getting interested.

'She's on the game!'

'What game?' I asked innocently.

Looking back, I find it hard to credit that I was ever so naïve. Syd obviously did as well, because he gazed at me incredulously for a while, clearly wondering if I was trying to tease him. Having decided that I wasn't, he leaned forward with a slightly reddened face and whispered hoarsely, 'She's one of the ladies, and that's her maid!'

I stole a quick glance at them, but couldn't quite picture the girl as someone with a title, and the maid looked more like a bodyguard. Syd seemed nearly floored when I looked at him blankly again. He scratched his head and seemed to be searching for words. Then, leaning forward once more and studying my face for signs of comprehension, he said, with suitable pauses:

'She's a business girl ... One of the birds ... A tart ... A prostitute!'

It was only his last term that I understood. He leaned back with relief when I blushed and gasped, 'Oh!'

I felt embarrassed. Syd was holding his glass out for another beer, and while I was filling it, I was relieved to see a couple of his friends arriving. I opened two more bottles, so all three glasses were lined up when they turned to the bar after greeting Syd.

I left them and wandered back along the bar. The dumpy woman was ready for another gin, and I was able to study the blonde at closer range.

I was utterly intrigued, but anxious not to make it obvious. I had never knowingly seen a prostitute before and I was filled with curiosity. Apart from her voice – which had a slight northern accent that she had clearly taken pains to disguise – the most noticeable thing about her was her hair, which was long and gleaming. In defiance of the upswept fashion of the time, it was a mass of loose waves and curls. She was pretty; but more than that, she was provocative and reckless-looking. She wore quite a lot of make-up, especially around her eyes, and I was struck by her resemblance to a bust I'd seen of an Egyptian queen, Nefertiti. Her sweater was simple but looked expensive: turquoise silk with a V-neck showing her cleavage. She had pushed the sleeves up to just below her elbows. As I watched, she swung her feet lightly to the floor and walked with easy assurance to the jukebox. Marilyn Monroe could have learned something from that walk. Her skirt was grey, tight and straight, with a slit at the hem; the waist was cinched tight with a wide black patent leather belt, and her extremely high-heeled shoes were of the same material. It was obvious that her flair lay not so much in the clothes she chose to wear as in the careless negligence with which she wore them. I somehow knew that she would look good even in a sack. She had all the qualities I lacked: glamour, boldness and an eye for fashion. In spite of all these assets, though, she was evidently unhappy.

Her companion caught my eye. She was dressed in a food-splattered red Moroccan frock and a black straw hat decorated with bunches of artificial cherries nestling amongst crumpled leaves. Somewhere at her feet was the disgusting matted fur wrap which I later found out was the reason for her nickname. Fumbling in her handbag, she produced a compact and smirked at her own reflection for a while. Then, leering across at me with what she obviously believed to be a winsome smile, she spoke.

'It comes to something, don't it, when the maid's better-looking than the mistress!'

I was saved from having to comment because Syd and his friends had run dry again.

A strange feeling came over me; everything seemed unreal. What on earth was I doing here amongst all these peculiar people, in this sleazy little basement club? I thought of my grandmother and blanched.

The blonde returned to her seat, and sat there looking stiff and aloof. I felt sorry for her. Then, to my horror, the maid lumbered down off her stool and came towards me with one elbow slithering along the counter. As she reached where I was standing, she treated me to another of her ghastly smiles and hissed in a stage whisper:

'She's muck – and she knows it!'

Then she pushed herself away from the bar to pass Syd and his friends and went through the archway that led to the toilets in the vaults below the pavement. I didn't know whether the blonde had heard, but when I looked, she was staring hard into her drink.

Just then, the jukebox got stuck and I went over to give it a remedial kick. Returning, I saw the woman reappear from the vaults, wearing a triumphant expression. She walked purposefully to where she had been sitting, and after delivering a few seemingly strong words to the girl, picked up her handbag and stomped out of the club.

I had just got back from serving the pair at the corner table and was dropping the used glasses into the sink when I was suddenly electrified by the sound of the blonde's voice, full of pent-up fury and exploding with venom.

Alarmed, I spun round, thinking for one awful moment that she was addressing me, but she was just sitting there with clenched hands, glaring belligerently into the remainder of her gin.

I watched her with growing sympathy as I swilled the dirty glasses in the sink. She looked up and caught my gaze, and a grin spread across her face as she realised I'd heard her. It was surprising how impishly different she looked when she smiled.

'Sorry, love,' she apologised. 'But I'm so bloody mad I could burst!'

'Well I hope you won't,' I replied, "cos I have to mop up at the end of the evening.' My remark actually produced something akin to a giggle, and she pushed the gin away from her with an expression of distaste.

'I don't think you like that stuff any more than I do,' I said. 'Feel like joining me in a lemonade?'

'Yeah, let's be devils!'

I poured us each a large glass and, not wanting to intrude too much, carried on working.

'What a life!' she sighed, making it obvious that she wanted someone to talk to. I moved towards her.

'Had a bad day?' I asked.

'Actually . . .' she said, lifting herself from the slump she had fallen into, 'actually, I've had a bloody good day. It's just that cow, Rabbits, who gets on my wick. That's my maid: the one who just went out. I wish she'd just drop dead and do everyone a favour!'

She seemed to take it for granted that I knew what her trade was.

'What's Rabbits done, then?' I asked, now full of curiosity.

'Nothing – as usual – and that's the whole damn trouble! Absolutely bloody nothing! She sits on her fat arse all day, and if I even want a cup of tea, I have to get it myself. She's filthy dirty and never bothers to clean the place or do a bloody hand's turn. It makes me sick!'

She sipped gloomily at her lemonade and went on:

'I could just about put up with all that, but it doesn't stop there. She thinks she's the boss: always trying to order me about. Talks about me behind my back, too. She takes the piss and pulls all sorts of faces she doesn't think I notice.'

She learned towards me, gradually getting angrier.

'Do you know, she's even stopped me having friends up to the flat because she reckons it wastes time – wants me to flog myself to death so she can get more tips. Tonight was the last straw, though; she's gone a bit too far this time!' She sat back, her eyes wrathful with the recollection.

'What happened?' I asked.

'Well . . .' she replied, settling herself more comfortably, with the air of one preparing to tell all. 'It's what she just said that really choked me, and I don't think I can stand the sight of her much longer!' She paused again, leaving me positively burning with curiosity.

'What did she say?' I asked breathlessly.

She took a deep breath and her nostrils flared slightly. 'She only called my bed a meat stand!' Her eyes filled with angry tears as she went on: 'And I'm not taking that from anyone!'

'Oh!' I gasped, relieved to know, at last, the cause of the friction, although puzzled as to why its effect had been so devastating. Her annoyance was sufficiently infectious for me to add, with feeling, 'She didn't!'

'She bloody did!' she said vehemently, though her temper was abating now she had someone to share her anger with.

'But why do you have to put up with all this?' I asked.

She sighed. 'In our business, love, maids sometimes go with the flat. I could find another place, but I'd have to find another lot of key money. Besides, I like the flat I'm in – it's in a good spot – but that old sod's driving me potty!'

She was chewing her lip with the frustration of it all, and I was searching around in my mind for some possible solution to her problem.

While the girl and I had been talking, I'd noticed two more of Syd's friends come in. Syd was taking an interest in my conversation with the blonde. He told his friends he'd join them later, and ordered another beer. In doing so, he stationed himself on a stool much closer to us.

'What about asking the agent or landlord if he could get Rabbits a job with someone else?' I asked. 'Tell him you can't work with her properly and soon won't be able to pay your rent. He can supply you with another maid and so he won't be any worse off, will he?'

'It's an idea,' she agreed. 'It's not as though the greedy cow's grateful for anything. I get good tips for her and I'm never out long before I bring someone back. Some maids have to wait for hours! And do you know ...' she leaned closer to me across the bar, 'I've been up and down those bloody stairs twenty-four times today already!'

'Oh!' I cried, caught between sympathy and surprise. 'Oh, your poor feet!'

Her jaw dropped open in amazement and she stared at me for an instant, then threw back her head and let out peal after peal of helpless laughter.

'My feet?' she choked. She tried to prevent more laughter and to regain her breath. 'Oh, you'll be the death of me – look, you've made my mascara run!'

She dabbed at her eyes with a little lace handkerchief

she had snatched from her bag. 'The funny part is that you meant it!'

Her amusement was contagious; even Syd was grinning and surreptitiously moving nearer. I was laughing too, although the full humour of what I'd said had escaped me. The laughter gradually died down and the girl's face began to resume its former sombre lines. Then she gripped the clasp of her handbag with both hands, as though preparing to leave.

'Well, I suppose I'd better be off. The old bag'll be sitting up there waiting for me and getting into an even worse mood.'

It dawned on me that she was as frightened of her maid as I'd been of my grandmother.

'I'd sooner stop here, though, and have a bit of a laugh,' she said.

'I wish you could,' I replied, feeling a little sad. 'But I suppose I ought to get on with some work too!'

'What's your name, love?' she asked suddenly.

'Barbara,' I answered.

'That's Babs to me.' She grinned. 'And I'm Mae.' She put her hand out to clasp mine and our eyes met in a smile. At that moment, I knew that she needed a friend as much as I did.

Not long afterwards there came a crashing of feet along the upstairs passage, followed by what sounded like an elephant plunging down the staircase. The bamboo curtain was swept aside with a mighty clash and Rabbits burst through. Her face was puce. For a moment she stood, hands on hips, surveying the scene and looking for all the world like Henry the Eighth's twin sister – and then she exploded.

'What the hell do you think you're playing at? Here's me, sitting up there like a bleeding lemon, and here's you, down here, getting bloody pissed. What do you think I am?'

All eyes in the club were riveted on the scene, while the jukebox carried on regardless with 'Stardust'.

Mae did not reply. Indeed, she was speechless and her face was ashen. Nor did she make any attempt to stand up; she seemed frozen. The maid obviously expected her to jump up and leave immediately. Infuriated at the lack of response, she fairly screeched:

'So that's how you want it, is it? Well leave your bleeding boozy friends and come along the alleyway and we'll have it out once and for fucking all. You've been asking for this for a bloody long time, you have. Now you're going to get it!'

Then, throwing her head forward, she spat on to the carpet, spun her ungainly bulk round, nearly tripping over her own feet, and mounted the stairs heavily. The other customers tactfully withdrew their attention from Mae — all except Syd and me, who were regarding her with concern. Syd drew closer.

'What are you going to do?' he asked gently.

'Her!' answered Mae tersely, from between clenched teeth. 'If I let her get away with that, my life won't be worth living!'

Much as I hated violence, I couldn't help but agree. Syd seemed to feel the same and was hovering in an uncertain way.

'Can I give you a tip?' he asked tentatively. 'I could show you a good way of getting the better of her.'

'How?' asked Mae.

Syd's face lit with enthusiasm and he stationed himself in front of her.

'Well,' he said, 'you know how two women in a barney always grab each other's hair, don't you? Well, take a hold of mine.'

He bent his head forward, and Mae grasped his orangey curls. Syd then clutched her wrist and took her hair in his other hand, which caused Mae to instinctively grab his waist. The other people in the club were all attention once more, and I watched Syd's demonstration with interest. It looked very clever, but I didn't learn a thing: it was all too quick, ending with no one holding anyone's hair any more and Mae in a helpless grip. Syd released his hold.

'See, it's easy,' he said. Mae laughed and called him a bastard as she rubbed her shoulder. However, Syd wasn't happy until she'd done the same thing to him. She was a quick learner. Then, smoothing her skirt, she said decisively, 'Right! I've got to go!'

At that moment, two sets of heavy footsteps could be heard coming along the upstairs passage.

'Blimey, she's got reinforcements!' said Syd, bristling. We stood stock still, watching the doorway, and I took a deep breath of relief when we saw it was only a couple of cabbies, who walked straight up to the counter and started jovially tapping on it with coins. The tension was broken and I went along to serve them. Mae thrust her handbag at me.

'Look after that for me, ducks. I'll be right back.' Then off she went at a brisk pace.

'I'll come along too,' said Syd, and he strode after her.

I felt rather shaky at this proximity to violence, but sensibly reminded myself that incidents of this sort must be taking place in Soho every night. I felt an affinity with Mae, and it made this particular fight a much more personal thing. I kept wondering how she was getting on and was glad Syd had gone with her; but I couldn't dwell on it for long, as all at once everyone seemed to be wanting more drinks at the same time. Added to that, Tommy – the pianist for Saturdays – had just arrived. Directly on his heels came two bookies with their girlfriends. I was turning off the jukebox ready for Tommy to start playing when Jim and Ronnie returned, closely followed by another small group of customers. Tommy gulped his drink down and, going over to the piano, loosened his fingers with a series of ascending arpeggios. The busy evening trade had begun.

I wasn't aware that Mae had returned until I heard her asking for her handbag. She was beaming over the counter from beneath a mop of dishevelled hair, amongst which was an angry patch of congealing blood. Syd was standing, jubilant, behind her.

'What happened?' I asked, relieved that the fight had ended and she seemed not too much the worse for wear.

'What happened?' she repeated, chuckling. 'This is what happened!' She stood back so I could see her full length, then she stuck her left foot well forward to display a shapely leg right up to the thigh, where the seam of her pencil skirt had ripped apart.

'Proper little Hackenschmidt she was,' Syd said. 'Went off a fair treat!'

'You tell her what happened,' said Mae, giving me a wink.

'Well, let's get a drink in front of me first,' Syd said. 'Let's all have one. Yours is gin and bitters, isn't it, Mae?'

'No!' said Mae defiantly. 'Me and Babs are going to have double lemonade. Aren't we, love?'

'Strewth!' said Syd. He declared that he, at any rate, was going to celebrate with a double whisky, and after a couple of sips, he embarked on a graphic account of the contest.

'By the time me and Mae got there, Rabbits had a fair crowd round her because she was ranting away and carrying on and they wanted to see some bother. Anyway, the minute she caught sight of Mae, she started shouting and went straight up to her. She puts her handbag down, ready for action, and screams like a mad thing. Mae started to see the funny side of it and just laughed in her face. Well, that really got Rabbits' rag up. It was just like I said it would be: each grabs a handful of hair. But Mae here' – he placed a hand on her shoulder – 'Mae done just like I showed her and Rabbits didn't know what'd hit her. Then Mae let go and Rabbits tried to hide behind the crowd. She got lairy like and started throwing her shoes, but all she done was hit a couple of ringsiders. Then she scarpered – and that was it! A right loony, that one!'

When he'd finished, Mae said admiringly, 'He should have been a reporter, shouldn't he?'

At this, Syd bowed low in proud acknowledgement and, after another sip of whisky, said to her, 'Why don't you tell Barb what you said to me just now?'

Mae looked at me intently. 'Well, it's like this . . .' she began. 'Well, perhaps you wouldn't want to, but . . . well . . . even if I had to find another place, I need another maid. There's nothing to it and it's two pound a day and tips. What are you earning here? A fiver a week? What do you think? It's not as hard as the job you're doing now.'

It had all come out in a rush and now she was watching my reaction. Syd was standing behind her nodding his head vigorously and mouthing at me furiously to take the offer. I was thunderstruck.

'But I don't know anything about being a maid,' I protested. Visions of my grandmother's face came into my mind. A maid meant something very different in her book, and to be honest, I was already imagining a life below stairs and a starched apron.

'Nothing to it!' she repeated airily – in reckless disregard of what I later found to be the truth. Then she added wistfully, 'And it would be nice to have someone I could have a bit of a giggle with sometimes.'

Of course, that more or less hooked me. I always had been a sucker for feeling needed, and somehow, I had already begun to feel a protective affection towards Mae. Besides that, she was offering me more money than I was getting from both my jobs put together.

'I've had no experience, though.' I knew I was repeating myself, but I wanted to make sure that she realised the fact.

'Honestly, you don't need any, love. It's just that a girl can't be on her own in the flat and someone's got to be there for clients who come while I'm out.'

'When do you want an answer by?' I asked weakly.

'Well, now, if possible. I want to get Rabbits out of my flat right away if I can. Or if I know you'll come, I need to find one without a maid.' She was smiling at me in the most beguiling way, with the wistfulness still showing through, and I began to smile back.

I took the plunge. 'All right. I'll do it!' I said. 'But I hope you won't be sorry you asked. By the way, you know I'll need to give notice here.' I wasn't worried about my day job, as I had long dreamt of leaving that.

Mae's face fell. 'Can't you just walk out?' Then she added quickly, 'Oh well, see what you can do.' She swung round to Syd. 'What's the time?'

'Twenty-five to eight.'

Thinking aloud, Mae patted a finger against the palm of her other hand. 'I wonder if Charley – he's the agent – will be at The Intrepid Fox yet. I'll go round and wait.'

She gently pushed past Syd and jauntily made for the door, twiddling her fingers in the air to us. 'See ya,' she called out.

'You've done yourself a big favour there,' Syd confided. 'You'll see. Your uncle Syd wouldn't put you wrong. The missus of one of me mates is a maid: that's how I know.'

'Well I hope you're right,' I answered dubiously.

I had to break off then because another party of people had arrived and a whole load of dirty glasses had accumulated. By the time I was through, Mae had come back. Her face was a mixture of emotions.

'Was he there?' Syd asked quickly, avid for news.

'Yes, he was there all right,' she said grimly. 'But you know that bloody Rabbits . . . she's only gone and beaten me too it. She's offered to help him by showing other flats to the girls, so she can get herself fixed up somewhere else, and badmouth me at the same time, I don't doubt.' Then she shook her head as though to banish her annoyance and smiled. 'Give in your notice?' she asked brightly.

'Well, not yet. I thought I'd better wait and see how you got on first.'

'Do it now! We'll start on Monday.'

Syd leaned over. 'Lovey,' he said to me. 'Tell Jim you'd like to finish up tomorrow. He can only say no.'

I looked round to see where Jim was. He was standing with a tray hanging from his hand, chatting with a group at a table he'd just taken some drinks to. When he came back to the bar, I put it to him as boldly as I could: I wanted to leave and would like to do so as soon as possible. I told him I'd had the offer of another job that would make life a bit easier for me.

'Well,' he replied. 'Can you see me through tomorrow night? There's stacks of girls looking for evening work. 'Spect I'll be all right.'

'Yes, I can do that. Thanks a lot, Jim.'

Brimful of joy, I hurried back to Mae, who knew from my face before I reached her that everything was settled. 'I finish here tomorrow night,' I announced triumphantly.

She fished in her handbag and produced a small white visiting card, which she handed to me. It read:'M. Roberts, Plumber. 2nd Floor', followed by the address.

I looked up, tentatively amused, and caught a broad answering look of merriment on her face.

'Well, I've got to give clients something to help them remember where to find me, haven't I? And if their wives go rummaging through their wallets, they're not going to worry about a plumber, are they? It's a damn good idea too, I reckon, 'cos it's whore frost that does your pipes in – innit?'

Syd was guffawing; I was semi-choking.

'I'm off!' Mae said abruptly. 'Got to get that lock changed before Rabbits gets any funny ideas. See you about four o'clock Monday, then. Okay?' Impulsively, she leaned over and kissed me. 'Be seeing you.'

As she moved away, I thought of something. 'By the way, what sort of clothes should I wear?'

She considered for a moment, then replied, 'Something shapeless, if I were you.' And with an urchin grin, she was gone.

Syd looked as though he would have liked to follow her, but hadn't quite the nerve. Instead he said to me, 'Cheerio, Barb. I'd better buzz off and see if I can find the boys. They'll wonder what's happened to me.' Then he left too.

I took a deep breath and went back to the washing-up, my mind a jumble of events. Ronnie, whose sharp little eyes and ears missed nothing, said grumblingly, 'It's your affair – far be it from me to interfere – but you do know what sort of people you're getting mixed up with, don't you . . .?'

Four

~

I arrived home that night grateful to be alone at last to think about the evening's events. Although it wasn't cold in my room, I felt that I wanted to see the comforting glow of the gas fire and knelt to light it. I filled the kettle and put it on the ring. While waiting for it to boil, I gazed contentedly around my little room.

With the permission of the landlord and the extra money from the club, I had managed great improvements. I had replaced the blackout curtains with bright chintzy ones, and I'd bought a pretty orange bedspread to hide the army-surplus blankets. The paintwork on the walls, which had been a nasty waiting-room shade, was now all a nice shiny white. Even the drab, worn lino, made up of different scraps fitted together, had received my attention. Every morning before going to work, I painted another square yard of it with liquid lino in a pleasant burnt-orange colour. For a shilling each, I had purchased two orange boxes, which I'd stood on end and covered with American cloth. Both had a strong central partition that served as a shelf. One was now my larder, and the other a bedside table.

In one corner was a large earthenware pot, which I'd joyfully found marked at sixpence in a junk shop. This was now filled with sprays of beech leaves, which were slowly turning a beautiful bronze. I had also been guilty of what I considered to be two extravagances – a small bedside lamp with an orange shade, and a little Bush radio. I had just paid the first month's instalment of sixteen shillings on the latter. This was a wonderful buy; it still works perfectly today and has never had a thing go wrong with it. So, with my books on a home-made shelf and my possessions dotted around, it was all quite cosy, though still nothing to write home about.

Not that I could write home anyway. My grandmother had been quite specific on that point, telling me that as far as she was concerned, from the moment I left her roof I was dead. When I walked out, she'd thrown my ration book after me and said, 'And may you never know a day's happiness in your life.'

At times, I still found solitude quite a fearsome thought, but it was something I knew I had to get used to, and common sense told me that, in truth, I was no more alone now than I had been before I left home.

The kettle boiled and I made some coffee. Taking it over to the bed, I curled up on my nice new bedspread and, once again, suddenly felt the jubilation of having escaped from my grandmother. I wasn't quite sure what I had escaped to, but the joy remained. No need to feel nervous, I told myself. Life had improved, and although I was still lonely, at least now I was free.

I went and raided my biscuit tin. Even this gave me a thrill: just to do so without a voice from the next room shouting, 'And what do you think you're doing?' Then I indulged in another of the perks of freedom: a forbidden cigarette. The fire had heated up by now; it was pink, hot and popping merrily amongst its broken bits of fireclay.

For the first time since I'd left home, I felt that I could really relax and think properly. Until now, I had always been too busy or too exhausted to do so. I thought how nice it would be if there was someone with whom I could talk things over – but there wasn't and never had been. It had always been impossible for me to form a really close friendship with another girl because of the very limited amount of freedom I had been allowed. All my contemporaries were the 'bright young things' of the twenties and had been brought up accordingly, having been given lots of latitude, spending money and smart clothes. Because my circumstances were so different, I was too embarrassed to accept invitations to parties and outings and, out of awkwardness, withdrew into a shell of studiousness and apparent indifference. At work also, I had not been able to make friends: my responsibility for discipline put a stop to that. It was clear that whatever decisions I had to make now, they must be made without help: that I was mistress of my own ship and must choose my own course, no matter how unreliable my steering was.

I made myself another coffee to help me think about one aspect of my new job that was causing me some anxiety: sex. It was a subject about which I knew almost nothing. At that time, my formal sex education consisted of one cryptic remark made by my grandmother in a rare expansive moment: 'Men only want you for one thing.' Although the experience with my boss had, up to a point, proved her right, I really had very little idea what that 'one thing' was. I had gleaned the rudimentary facts from the girls at school, but these were of the most basic nature. Later, at art school, I had been far too engrossed in my work to give the matter much thought. Most of the other girls were beginning to go out with boys and, no doubt, learning quite a bit. I think I must have been one of the most ignorant young women of my age. I knew this, and it worried me that Mae did not. I wondered if I'd been unfair to her in accepting the job.

But then, I thought, brightening, surely a maid doesn't need to know anything about sex. I anticipated that one of the things I would have to do was take the various callers' hats and gloves, and that that was what earned the tips Mae had mentioned. As well as that, I supposed, I would keep the place clean, pour liqueurs or coffee as required and do bits of mending and such. Nothing to worry about there: these jobs were all familiar to me. And twelve pounds a week – riches!

I recalled some of the language I'd heard tonight – especially from Rabbits – and I grinned. It was almost poetic. At home, under extreme emotional stress, I had been allowed to say 'Blow!' and 'Dash!' How satisfying it must be, I thought, to really let rip as she had done.

I never once considered the fact that most people would have regarded the new life I was embarking on as the steep and slippery road down into hell. Mae seemed so bright and spirited that I regarded Ronnie's gloomy remark about the people I was getting mixed up with as peevishness at my leaving. It was so typical of the sort of thing my grandmother would come out with that I thought no more about it. Grandmother had always maintained that my mother had had to get married because of me, and that because of this, I was bound to inherit her morals and would need watching. Perhaps she was right.

A favourite teacher at art school had said that artists such as Renoir, Goya and Hogarth had lived, seen, thought and suffered. 'That,' he said, 'is what makes them great painters.' At that time, I would have got fairly high marks for the suffering and thinking bits but that was all. In my case, the sort of living and seeing my teacher meant had – until a few weeks ago – been strictly second-hand. This, I thought, is my great chance to really live and see. I would be foolish not to take it. The way I saw it, I would serve as maid and the experience would serve me.

The thought of being a maid presented a picture of myself in a frilly white cap and apron. I smiled at the image, though my stomach turned over at the thought of what my grandmother's reaction would be if she were ever to know. One of the things she was totally against was any of her family going into domestic service; she would have had hysterics had she known what I intended. But it only added extra appeal to me – here was an opportunity that I saw as a gesture of defiance against the thousand and one thou-shalt-nots that had hemmed my life in.

I decided that on the following day I would write a note to my boss at the studio, telling him that I had left and giving him the name of the best girl on the staff to replace me. The next day being Sunday, the studio would be empty and I could collect the few private possessions I had there without a fuss. I breathed a sigh of relief at the thought that soon I really would be free of the past.

I undressed and turned out the fire, which gave a few protesting pops as I climbed into bed. My thoughts turned towards Mae. I remembered the impetuous way she had leaned across the bar and kissed my cheek. Perhaps at last I had found a friend.

Five

~

On Monday afternoon, with butterflies in my stomach, Mae's address in my handbag and, as instructed, wearing my most shapeless dress, I arrived at what I thought to be the nearest underground station.

I'd allowed myself plenty of time, and for the first time, I found myself wandering around in Soho. My route to The Mousehole every evening had been through comparatively deserted streets in a quieter part of the outskirts. Now I ventured into the heartland and fell under the spell of a sordid magic that to this day has never faded for me.

I was overwhelmed by the noise, the smells, the teeming squalor of its life and its disregard for order. I passed fascinating little shops whose windows were hung with peculiar cheeses and strings of queer sausages, the barrels on the pavements filled with pickled herrings, olives and unrecognisable things, the racks holding newspapers from all over the world; Chinese shops with flattened, varnished ducks and cardboard-like dried fish hanging from cords amongst paper parasols and incense; rowdy street markets selling vegetables and fruit, some of which were completely unknown to me; dirt and debris everywhere; the many foreign restaurants and cafés, exuding pungent smells of herbs and garlic, and the raucous but melodic sounds of waitresses shouting orders in Italian down to long, dark kitchens. I was enchanted by it all.

I could have lingered indefinitely, drinking it all in, but there would be plenty of time to explore on other occasions and I thought I'd better find Mae's place. In the end, it wasn't so much a street as an alleyway – and a very dirty one at that. It clearly hadn't been swept for some time and then, probably, only by the wind. It was just a pedestrian way, partly cobbled, partly paved and with a slight dip in the middle. Whether this was by design or the wear of centuries, I didn't know, but it acted as a trap for rain and rubbish. Apart from that main furrow, there were other hollows, all full of sludgy water. I would hardly have been surprised had a window overhead been thrown open and more filth been hurled out to join it.

Looking up, I saw that all the buildings were three or four storeys high and the windows blind and grey, with many panes broken and replaced by cardboard. High above me was a narrow strip of sky, and if any sun ever penetrated this noisome little lane, its light would have been fleeting.

On one side were small shops with grimy windows, while the buildings opposite had railings in front where, looking down, you could see open basement areas full of refuse. Pigeons were everywhere, adding to the squalor. They were on every parapet and window ledge: a dirty, dishevelled, sinister little lot, covering everything with giant white droppings. Some were pottering about on the ground, scuffling amongst the debris. They somehow reminded me of the people I passed. Many of those I saw were lounging against the empty shops or railings, one old lady was rummaging in a dustbin, and in a doorway, another was seemingly taking an afternoon nap with all her worldly possessions in bundles beside her.

I nearly turned back, but just then, glancing down into

one of the basements, I saw such a pretty sight. Framed inside a sparkling, clean open window, hung with spotless lace curtains, a white-haired old lady was sitting knitting. Above her was a cage in which a canary sang merrily, and on her window ledge were two sleek old cats: one washing while the other snoozed. There were many potted plants on the steps leading down to her door, as well as others hanging from nails everywhere.

Mae's place is probably nice too, I thought. Some people just choose to live in unusual places.

Looking around, I saw that I had almost reached the end of the alleyway and must have missed the house I wanted. I turned around and retraced my steps a little way until I found it.

By now, I was having not just second but third thoughts. I shuddered as I took a step through the open street door into the hallway. The long, dark bare boards stretched ahead covered with almost as much debris as there was in the alleyway outside, and it smelled just as bad. The grubby wallpaper hung in strips and the exposed plaster was covered with scrawls and graffiti. At the far end I could see a split and broken staircase turning in a dogleg and disappearing from sight. Beyond that – what? I wasn't sure that I wanted to know. Just then, I heard a low voice in my ear:

'Looking for someone, my dear?'

A man had sidled up to me and was blocking the doorway. On his face was the look my boss had worn a few weeks ago. I didn't know quite how to get rid of him without being rude, but I knew that look well enough to know the difficulties that could ensue. I muttered, 'I'm all right, thank you,' and self-consciously traversed the passage, praying that he wouldn't follow. At the bend in the stairs, I stole a glance back and was relieved to see that although he hadn't gone, he had remained standing in the doorway. I carried on until I reached the first-floor landing, where a boarded-up window was lit by a very dim naked electric light bulb. There were two doors, secured by massive padlocks. The rubbish began to thin out as I climbed the next flight, possibly because a small lidless dustbin was handily placed on the next turn in the stairs.

The second-floor landing was much like the first, but the dirt had been swept over the top step, where it lay in an untidy ridge. The window here was not boarded up, and light struggled through panes that were covered in transparent paper, ornamented to look like stained glass: no doubt to afford some privacy from the buildings to the rear. The doors here were not padlocked; the one to my left was ajar, and fixed to it with four drawing pins was a piece of cardboard bearing the name 'Mae' written in nail varnish.

I knocked.

'Come on in, love,' I heard Mae's voice call. I pushed the door and went in.

Along a short hallway and through a second open door ahead, I found her sitting on a divan bed and pulling on a pair of stockings. She looked up and grinned at me.

'Hallo, lovey! So you got here! I wondered if you would.'

Me too, I thought. Out loud I said, 'Hello – yes, it wasn't too difficult.'

'Now what about a nice cup of tea and I'll show you everything before we start.'

Start what? I thought, following her back into the hall and into a tiny kitchen. I still had the idea that being a maid involved some sort of domestic work.

From what I could judge, the entire flat had once been a single large room, one corner of which had been partitioned to make the small entrance hall and kitchen and creating an L-shaped bedroom. In contrast to the staircase I'd just braved, this little flatlet was a paradise, though compared with anyone else's idea of a home, it wasn't much. The block must have been built about a century ago and Mae's bit was in need of a little care. The hall and kitchen had been painted in cream and fitted with brown linoleum. Opposite the kitchen door stood a low, old-fashioned unit with two drawers above and a cupboard below. On top of this was the big brother of the gas ring in my bed-sitter: a double one. On it, an aluminium kettle was just beginning to sing. Mae was chatting away, showing me where things were kept, as she prepared the tea.

At the end of the kitchen, in line with the outer door, was a window overlooking the backs of surrounding buildings. It provided no sight of the sky: just white-splodged bricks, water pipes and, of course, a row of the same vile-looking pigeons lining every window ledge. Below the window was a deep chipped stone sink full of dirty crockery, from which Mae produced a teapot. I would have liked to have washed it, but was too late. She put it on the small enamel draining board and wiped some grease off the lid with one of the dirty tea towels that were strewn everywhere. She seemed oblivious to the matchsticks and cigarette ends covering the floor, and added another butt to them after absent-mindedly attempting to put it in the overflowing bucket underneath the sink. The two chairs were piled high with clothes and the walls were splashed with grease and dirty water. I rescued two cups and saucers from the sink and washed them. Mae was still chattering:

'See what I mean about Rabbits?' she said. 'Just look at this place. Makes you sick, don't it?'

I cast my eyes around again dutifully and agreed. I dreaded even to think what the cupboards and drawers contained. Mae continued:

'I'm that pleased to get rid of her, I tell you straight, love – filthy old pig! Come on, let's have our tea in the other room; it's more comfortable in there.' Picking up our cups, we left the foul hole and shut the door behind us.

The other room was more comfortable – marginally. I noted that the filth was less concentrated as I shifted a heap of clothes off a basketwork chair, sat down and cleared a space for my cup on the cluttered dressing table. Mae sat on the bed and deposited hers on the little bedside table. I looked at the rose-pink Regency stripes and wondered whether it was Mae who'd decided on this touch of glamour. Instinctively, I compared her efforts at home-making to my own, noting the cheap but newish wardrobe, the chest of drawers and dressing table. I decided that one of the first jobs I would undertake would be to tidy this: I wondered how anybody could be so nonchalant about the festoons of stockings and bras that hung from its open drawers.

Although it was still daylight, the pink brocade curtains were closed. I supposed, correctly, that they were never opened, but at least they gave the room a certain cosiness. My artist's eye for colour took in the warm glow from the pink-shaded bedside light, added to by another from the standard lamp round the corner and one from the kitchen's electric fire. I put my feet on one of the two fluffy rugs, carefully avoiding the screwed-up paper tissues and the odd stocking strewn on their surface. On the bedside table – amongst a welter of dirty cups, several overflowing ash-trays, empty cigarette packets and make-up – stood a large dark-blue cardboard box with the word DUREX printed across it in bold white letters.

I drank my tea, listened to Mae and wondered when a cap and apron would be thrust at me, or, more appropriately, a mobcap and dungarees. I was already absorbed in planning a campaign for cleaning up the place, but Mae was still chattering away, obviously in a party mood. I could tell from the tone of her voice that she was leading up to something special. I shook my mind free of brooms and dusters to give her my full attention.

'... but – here – do you know what? After I left you on Saturday, I couldn't do any more work till I got someone in to change the lock, so I thought I'd go and get a meal in Luigi's place – and guess who was in there.'

'I've no idea!' I answered, knowing it would be Rabbits.

'Rabbits!'

'No!' I gasped, impressed with my ability to act my part. 'What did you do? Walk out?'

'Me? I don't think so. She's the one who should've walked out.'

'What happened?'

Mae chuckled. 'Nothing, for about ten minutes – until I'd got me grub served. She had to wait till then, didn't she? I was having spaghetti and she couldn't resist it. So I got the lot in me face!'

'Strewth!' I said, using Syd's catchphrase. 'Then what?'

'Well, you can imagine: I fairly boiled over. I fetched her such a clump behind the earhole it spun her round. I got both hands in her hair from behind and nearly pulled her bleeding head off. You should have heard her scream! But the bitch kept kicking back at my shins and I didn't know what to do about that. Just look at my legs!'

I looked, and through her nylons I could see that both legs were black and blue, with several bumps and a gash.

'*Ugh!*' I winced. 'Nasty!'

She leaned over, picked up the cup in front of her and took a swig, which she hastily spat out. It was the wrong cup, containing dregs from goodness knows when.

'I bet that's her cup too!' she said. 'Anyway, Luigi came

up and put a stop to it and threw her out. He offered me another plate of spaghetti after I'd cleaned myself up, but somehow I didn't fancy it.'

'Do you think you'll have any more trouble with her?' I asked.

Mae shrugged. 'I'll try to keep out of her way, but if she comes here again, she'll be sorry, 'cos I'll be ready for her next time.'

She reached for her handbag and, opening it wide, held it out for me to see inside. There, besides her purse, keys and miscellanea, lay a large penknife. She removed it and clicked out a wicked-looking blade.

'Next time,' she said ominously, 'I'll carve her, I swear I will!'

Ronnie's words came back to me as I watched Mae retract the blade and drop the knife back into her bag, but this time I feared his warning might have been well placed.

Mae took a sip out of the right cup and said, 'We're going to have such fun, us two!'

It sounded a weird sort of maid-and-mistress relationship to me, but I was all for democracy.

I pushed the thought of the knife to the back of my mind, hoping it was just for show. 'I'd like to do a bit of spring-cleaning,' I ventured. 'You know: get the place more comfortable.'

'Go right ahead, love. Anything to make you happy. That is, if you have the time; we get a bit busy, you know.'

Surely, I thought, all the clients don't come at once. Aloud, I said, 'Do we?'

'Well, let's hope so,' she answered, lounging back on the bedspread and puffing out great clouds of cigarette smoke. 'As soon as I've finished this fag, I must put me face on and get cracking.'

And get cracking she certainly did. It wasn't long before

she was made up and ready for action. I was in the tiny kitchen, trying to decide how to tackle its filth, when she went shooting past me out of the door and clacking down the stairs, tossing a breezy 'See you, love' over her shoulder as she went. I was alone in the flat. My mind, I think, still refused to get to grips with what was about to happen. The entire flat was hardly large and the wall was only a partition, with plasterwork on one side and bare on the other. Sounds from one room were almost as audible in the other. Mae was about to . . . to do *it* . . . and all I could think about was whether to deal with the sink first, or the floor, or the overflowing bin.

I had made some sort of start on the clutter when, in what seemed an astonishingly short time, I heard footsteps ascending the stairs, a male set closely followed by Mae's own. I swept the cigarette butts on the floor into a pile, using anything that came to hand to do it. (There was, of course, no broom). Then the door to the flat shot open, and the two pairs of footsteps swept through into the bedroom. Encased in my little kitchen as I was, I saw nothing.

I began to tackle the detritus littering the sink and its surround.

There must have been sounds from the room beyond, but I think I can honestly say I heard none of them, so intently was I concentrating on the task at hand. I was thankful to have my work in the kitchen to focus on. Then Mae's voice sang out to me and her arm appeared through the bedroom door, bearing cash. I took the money and scuttled back to the safety of my kitchen, feeling like a rather nervous stage hand. I continued to make a tiny dent in the mess surrounding me.

In what again seemed like a remarkably short space of time, doors opened and closed, and I heard male footsteps leaving the apartment, followed very soon after by Mae, who shot me some cheerful parting expression – 'cheerio', 'see you', 'bearing up?' – as she darted away. Apart from these few moments of friendly contact, and always of course the moment when her hand appeared through the bedroom door to bring home to me the money that lay behind all this, I saw neither Mae nor her clients, and avoided thinking about what was happening. The sink and the floor and the stains on the wall and the piles of rubbish occupied me completely.

After half an hour or so, Mae had seen three clients. Within an hour she had dealt with half a dozen all told. It was towards this point, and utterly bewildered, that I began to realise what prostitution really was.

'But Mae,' I wailed, as she started for the stairs once more, 'I read in a book once that eight or nine men in succession could kill a woman!'

She paused with her face just above the banister rails. 'It's a good thing they're wrong then, isn't it?' she said, grinning at me. 'Ta-rah, love; see you.' And she clattered off again.

When she returned with the next client, I could hear her laughing like mad and repeating my words. On the way into the bedroom, I caught sight of 'the punter' for the first time. He seemed like a very ordinary man of about thirty, suited and safe-looking – certainly nothing like the picture my imagination had created. He glanced at me and smiled. Afterwards, he saw fit to lash out with a ten-shilling note as a tip for me.

That was another thing I'd got wrong: I had thought that the wage of two pounds a night was to be my main income and the tips would be tiny extras. In that first hour, it would have taken a brain a lot denser than mine not to realise that the truth was the reverse. Every time Mae's arm shot out at me with her fee of a pound or more to protect, there, amongst the paper money, was silver for me, usually half a crown's worth.

I was determined to be a proper maid and bring some sort of order into the place in the incredibly short space of time it took her to come bustling up the stairs with another 'boyfriend'. As I became braver, whenever she left the bedroom to go on one of her swift sorties into the street, I dashed in, madly collecting armfuls of the accumulated rubbish. After the rush of that first hour, Mae started not to slow down exactly, but to allow breaks for cups of tea and gossip and sly comments on the quirks and peculiarities of the men she'd seen.

On that first day, I ran the gamut of every known emotion. When at last, somewhere around midnight, Mae shoved me into a taxi and sent me home, I threw myself back on to the seat in a state bordering on bewilderment. I thought I ought to feel thoroughly shocked, nauseated and dirty, but I was amazed to find that I didn't. All I could feel was the ache around my stomach muscles caused by laughing at the flippant way in which Mae conducted her business. I had learnt a lot that day, but the most wonderful thing was that I'd learnt how to really laugh.

Six

~

The following day, when I arrived at the little alleyway, I was surprised to find myself regarding it with something like affection. Nothing had changed, but in some subtle way, I had. The rubbish still lay about in rotting heaps; in their aimless shufflings, the pigeons and the people were just as uncouth as they had been the day before, but I no longer regarded them with distaste. It was as though I had finally found my own people. I walked slowly along, relishing this fact. I was amongst fellow outcasts. That day the flat felt homely and lived-in, and it was warm with yesterday's laughter. Mae, who had arrived only a few minutes before from where she lived in Paddington, had already put the kettle on and greeted me cheerily. Everything felt good.

'You know,' I reflected, as we were drinking our tea in the bedroom, 'if I had a key, I could get here before you and do some cleaning. The stairs and this room, for instance: I could never do them while you're working – at least not the way you work. The place gets like Victoria station!'

'Well, don't kill yourself; it's already looking miles better than it did.' She glanced at her bedside table, which now held only one cup and one ashtray. 'I'll get another key cut if it makes you feel any better – had to give Charley the spare one. Let me know what cleaning things you want – I don't s'pose there's any there – and I'll drop a list in at the oil shop.'

On her first trip out, I reminded her of this, and an hour later, I was presented with a shiny new Yale key (as we were the only people in the building, only the front door was ever locked). I then listed all the things I needed to assist me in my battle for hygiene. It was a long list. Mae had been right: we had nothing. The only cleaning implements consisted of a mop in a bucket of turgid liquid – as I pulled it out, its strands fell off with the weight of the water – and an old broom whose bristles were practically worn down to the wood. She took the order to the shop at the end of the alley, and during the afternoon, an elderly man in a grey overall delivered everything I needed.

'Looks as though someone's going to do some cleaning,' he said, as he dumped the large cardboard box on the kitchen floor and divested himself of the new broom and mop. When he straightened up, he spoke the words I was going to hear over and over again during the next few weeks;

'New here, aren't you?'

'Yes,' I said. 'It's only my second day.'

'You're on to a good thing with that girl; she hustles like nobody's business. The wife and I watch her sometimes. Cor blimey, must be in and out like a fly!'

Just then, we heard the 'fly' returning. After tactfully letting her and her new acquisition get into the bedroom, and with a wink in my direction, the hardware man left.

He was right: Mae *was* in and out like a fly. There was something metronomic in the way she worked. She marched up the stairs behind each man – never in front of him, in case he changed his mind halfway up and ran off.

When she had safely landed him in her room, they would stay there on average for five or ten minutes, and then the man would depart on his own. A couple of minutes later, he would be followed by Mae. Only a minute or two would elapse before the process was repeated.

During those first days, I drew a sort of blackout curtain over my thoughts: at least in regard to what went on in the bedroom. Mae, without knowing it, made it easy for me to do this, or perhaps I had Rabbits to thank, because out of habit, Mae was still working to the rigid rules that her tough former maid had laid down. This state of affairs was to be short-lived, but it did help me over the initial stages of what was to become an extraordinary partnership.

On this, my second day, some of the initial startling strangeness had worn off, and not receiving any further shocks to the system, I began to sit up and take notice of everything going on around me.

Now aware that men who consorted with prostitutes were not the outwardly sinister and debauched creatures I had supposed, I no longer tried to keep out of sight. After glimpsing the first customer by accident, I had realised that one of the reasons I was there was to be seen, so that the clients would know Mae wasn't alone. I began – albeit it with extreme shyness – to glance at them as they passed the kitchen door.

To my bewilderment, one after another turned out to be as unthreatening as the first. These were men I had seen all my life, on buses and trains and out shopping with their wives. I saw men who had been sent out in the morning in clean shirts and polished shoes – men who had kissed their children and their wives a fond goodbye as they left for work. Some wore trilbies; some wore caps; some even wore bowlers and carried rolled umbrellas. I was shocked to realise that any of the men I had ever known, even my own relatives, could be doing this.

In they came and out they went, all these respectable men. Here and there, a roughneck was thrown in for variety. Gradually, the shock I felt metamorphosed into the attitude most women adopted towards the opposite sex. I quickly came to know the meaning of that shrug of the shoulders and the scornful utterance: 'Men!'

During the afternoon of that second day, I was somewhat disconcerted by a man who came up during Mae's absence. He breezed up to the landing door, eyed me up and down, and said crisply, 'How much?'

When I realised what he meant, I blushed furiously. For a moment I was speechless with indignation.

'I'm the maid!' I said at last.

He retreated hastily, leaving me feeling that I had narrowly preserved myself from a fate worse than death. I decided that a shapeless dress wasn't effective enough. It was evident that this kind of maid *did* need a uniform after all: an apron at least. With some regret, I also decided to abandon my new toy: my make-up.

By the time the day was about two thirds over, I was really getting into the swing of things. I even had a little notebook of tear-out pages in which I could jot down the takings. I was sure that once I got the place clean, everything would run on oiled wheels.

Mae came tramping up once more, this time with a sad and worried-looking man in a Homburg hat. I stationed myself outside the bedroom door, waiting for the money to be passed through, and complimented myself that I was already acting like an old hand at the game.

Why, I thought – somewhat prematurely as it turned out – there's nothing to it.

There was some discussion going on inside the bedroom,

and I waited for longer than usual for the door to open its accustomed six inches and Mae's undraped arm to come out.

'He's staying for a bit,' she hissed. 'There's fifteen bob for you there and a fiver for me.' Then she shut the door.

Ah, I thought, a chance for me to get a few jobs done if I'm lucky.

I unpacked my cleaning materials as lovingly as if they had been pieces of Spode china, and made the beginnings of an onslaught on the dirty crockery. In the midst of all this happy domesticity, I heard footsteps mounting the stairs, and presently a man rounded the corner. He was very large, with a red face, and he looked as though he belonged to a road gang. Breathing adenoidally, he entered the little hall.

'Where is she, then?' he asked in a hoarse whisper that shook the walls.

'In there,' I answered, pointing to the bedroom door. Turning on my best maid's manner, I added, 'She's busy. Will you come back again later?'

'Not going down there again – fed up with hanging around in the street. I'll wait.'

With that, he pushed past me into the little kitchen and, with a gusty sigh, lowered himself into one of the chairs.

My self-assurance was gone: this was something I wasn't prepared for. To be closeted in a small space with a large man who was waiting for sex just didn't feel right, even in this new world of mine. I felt flustered, and turned back to my washing-up, only to feel my neck crawling as I felt his eyes on me. I thought about escape: all of a sudden, the banisters on the landing seemed to cry out for my new feather dusters. But lead settled in my stomach as I realised I couldn't very well leave him alone in the room where the money was. I feared he might clobber me while I wasn't looking. Nervous, but putting on a brave face, I turned to face him again. So far, he hadn't taken his eyes off me. Suddenly, he spoke.

'You're new,' he said, as though I was guilty of a wilful deception. He returned to his oafish staring. After a while, he made another discovery: 'Bit young, ain't you?'

I was trying to think up a suitable answer when I heard stealthy movements on the stairs.

Oh Lord, not another one! I craned my neck round the kitchen door, just as a timid little man wearing glasses and a raincoat appeared at the top. My relief was palpable; I was no longer alone, and at least this one looked inoffensive.

'Is she in?' he whispered, darting little nervous glances about the place.

'Yes, but she is busy,' I answered, in a voice that I hoped would be loud enough for Mae to hear.

I was lucky. There were movements from the bedroom, and Mae's voice sang out, 'That someone for me? Tell him to wait a few secs. I'm just coming.'

I ushered the little chap before me into the kitchen. At the sight of the other man, he froze, and would have bolted except that I was behind him, resolutely blocking his exit.

So there we were: jammed like commuters in the rush hour, trying not to look at one another – until Mae got rid of her long-playing customer.

'What's this, a bleeding orgy?' she exclaimed when she saw us. 'Well, who's first?'

The large man managed to squeeze his way through, and after taking a deep breath, I asked the timid one to sit down.

He spent this waiting period studying his nails and casting surreptitious fleeting glances in my direction whenever he thought I wasn't looking. My jangled nerves began to calm down, and something akin to confidence took over as I lit a cigarette.

When the two men had been seen to and dispatched, I rushed into the bedroom, where Mae was pulling on her skirt.

'Did I do the right thing?' I asked anxiously, feeling very inadequate. 'Or if there's two, should I send one away and tell him to come back later?'

'Just stick one of them in the waiting room,' she replied, zipping herself up.

'Waiting room!' I gasped. 'What waiting room?'

She stared at me, nonplussed. 'Didn't I show you the waiting room? I must be going round the bend.'

She went into the kitchen and I followed her. Opening a meat safe, she stuck her head in, fished around a bit and finally emerged triumphant, holding a mortise key.

'Here, follow *me-ee*,' she said, in deep, sexy tones. She made her way in sinuous style across the landing to the battered door on the other side. This she unlocked and threw open with a loud crash.

'*Voila!*' she announced.

She stood back to allow me to peer in. My eyes took in a room of about eight feet by ten. I couldn't help but wonder at the odd contents: a fitted cupboard, open and stuffed with ropes, strange old garments, a few tattered books and a number of rather bizarre objects. I decided to ask about this another time. Taking up about a third of the total space was a large office desk, and though I hadn't exactly expected anything resembling the dentist's or the doctor's, I was glad to see that the waiting room did at least contain various chairs for those who would have to wait: a real granny's armchair, covered in grubby chintz, a basketwork chair and a wooden stool. There was also an oil stove and an electric fire. In here, as in the bedroom, the curtains were closed.

'Well that is handy!' I said at last. I was relieved that at least the crush in the kitchen need never be repeated.

'I should say it's handy. Don't know what we'd do without it some Saturdays, and as for kinks and things, well . . . !' She paused eloquently.

My growing confidence wilted somewhat with her last sentence. There were innuendoes there that I didn't understand, and I had a nervous feeling that it wasn't all going to be as simple as I had supposed.

As the second day melted into the third, I gradually became acclimatised to the conveyor-belt system. I was glad I now had a key, as it was evident that during the working day, I could do nothing but attend to Mae; the sink was still crammed with the same crockery it had held when I arrived. Numerous cups of tea seemed necessary to her existence; they were mostly left untouched, though, as they served largely as an excuse for a pause and a chat. I became a tea addict myself, and found something comforting and basic about making and drinking a pot. Basic comfort was needed in this new life of mine.

While we were having a rare proper tea break, with the door to the flat shut, we heard a gentle but steady tramping of feet on the stairs. It sounded as though we were being invaded by an army of orderly soldiers. The steps halted outside our door and were followed by a polite knock. We stared at one another, then both made for the door, Mae slightly ahead. When she opened it, over her shoulder I saw a row of anxious choirboy-like heads, each surmounted by neatly slicked hair and balanced on top of a tidy navy-blue serge suit. There was a long silence as we all gazed at one another. The leading alto tried to say something but failed. Mae broke the silence.

'Look, duckies, I'm just having a cup of tea.' She paused.

'Come back in a couple of years.' She closed the door and leaned against it weakly.

'Well, did you see that? Can't have been more than sixteen years old, any of 'em. One would have been bad enough, but four! Blimey!' She brooded over her tea for a bit. 'I don't know what kids are coming to these days. It's bloody disgusting!'

At the venerable age of twenty-one, I agreed.

Seven

~

The next day I arrived almost at the crack of dawn. First I examined the wallpaper along the hallway, and decided there was so much of it missing already that there wasn't much point in trying to stick back the loose bits. So I had a jolly quarter of an hour ripping it all off. While I was doing this, for the first time I noticed the array of ancient fuse boxes high up towards the ceiling. They hung off the wall, dangling a plethora of bare cables and cobwebs – surely they couldn't work in that state. Then my eye caught sight of the thick black electric wire running along the angle of the ceiling and disappearing through a small hole in the wall into the building next door. So that was the secret! I shook my head and returned to my work.

It was eerie, alone there in that large derelict building with all its locked rooms. Even the shop on which it all rested was boarded up and empty. But for the sound of a dripping tap somewhere, it was as quiet as the grave. The noises I made with my cleaning seemed out of place, and I could feel the ghostly inmates of the past watching my efforts. The pigeons on the window ledges outside didn't help my nerves much either: several times I jumped with fright as, in sudden clattering batches, they launched into flight.

Amongst the litter on the hall floor were a number of

flyers in varying stages of decomposition, the tattered remains of a rates demand and a couple of mildewed Inland Revenue envelopes, optimistically addressed to 'The Occupier'. I swept them up with the rest of the rubbish, then scraped away at the numerous lumps of chewing gum. Finally I scrubbed the stairs and passageway with strong pine disinfectant. I had just had time to wash the grime off myself when Mae arrived.

'Crikey!' she gasped. 'I thought I'd come to the wrong house – smells like a bleeding hospital!'

'By the way,' I said, 'did you know that we are using next door's electricity?'

'Go on! Is that a fact?'

I took her down to show her the disappearing flex.

'Well, what d'you know!' She stared up at it for a while, then burst out laughing, 'What a stinker! That bastard Charley has just had twenty-five quid out of me for electricity.'

During the course of the following mornings, I spring-cleaned the bedroom and waiting room, polishing the furniture and the floor, shampooing the rugs and cleaning the paintwork. What had appeared to be brown lino in the little hallway and kitchen turned out to be cream tiles.

With rubber gloves and a strong stomach, I turned out the cupboards and drawers in the kitchen. I found milk bottles with thick mould swimming on an inch or two of liquid; potatoes rotting among their own tendrils; smelly, lumpish dishcloths and other things I couldn't even put a name to.

After cramming all this into other people's dustbins along the alleyway, I scrubbed everything in the kitchen and arranged my new cleaning materials on the shelves under the sink. Of provisions I found nothing, beyond the half-empty packet of tea, the tin of milk and the tiny amount of sugar that were in use, so I wrote out another shopping list and presented it to Mae.

'You'll break me!' she said affably.

The next time she went out, she dropped the order in at the nearest grocer's. He soon turned up in person to satisfy his curiosity as to what had prompted this unprecedented demand.

His first words were, of course, 'You're new here, aren't you?'

He scrutinised me carefully. 'Haven't seen you around the area before neither, I don't think,' he said, continuing his bird-like examination. I made no reply, and he rambled on. 'Well, let me tell you, you're on to a right gold mine with that one. They call her the Queen of Soho round here, you know. They say she can earn more than any other two of 'em put together. Must say, I've never known anything like her – and I've been around a good few years. Heart of gold, too: real ray of sunshine. Oh well, better be off; this won't buy the baby a new bonnet, as they say!'

With this, he nimbly trotted off down the stairs. Though I made allowances for exaggeration, I felt impressed and pleased with what I'd heard. To me, Mae had seemed to be special from the start, and it gave me great satisfaction to know that others regarded her that way too. So I, with my complete lack of credentials, was working for the Queen of Soho!

Still musing on my new position in life, I began stacking the groceries into the meat safe. As I put the last couple of things away and stood admiring the effect, I heard Mae's voice behind me:

'You're just like a bloody squirrel, you are!'

I swung round in surprise. She had crept out from the bedroom and had been watching me. The way I saw her then is the way I so often see her now in my memory. It was such a characteristic pose: she was leaning against the door jamb, pulling on her gloves – she never went out without them – and squinting through her cigarette smoke. I will never forget her careless elegance. She was wearing a beautifully cut suit of mushroom gabardine, but whereas most women would have chosen a smart frilly blouse or a turtle-necked sweater to wear with it, all Mae had on underneath was a bra; between the immaculate lapels, her wonderful creamy cleavage was visible. Consequently, although she was dressed in the clothes of a lady, she looked like a tart – which, after all, was what she intended.

'You look so nice,' I told her.

'But of course I do!' she said with mock haughtiness, striking another elegant pose. Then, twirling the bunch of keys she always took with her, she was gone.

I put some sugar in a bowl, made some sandwiches and cut the cake the grocer had brought. Later that afternoon, we sat down to tea like ordinary, respectable people. Laughing at the scene, Mae said that perhaps she'd been wrong about her flat being like a hospital: it was more like a vicarage.

Despite her jokes, she must have caught the home-making bug too, because she started to bring in little things to improve the place – a couple of scatter cushions from home, an ornament or two. Now and again, when she came back with a man, she also brought something that had caught her eye in a shop. Once, it was an antique toasting fork – what she intended to do with it was a mystery – and on another occasion she produced an embroidered tea cosy and a pair of sugar tongs. All in all, we were really getting quite 'refeened', as Mae put it.

The toilet we used was down on the floor below, and so that no one could lurk in there or leap out at us, we kept the key for it hanging in the kitchen. Clients who wanted to use the toilet were handed a bucket – 'Because,' said Mae, 'if I let them go down there, they might suddenly change their minds about coming up again and scarper.'

I was now wearing an apron: not exactly a typical frilly one, but enough to prevent the clients from being confused about my role. Furthermore, I wore my hair primly wound in a tight bun, high on the back of my head. I had reverted to the Sunlight-soap-and-no-make-up image, hoping that this might also help to make me appear just a little forbidding.

I finally felt I had things under control. By arriving earlier than Mae each day, I could maintain things in reasonable order. By now, I had begun to turn out the drawers in her bedroom, and had mended a mass of various garments. I had also jettisoned about a hundred laddered stockings and was at last able to close the drawers properly.

Now that I'd tidied up, I had more time to think during Mae's frequent absences. This wasn't altogether a good thing. I began to realise just how nerve-racking it was to be alone in that building – especially if Mae was out for longer than usual. The street door was always left open after she'd started work, and there was always the possibility of Rabbits coming up to vent her spite on me. Rabbits, though, was at least a known quantity; what I feared most was the unknown. Whenever I heard the slither of a man's raincoat brushing against the sides of the narrow staircase when I was alone, I felt a mounting terror, rising to panic the moment before the customer came into view. When they had actually appeared and I could get a look at them and see that they were far more nervous than I was, my fears would subside.

I had to make sure I listened out for anyone who came up, because, if someone did manage to get past our landing unheard, he could hide round the bend of the stairs above us, listening for Mae to go out, and get me on my own with the cash. There was a lot of money in the place, and the danger grew greater as the evening wore on into darkness and even more accumulated. The clients I had to be most wary of were the first-timers. Some were potentially nasty, and I often prayed that Mae would return before they became unpleasant.

My anxiety didn't end when the men disappeared into the bedroom with Mae. Though she always closed the bedroom door, it was left unlocked so that I could rush in if violence erupted.

What I had come to regard as the 'Rabbits Regime' was still in full force, and I was getting used to the constant stream of men in and out. That is not to say I didn't get the odd jolt. For example, Mae was closeted in the bedroom with a client one afternoon when I heard a tap on the entrance door. There had been no sound of footsteps and I looked up, startled, to see a vicar standing there, smiling benevolently. He looked so pure in contrast to the surroundings, with his honest, open face, fair hair and brilliant white dog collar. I was filled with confusion and felt pangs of guilt.

'Is Mae in?' he asked with a smile.

So he knew her! Mae had never mentioned that she had any religious convictions: if she had, it was odd but not impossible. I stammered out that she was engaged for the moment. My hopes that he would go away were soon dashed.

'Well in that case I'll sit and wait for her, if you don't mind,' he said serenely. After a while he added: 'I haven't seen you here before, have I?'

'No,' I agreed in a small voice. 'I've only just started.'

I busied myself at the sink and hoped that Mae wouldn't

be long. I supposed the man to be the saintly sort who was willing to risk censure by calling on a prostitute to give counsel or advice. Perhaps Mae was in his parish and he was determined to make no distinction between the members of his flock.

At last Mae released her previous client and greeted the vicar cordially, before taking him into the bedroom. Considering this to be a parochial visit, I didn't bother to stand outside the door as usual. When Mae opened it a few minutes later, I thought it was to summon me in to share the vicar's words of comfort. But when I left the kitchen and turned towards the partly opened door, there was Mae's arm, rising up like a beautiful swan's neck with money in its beak.

I felt cheated and strangely angry. Who could you trust if not a vicar? I couldn't look at him when he left . . . but then who was I to throw stones? I stood there deliberating; perhaps he was an actor – this was, after all, the centre of Theatreland. As soon as he had gone, I ran in to Mae to ask if he was real.

'Is he a real vicar, do you mean? Course he is! They are men like all the rest. True, I do get kinks who come dressed up like vicars, but you know them straight away. They act all sanctimonious and start preaching while they're on the job. I've got several real ones – they never say a word about religion.'

I resolved never to be surprised by anything ever again. It was to be my saving grace.

The speed with which Mae worked had worried me right from the beginning, and I soon talked her into slowing down a bit. Consequently, our life became noticeably more leisurely, and we spent a little more of our time in chatter and, more often than not, helpless laughter. Whenever a client left, Mae's voice would sing out from the bedroom, 'Where are you, y'sod? Come and talk to me!' Then she would begin rummaging through drawers and cupboards, looking for a dress or suit to show me, or ask if I thought she looked better in the blue earrings or the gold. Or she might be in a reminiscing mood and recount some childhood anecdote, or a yarn concerning some 'geezer' she'd known.

Often during these interludes, while we were still sitting in the bedroom with our heads together – she clad in only a bra, suspender belt and stockings – a client would venture upstairs. 'That's a bit of luck,' she would say to me under her breath. 'Now I won't have to get dressed.' Then to the new arrival she would give a joyous 'Hello, love! You're just the one I was hoping to see. I've been talking about you to Babs. Haven't I, Babs? You haven't met my new maid yet, have you? Now don't you forget, any time I'm busy, you come up and Babs'll make you a nice cup of tea – won't you, Babs?'

Smiling, I would then stand up to go. Often the men would grin wolfishly and suggest that there was no need for me to rush off. Mae would scold them fondly: 'Cheeky bugger. Want two for the price of one, do you?' As I returned to the kitchen, I would hear her demanding to know why whoever it was hadn't been to see her for such a long while and saying she'd missed him and he mustn't leave it so long again or she'd think he didn't love her.

It was this sort of treatment that made her so successful. Each one of her clients thought he was someone special, and she had a long list of regulars. The grocer hadn't exaggerated after all: she was a queen indeed.

Though she never said much about her background – and I quickly learnt that it wasn't the done thing to ask – it was during our many tête-à-têtes that she told me that she'd been married very young, and that at eighteen, her husband had gone off, leaving her with a baby to support.

'So that's what really started me on this life,' she said.

She had eventually allowed a couple to foster the baby while she found work. Gradually she discovered that she was good at the profession she'd chosen, and even enjoyed it at times. Eventually the couple had adopted her child and Mae had made this new life her own.

She told me bits about her love life – which she kept completely apart from her work. Apparently she was 'almost between lovers' at the present time.

'What do you mean, *almost*?' I asked.

'Well, it's difficult to say,' she mused. 'I'm sort of finished with Alphonse and I haven't really got started with Tony. Fact is, I don't know whether I ever will. Tony's a Malt, you see, and I don't trust the Maltese. Haven't had one yet, and, from what I hear of them, it's just as well. But he says he loves me. Oh, Babs, if you could hear the way he says it!'

I didn't pursue it. I have always been of the opinion that if somebody wants me to know something, they'll tell me. Perhaps this is down to my upbringing, or perhaps some instinct told me to leave the subject alone. If instinct it was, it was an accurate one. Tony was to prove to be bad news.

Eight

~

Saturday came, and I felt like an old hand. Finding it hard to believe I'd been working at The Mousehole and the studio only one week ago, I walked to the flat through the late July sunshine. I found it even harder to credit that it was less than two months since I'd left home. I had learnt so much in that short time that it seemed incredible. And to crown it all, I'd finally discovered all about sex.

My carnal education had mainly come about by accident. During my assault on the chaos in the bedroom and waiting room, I had unearthed a massive quantity of photographs. It was from these that, in the crudest way possible, I was enlightened about the birds and the bees and finally learnt what lay beneath the statues' fig leaves and the models' posing pouches. I also found out – graphically – the number of uses to which it could be put.

Some of the photographs were extremely old. I recall one in particular, in which *he* wore a striped pyjama jacket and socks, fastened up with garters and suspenders, and *she* wore stockings, rolled down to below her knee. He had a Hitler-like moustache, and his hair, parted in the middle, was plastered down on each side, his face bearing a ferocious scowl. *She*, obviously a flower of dutiful Victorian womanhood, was simpering compliantly. She must have needed considerable fortitude, because they were performing on a very jagged lump of rock.

Some of the photographs, though, included such a mass of people and such a complicated plaiting of limbs that I found it impossible to make either head or tail of them. I resolved to decipher these later when I had more time. Amongst this biological bonanza, there was a fair sprinkling of studies of ladies' torsos. Again, there is one in particular that comes back to me clearly over the years. It was an upward shot of a lady smiling lasciviously down at the camera from between two of the most enormous bosoms I have ever seen – and still don't believe.

Further finds under the bed and in the cupboard above it were a huge assortment of canes and leather straps that quite mystified me. Nevertheless, in my zeal for tidying and making things look pretty, I put all the canes into an old vase and stood it in a corner of the bedroom. It looked rather arty, I thought, and was almost as effective as the pot of beech leaves in my bed-sitter. One morning, while brewing our first cup of the day, I asked Mae what the canes were for.

'Well, whacking 'em, of course!'

I stopped what I was doing and stared at her.

'The men?' I asked. 'Don't they mind?'

'I never hear them complain – only when I don't hit 'em hard enough. Haven't you heard me at it?'

Thinking about it, my mind went back to my first day and the strange cracking noises I'd heard coming from the bedroom. I'd heard them again often enough but hadn't really paid any attention, supposing them to be caused by the bed springs. I sat down weakly on the other chair.

'Oh you are funny,' she giggled. 'Come on, where's that cup of tea?'

Despite occasional revelations, like the canes, I was

beginning to feel as though I knew what I was doing. I was the mistress of my trade; at last I could look this Soho in the eye.

Later that day, waiting for Mae to return from one of her sorties, I peered out of the front window at a man with a crowd around him. He was making a lucrative living with a folding table and a pack of cards, while his gullible audience attempted to 'find the lady'. I watched until there was a shrill whistle from his confederate further along the alley, who'd spotted a policeman approaching. Then he and the crowd melted away as though they had never existed.

I tried to settle down to read a book. I was just beginning to worry, when I heard Mae's steps on the stairs. As they got nearer, I could hear that they were accompanied by a funny scrabbling noise and the sound of panting. I shot out on to the landing just as, round the bend of the stairs, two eager half-grown poodles appeared. Behind their jewelled collars and taut leads they were tugging a breathless Mae. Her face was flushed and excited.

'Look what I've got for us,' she announced triumphantly. 'Aren't they gorgeous? I just couldn't help it, they looked so sweet in the shop!'

One was black and the other white, and being still too young to be clipped, they were a mass of curls. She had already named them – Mimi and Fifi.

'I thought that, what with the place looking so nice now, they'd add the finishing touch!' she said. 'Anyway, it's nice to have animals about the place.'

I loved animals too, and we had a happy half-hour watching them while they cautiously explored. But they soon started to feel at home, and all their natural *joie de vivre* became apparent as they scudded about everywhere, shooting rugs from under them and jumping on to everything they could reach. Then one of them made a neat little puddle on the polished floor, and a measure of gloom stole over me as I realised the place wouldn't be looking nice for much longer.

While we drank our tea and they continued dealing out destruction to every object they encountered, I wondered how Rabbits would have taken to this invasion. I guessed she wouldn't have taken to it at all. In fact I had a feeling the 'Rabbits Regime' was rapidly coming to an end.

Thinking of this prompted me to ask Mae if she had had any more trouble from Rabbits.

'Oh, didn't I tell you?' she replied, pausing in applying her lipstick. 'She's gone. Dead.'

I went cold. I remembered the knife in Mae's handbag and my chest felt tight.

'What did she die of?' I asked, trying to sound casual but finding it difficult to speak.

'Oh, I don't know,' she said with complete indifference. She smoothed her lower lip with a finger. 'Heart attack, I shouldn't wonder.' She gave a little laugh. 'Good riddance anyway.'

I never did find out what had actually happened to Rabbits. In the back of my mind I debated for a second or two whether Mae could really have had anything to do with her demise. It wasn't likely, and besides, I was under Mae's spell and could think no ill of her. Protected by my growing love for her, and her irresistible charisma, Mae probably knew that as far I was concerned, she could − metaphorically, if not literally − get away with murder.

If Mimi, Fifi and the coldly rendered death of Rabbits were the first signs that I was not, in fact, as in control as I thought, then much worse was to come. Even now I shudder at the recollection of that hectic first Saturday. There were other days like it, and many far worse, I suppose, but that one remains in my memory as a day of utter chaos. A combination of reasons made it so: the arrival of the dogs, the uneasy feelings about Rabbits' death and the fact that I'd only just been congratulating myself that I could now handle my new job with efficiency, if not verve. Nevertheless, even without these considerations, Saturdays, I was to find, were always overwhelming, and the first one of them to hit me seemed like a tidal wave.

In the hurly-burly, my worries about my predecessor were forgotten, but my new-found confidence had taken an awful pasting. Had it not been for the dogs, things wouldn't have been quite so bad, but with them, the tempo was beyond belief and I felt myself inwardly becoming a gibbering wreck.

We decided that for the time being, the only place for our new pets was the bedroom; that being the only door that could be more or less kept shut. Mae made them a bed with one of her fur coats in the corner. As it was mink, it should have been very comfortable, but the two dogs seemed to have a yen to get back to the pet shop (I can't say I really blamed them). Every time someone opened the door, they shot out in a blur. I must have gone down those stairs to retrieve them as often as Mae did in the course of her business.

They created havoc in the bedroom, and after only a couple of hours, it looked as bad as it had on my first day there. The only thing to be said in the dogs' favour was that they didn't like men. When one arrived, they nearly always slunk back to their mink. There were exceptions to this rule: sometimes they disliked a man so much that they attacked his ankles while he was getting his money's worth, which didn't go down well.

Mimi, the black one, was always the ringleader.

'Who's my limb of Satan then? *Who is?*' Mae would coo,

holding her high in the air like a child. Mimi, getting a nice aerial view of the wreckage she had caused, would wag her tail happily.

Had anyone had the time to train them, they could have been turned into perfect pets, but we hadn't the time. They were – and remained – completely untamed.

As I grew to know her better, I discovered that Mae thrived on chaos. It was characteristic of her that she should buy her two canine hoodlums on a Saturday, the busiest day of the week. It was the day on which every worker was keen to spend his hard-earned wages. It seemed that the whole of Soho's male population was making its way up to Mae's flat. The tramp of feet on the stairs was endless. When Mae picked up a man, others would watch where she went and follow. It was incredible. No time for tea breaks on a Saturday! There was a slight lull between five and six o'clock, when the afternoon crowds began to go back to the suburbs and the evening ones had not yet arrived. Even so, business went on at a steady gallop, the only difference being that for an hour or so, the waiting room was empty.

At other times, every chair was occupied. It looked like a doctor's surgery, although the thick pall of smoke from nervously puffed cigarettes marred the effect. I felt more like a nurse than a maid as I stood courageously in the doorway saying, 'Next, please.' There was no time to feel embarrassed by this sea of strange faces; it was all far too brisk and clinical. By nine o'clock it was standing room only, and I began to wonder if some of the straps and belts I'd found couldn't be fixed to the ceiling for the men's benefit as they jostled past each other.

Around ten thirty, Mae shouted to me from the bedroom, 'Babs, quick! Run down and shut the front door, there's a load of drunks coming along!'

With the desperate knowledge that I couldn't handle a load of drunks lending wings to my feet, I flew down the two flights of stairs at top speed. I skidded in a large puddle halfway along the hall, grabbing the edge of the front door as I fell and ramming it shut a fraction of a second before the rowdy, singing mob came level. They began to kick the door and call me colourful names. Although I had heard the click of the Yale, I thought I'd better slip the bolt in at the bottom as well. As I straightened up from doing this, the flap of the letterbox was pushed open and two beady eyes peered in at me.

'I can see you!' said a beery voice.

This was followed by the sound of raucous laughter and more loud kicks as I went running back to my gentlemen in the waiting room to see if they were still behaving themselves. I was surprised to find that, by contrast to the lot downstairs, these seemed to be models of propriety. They all congratulated me warmly and were evidently relieved at my success. Cigarettes were offered from all directions and we fell to chatting in an amiable way.

Although the battering on the front door ended fairly soon, there were so many other drunks about that Mae decided we'd better leave it locked. Our little party in the waiting room gradually dwindled as, one by one, they were ministered to and, one by one, I accompanied them downstairs to lock up again behind them.

By about eleven thirty the last one had gone and Mae said wearily, 'Put the kettle on, love, I think we've had enough for one day, don't you?'

She looked exhausted and was leaning against the door, her face shiny with perspiration and all her make-up gone. As I filled the kettle I said, 'Mae, you are dotty, why on earth do you do it? Why so many?'

She flopped on to a chair like a rag doll.

'Oh, I dunno, love,' she said in the same tired voice. 'The poor sods are there and they want it. What can you do? How many did I do, anyway? I've lost count.'

She rested her chin in her hands and waited while I got out my notebook and started adding.

'Seventy-two,' I told her at last. 'And you've made eighty-five pounds ten.'

'Not bad, I suppose,' she mumbled through an enormous yawn.

We both collapsed with our tea amongst the debris in the bedroom and kicked our shoes off. The dogs were at last curled up asleep and snoring in their glamorous bed. Mae and I rested in the tired companionship of old campaigners who have come successfully through a major battle.

I glanced around me at the mess. It looked like we had been vandalised. There had been no chance to tidy up between clients all day, but I was too tired to care. Then my eye caught the glitter of coins scattered on the rugs and tiles.

'Lots of money on the floor,' I observed lazily.

'That's for the sweeper,' she said through another yawn. Then, looking at my questioning face, she added, 'I mean you, you silly sod! Always get a lot of change when I rush 'em in and out – falls out of their pockets when they take their trousers off.'

She was now lying sprawled on the bed, one leg and an arm hanging heavily over the edge. Her eyes were closed and a cigarette was smouldering, undisturbed, in the ashtray at her side.

I gazed at her in astonishment. Seventy-two men! And I had worried that eight or nine might kill her.

I thought, too, of all the money. In this one day, Mae had received what an ordinary girl in a fairly well-paid job would earn in months. It was a staggering thought. Even my tips for today came to about twelve pounds; add to that my wages – Mae had agreed five pounds for a Saturday – and ignoring the nubbins on the floor, and I realised with a shock that in one day I had earned what it would have taken me over three weeks to make at the studio.

I mulled over the past week. So far, fate had been kind enough not to send along a client I knew. I thought of my old boss, the little man from the grocery store opposite my bed-sitter, my landlord or – the most horrific thought of all – one of my relations. It didn't make me feel easier when I told myself that they would be more embarrassed than me. With an average of three hundred men a week teeming in and out, I thought, an uncomfortable reunion was bound to happen sometime. But I was wrong; luckily for me, it never did.

Mae's voice broke across my thoughts: 'Let's have another cuppa, shall we? Then we'll buzz off.'

'By the way,' I said, 'there's a big puddle in the hall, and it's not the dogs.'

'Oh you'll soon find our passageway's a real little gents' toilet,' said Mae with a grin. She was beginning to rally. Then, changing the subject, she said – rather shyly, I thought – 'I'm supposed to be meeting Tony tonight: well, round about one o'clock or so.' She glanced at her watch.

'Have you made up your mind about him, then?' I asked.

'No, not really. But he's definitely got something – don't know what it is, but I think I'll have to find out.' Then, after a pause, 'You don't feel like taking the dogs home with you tonight, do you?'

I had been ready for this. After only a week with Mae, I was beginning to understand her thought processes. From the moment she'd brought those dogs in, I knew it was only a matter of time before she tried to lumber me with them, though I hadn't expected it to be so soon. But being in the jungle, I was learning its rules, the first one of which was 'Protect Thyself'. I answered with what I hoped sounded like real regret:

'Sorry, I really can't. My landlord doesn't allow animals.'

'Ah well,' she answered, quite unperturbed, 'I can put them in Tony's car while we're in the club. He won't mind.'

The last job of the day was to empty the bin by the side of the bed into which the tissues and neatly knotted used condoms were thrown. I brought in a newspaper and opened it out on the floor; Mae tipped the bin out on to it. The crackling of the newspaper woke the dogs and they came bounding over to see what was going on. Mimi darted in, snatched up a rubber that was lying near the edge and ran off with it. Fifi thought this was great fun, so she grabbed the other end and started a tug-of-war. Mae and I watched, appalled. The rubber stretched and stretched, and then the fiendish Mimi suddenly let go. Fifi got such a thwack on the nose that she yelped back to the mink and sat there blinking, with watering eyes. She never touched Durex after that, and ran whenever she caught sight of one. Mimi, on the other hand, seemed to have become enamoured of them, and was almost never without one in her mouth. If I tried to remove it, she would attempt to play the same trick on me as she had on Mimi. I didn't respond.

We clipped the leads on to the dogs, collected our things together and put on our shoes.

'I don't know about you,' I said, 'but *my* feet are killing me tonight!'

'Cheeky sod!' gurgled Mae, giving me a playful punch. 'Come on, you soppy 'a'porth, let's go.' Then her face changed, as something dreamy came into it. 'It's time for Tony.'

Nine

~

On Monday, Mae arrived with flushed cheeks and sparkling eyes, full of the news that she and Tony had spent the whole of Sunday in bed together.

'Ooh, he's lovely, Babs! You'd like him.'

I wondered how she could see sex with any man as special and romantic when she spent her life on a virtual conveyor belt of men.

'Them?' she said. 'They're not sex: they're work! Tony's real.'

An hour later the first lot of red roses arrived; the next day, another dozen, and so on for the rest of the week. Each bunch was accompanied by a little note in which Mae was smothered with endearments and referred to as 'my princess', 'my angel' 'queen of my heart' and so forth. I was still unaccountably uneasy at the thought of this affair, but Mae was bowled over, and went around looking dewy-eyed and dreamy.

By Thursday it had become the romance of a lifetime; on the following Sunday, Tony moved into Mae's little Paddington flat. His luggage consisted of one suitcase and six dozen more red roses. These were to be the 'last roses of summer': no more were to follow.

Not much work was done during this time. Mae was besotted and wanted only to sit and talk about Tony. She also told me how her affair with Alphonse had ended.

The couple used to spend a few hours every night after work in an all-night rendezvous where most of the Soho characters congregated to relax after the evening's slog. According to Mae, Tony – from somewhere behind Alphonse's back – had made love to her with his eyes.

'Not in a nasty way, you know: not undressing me,' she said. 'It was as if he was longing for me. His whole heart was in his eyes.'

After a few days of this, Tony produced a friend who happened to know Alphonse and who asked if they could join them.

'Rabbits told me about Tony,' Mae went on. 'She'd heard he came from a rich family in Malta but came over here penniless because he wanted to make his own way in life. She said all the girls were made up about him but he's very choosy.'

Choosy Tony spent the whole time burning Mae with his eyes and scowling at Alphonse; and the scowling was gradually augmented with growls. Eventually Alphonse suddenly remembered an appointment he had to keep. While he was paying the bill, Tony lounged in the doorway. Alphonse approached to find him leaning nonchalantly against the door jamb with a flick knife in his hand, paring his nails.

'Alphonse was petrified,' Mae chortled. 'When I got home that night, all his stuff was gone and I haven't seen him since.

'Tony's so nice, though,' she went on. 'He reckons he'd fallen for me so hard, he couldn't bear to see me with someone else. He didn't remember anything about getting out the knife – I had to tell him about that – and he's so scared about how violent he could get without knowing it, he gave me the knife to look after. That was the one you saw in my bag that time.' She leaned back, smiling fondly at her thoughts of true love.

Not long afterwards, I was doing some job in the kitchen and Mae, who had just seen off a client, was mooning over her roses. She was calling out to tell me how lovely the scent was in her room when I heard a tap on the outer door. Drying my hands, I went to see who it was, while Mae came to the bedroom door thinking it was another client.

We were confronted with an immaculate blue uniform on a very large policeman. I knew right away that he was not a beat bobby: he wore a flat cap and looked efficient and terrifying. My heart began to pound and my mouth went dry. What had we done? Why was he here?

'Do you mind?' he said, addressing Mae. 'I'd like to have a few words with this young lady here.' He nodded towards me. Very scared now, I glanced towards Mae for reassurance.

'Of course, Officer,' she answered. Then, to me, 'I'll keep the door shut while you're gone.' She came closer and gave my arm a comforting squeeze. Evidently she thought that an untold secret from my past had caught up with me and that I was, after all, a bit of a dark horse.

I took my apron off rather slowly, thoughts tumbling through my mind. Why me? What awful thing had I done without knowing it? Why hadn't I tried to find out if being a maid was illegal?

I asked the policeman if I needed my coat, and he told me I didn't; that it would only take a few minutes. Then he stood aside to let me go downstairs in front of him. My legs were shaking as I went, but I was slightly comforted by the smile he gave me as I passed. I reflected that there'd been nothing very officious about his manner, and on the way down he made a friendly remark about the weather, which helped to lessen my fears.

As we walked together along the alleyway, everyone was staring at us. At the end, we turned left to where a police car was stationed at the kerb. Another policeman was at the wheel and a policewoman was in the back. As I approached, she wound down the window, smiled and beckoned to me.

'I won't ask you to get in,' she said. 'I think you'll find it less embarrassing to talk through the window; it looks more casual that way. I hope you don't mind us fetching you out, but I wanted to have a word with you in private.'

Not very private, I thought. I could feel the gaze of curious passers-by, some of whom stopped to try and work out what was going on. My escort had obligingly stationed himself to one side of me, with his elbow resting on the roof of the car, so at least I was partly protected from their view.

'No, that's all right,' I answered. 'What have I done wrong?'

'Nothing at all, dear. Don't worry. It's us who are worried about you.'

That was a relief, but I was still puzzled.

'The fact is, several of our men have noticed you, and though you wouldn't have known it, one of our plain-clothes officers has also spoken to you. They are all very concerned.'

So that was it. I tried to think who the plain-clothes man could have been. It must have been one of those nice men in the waiting room on Saturday.

'What are they worried about?' I asked; although I think by then I knew.

'They're worried because you're much younger than any of the other maids and because you aren't the usual type. They said it was obviously not your sort of life and it would be a shame if you got mixed up in it any further.

They think you're too nice a person to waste your life like this.'

'But I'm only on the edge of it,' I argued. 'And I don't intend getting any more involved than this.'

'It isn't that easy,' she answered. 'It's only a very short step from what you're doing to what she's doing.' Here she nodded in the direction of the flat. 'Leave it, dear, while you can, won't you?'

'I couldn't do what she's doing!' I was horrified. 'I don't even like men very much.'

'Do you think she does?'

'No-oo,' I answered uncertainly.

'People can get used to anything for money, you know.'

'Not me,' I said with vehemence. 'I'll be all right, I promise you. But I can't leave Mae; she's my friend and she needs me.'

'You're very loyal,' the policewoman said with a sigh. 'But promise me you won't waste your loyalty. Don't throw it away on something worthless.'

'Mae isn't worthless!'

'Just wait and see; you'll learn in time. And be careful, dear.'

'I understand – and thanks for checking. It was very kind of you.'

As I turned to go, I saw the three of them looking at me in a rueful sort of way.

When I got back to the flat, Mae was nervous and burning with curiosity.

'What did they want?' she asked, almost before I was inside.

'Oh, they were worried that being here might corrupt me,' I told her. 'They think, given time, that I might take over your job.'

'Hey, that's not such a bad idea,' she laughed. 'Then

I can take it easy and you can keep me in my old age. Your feet are younger than mine anyway.'

The next day I was summoned to another meeting I wasn't keen on.

'Tony wants to meet you,' Mae announced when she arrived. 'I've told him so much about you and he's still never even seen you. He says why don't we all have a coffee together when we finish and then we can drive you home in the car; it will save you taking a taxi.'

At the end of the evening we met in one of those quiet little Italian cafés that never seem to do much business but stay open at all hours doing it. It was raining. I arrived carrying Fifi, while Mae carried the Limb of Satan, who was fast becoming her favourite. I was still apprehensive, but agog to meet this supposed prince amongst men. I reassured myself that he must be something special to have been able to capture Mae's heart.

Tony stood up to greet us from one of the tables. He was a short man of about twenty-eight, with a pasty face – he had olive skin but clearly saw little daylight. As we sat down and pushed the two dogs out of harm's way under the table, a gold tooth glinted as Tony gave me the first – and almost the last – smile I ever received from him.

It was dislike at first sight. To think that Mae, who could have had anybody, should have fallen for this pallid little thing completely floored me. His only redeeming feature was a kind of melancholy and liquid-eyed Latin charm.

I had to admit he was beautifully turned out, in his expensive suit, immaculate shirt – with just the right amount of cuff showing – navy tie and the diamond sparkling on his little finger. The hair above his puffy face was jet black and teased into short waves and curls, oiled to a sparkle, which gave him a slightly piratical appearance.

He and Mae were gazing at one another in an embarrassing way, but they pulled themselves together when the waiter arrived. Mimi and Fifi, who were getting caught up in their leads, began snapping at each another. Tony growled something that sounded like '*Mella!*' and peered under the table at them. I was often to hear him use this word; eventually I discovered that it was an abbreviated expletive that all the Maltese larded their sentences with. The admonition worked like a charm and the dogs were immediately quiet. I made up my mind to practise the sound myself, for use in dire moments.

We drank coffee and talked. Tony seemed like a man trying to be pleasant with a child he didn't much care for but whose parent was present. His accent was pretty enough, but he had no real conversation and peppered his speech with long, expressive silences. It was after one of these that he finally found something to say.

'Mae tells me the police wanted to talk to you yesterday.'

'Yes,' I said. 'I was scared stiff.'

'What did they want?'

The liquid brown eyes had changed and he was watching me with hard black stones. The change was unnerving, and I saw then what Alphonse must have seen: this was a man without scruples and potentially dangerous. Puzzled by his question and by his attitude, I told him the rough gist of our conversation, during which time he never took his eyes off me. When I'd finished, he snapped:

'Did they ask you anything about me?'

'No, of course not.'

'You're sure?' The eyes were still riveted on me.

'Of course I'm sure. What would they ask me about you for?'

I was beginning to get annoyed; I sensed the meeting had been arranged solely for this purpose. The liquid eyes returned and there was a gleam from his gold tooth.

'It's all right; I believe you,' he said with great magnanimity, and the diamond glittered as he flapped his pudgy white hand. Mae gave a little laugh.

'Tony's got to be careful, you see, love. He could get into a lot of trouble being with me. I told him it's too soon for them to have got on to him yet, but he gets nervous – don't you, love?' She patted his hand comfortingly and he flashed her an agonisingly false smile, and I knew in that instant that he had no more love for her than he had for me.

Ten

~

With the advent of Tony, there was a subtle but definite change in Mae. Almost overnight, she became more audacious: more bouncy. She spent hours in front of the mirror, making up her face carefully with masses of new cosmetics, trying out different hairstyles, or merely staring at herself from different angles. The dogs came in for a lot of extra affection and were forever being swept up into her arms and smothered with kisses; and not only the dogs, me as well. She was blissfully happy and the whole world was wonderful. At times like this, there was no one more magical to be with than Mae; she shone like the sun.

Soon after my first meeting with Tony, she arrived waving her left hand at me so I could see the ring on her third finger. She was literally dancing with joy, but calmed down sufficiently to give me her hand so I could examine the ring. It was a pretty gold one, formed of two snakes entwined together, with tiny diamonds for eyes.

'Isn't it lovely?' she breathed. 'And do you know what Tony said? He said that the very first time he ever saw me, he went out and sold the gold cigarette case his father had given him so he could go and buy this for me. He said he dreamed of the time he could put it on my finger. Isn't he wonderful? Don't you think he's wonderful too?'

She was always asking me this and I always had a struggle to reply. I longed to tell her that I thought he was a stinker, but instead I made vague enthusiastic noises, which were enough to satisfy her. She rattled on:

'I've managed to worm out of him when his birthday is and it's only two weeks away. So do you know what I'm going to buy him?'

I was dying to say, 'A gold cigarette case,' but it isn't always kind to be clever. 'No. What?' I said instead.

'A gold cigarette case! And I think I'll have his initials put on it. What do you think?'

'What do I think about the initials, do you mean? Well, it might make it less valuable if he ever had to sell it. I don't suppose anyone would be very happy about a cigarette case with someone else's initials on it.'

'In that case, it's having initials on, 'cos I'll have his guts if he ever tries to sell anything I give him.'

Later that same day, while she was doing her face for the umpteenth time, Mae came out with further thoughts on Tony's birthday. With terrific excitement and eyes shining, she suddenly swung round on her dressing table stool.

'Right. Know what I'm going to get Tony for his birthday, Babs?'

'A gold cigarette case, you said.'

'Ah, yes. But I've thought of something better. I *will* get him the cigarette case and give that to him first, so he thinks that's all he's getting. But his real present is going to be a car.'

'But he's got a car.' (Oh, never was money for a little snake ring better spent.)

'No, love, that's not *his* car. It belongs to a friend of his who's abroad for a few weeks. The other day, we were out driving and Tony was telling me about his ambitions and what he wants to do with his life. And then he said, did I want to see the first thing he'd buy when he got enough money? So I said, "Yes." Well, he drove to this showroom and he made me get out and look at a car they'd got there. I forget what make it was, but it was a lovely pale blue and he got so excited talking about it, and what with that and his nose pressed to the window, he looked just like a little boy. What you do fink?' She always said 'fink' when she was getting carried away.

'I think ...' I said slowly, 'I think it's an awful lot of money to spend on someone you've only just met. I think he'd be thrilled to bits with just the cigarette case.'

'Pooh to that!' she exploded. 'Now that I've thought of a car, it's got to be a car.'

She turned back to the mirror to do some more to her face, sulky because I hadn't been more enthusiastic.

'You don't understand. Tony and me will go on for ever. We might even get married. You wait till you fall for someone!' She was grinning mischievously at me in the mirror now: good-humoured again. 'Then you'll want to give him everything he wants too.'

'If you say so.' I smiled back. 'Mother knows best.'

'I should bleeding think so,' she mumbled, pressing her freshly painted lips together and staring at the finished result.

I watched her, thinking how this generosity, which I'd known she had, was a surprising contrast to her bouts of thrift, which I'd also seen. She was cheerfully − in fact, eagerly − lashing out many hundreds of pounds on a car, but had resisted spending a pound or two on the front door, which had needed attention when I arrived and was getting worse by the day. When we left at night, she would hold the handle and I would put my hand in the letterbox before we went through a 'ready-steady-go!' routine that had to be repeated several times. We were surrounded by odd-job men, any one of whom would have been glad to fix it, but Mae wouldn't hear of it. 'Something'll turn up soon,' she would say confidently – by which she meant that some client would do it for nothing.

The 'something' that turned up eventually was the meat porter, Syd. He was spruced up in his best clothes and making his first call since I'd been there: probably his first ever. It was a Monday afternoon and quiet – a fact he had probably foreseen.

'Just thought I'd pop in to see how you two girls was getting on together,' he said. But his careless tone was hiding nervousness. We offered him a cup of tea. 'Well, I don't wanna take up your time,' he said. Mae insisted and he relaxed a bit. When he was halfway through drinking it, she pretended to allow a bright idea to strike her.

'Any good with doors?'

'Doors?'

'Yeah, doors. You know, those things you open and shut – with handles on them.'

Syd smiled in a chagrined sort of way. Swigging down the rest of his tea, he rose to his feet, his face slightly flushed.

'What's the hurry?' Mae demanded.

He seemed confused by this.

'I thought you was giving me the hint I'd outstayed my welcome – that I was keeping you from your business, like.'

'Don't be such a Charley,' she said. 'I wondered if you would fix a wonky door for us, that's all.'

You could see Syd's relief. 'I'll go and take a look,' he said.

He was back a moment later, to announce that the top hinge was loose and ask if we had a screwdriver.

I produced all the tools we had, now collected in a carrier bag. Syd gazed inside with growing amusement. There was a hammer with a broken shaft; a bent screwdriver; an assortment of rusty screws; a pair of pincers with no pinch, and a keyless padlock. Syd took out the screwdriver and tried to hammer it into a better shape on the windowsill, then disappeared downstairs again. He was back to say the screws were too small and had we some matches to plug the holes with? Eventually he managed to get the door functioning properly and earned himself another cup of tea.

From then on, just like so many others, Syd was a marked man in Mae's book. I had taken notice of this: if a tap needed a new washer, it dripped away until plumber-client paid a visit. If anything went wrong with the cooker, we would eat raw food till an electrician-client came again. I got so fed up with the inconvenience that I eventually bought a few tools and learned to mend things myself.

Naturally Mae had also got the purveyors of merchandise well logged; woe betide the wine merchant who didn't arrive with a sample of his wares at Christmas, or the traveller in ladies' underwear who didn't come across with a few pairs of stockings. One day she discovered that one of her clients worked for the GPO, and in no time at all there was a telephone installed in the flat and another at my place – so she could always get in touch with me if she needed to. This was at a time when the standard waiting period for fitting telephones was several months.

I was beginning to know the faces of a few of the regular clients, especially those who had the same calling day each week. These now automatically made their way to the kitchen for a chat until their turn came round. Some of them were pleasant and friendly; others not so.

Mr Tucker, was 'something big' in the Stock Exchange.

He was a Friday-night regular. When I first met him, it was after he'd spent about three hours drinking at his club. He was 'posh'; he was fat; he wore thick horn-rimmed spectacles and his round, elderly face squatted under a bowler hat. He gripped the *Financial Times*, his gloves and a rolled umbrella in one hand and left the other hand free to clutch at the banister rails. Even so, he kept falling over on his way up.

'Gotter see me l'il girl ... Gotter see l'il Maezy-wayezy b'fore I g'ome to wifey-pifey.'

We always had to go down the stairs to heave and push him up. Even then, he would frequently collapse on the steps, swearing that Mae moved her flat further up the house every time he was expected.

'He's always like this,' Mae told me. Then, to him, she said, 'According to you, we work in a bleeding skyscraper.'

He gazed at her through unfocused eyes, hiccuped a giggle and attempted a feeble smack at her bottom – which missed.

He drank two cups of black coffee while Mae went on working, during the course of which I was instructed to make sure he didn't fall off the chair. This duty would have been easier had he not kept making futile lunges at me, saying, 'You're a nice l'il thing too. Why doncher come here, you fuckin' l'il beauty?'

Eventually Mae shepherded him, still staggering, into the bedroom, where she later told me she'd spent twenty minutes unsuccessfully trying to bring him to the point. On this and subsequent visits he left quite happy, still needing our aid to get him into the street.

Fred, on the other hand, was quiet, polite and really nice. Rather than being a standard regular, in his eyes he was actually courting Mae. Fred was a bachelor who desperately wanted not to be. His hobby was judo, which he took very seriously indeed. In fact, other than when he came to see Mae, I think he spent every night at his judo club – he was some kind of 'dan' and had a black belt. I liked him very much indeed and thought what a wonderful thing it would be for Mae if she could have seen her way to accepting his advances. But though he vaguely amused her, she didn't give him a moment's serious thought; to her he was a client, like Mr Tucker, and increasingly her heart belonged to her dreadful Tony.

Soon afterwards, I was to meet Tony's predecessor. Though Mae and I laughed about the evening many times, it is one I still look back on with misgivings at my part in this poor man's humiliation. It would be the first time I saw for myself Mae's easy capacity for cruelty and her desire to hurt. The first, but by no means the last.

Eleven

~

Something was up: Mae had come back to the flat without a man. Her face was full of mischief.

'What do you know? I've found out where Alphonse is. He's gone back to his old job: he's a waiter again, at a snazzy restaurant in Lancaster Gate. You and me are booked for a giggle. We're going tomorrow – it's about time we had a night out – so bring a party frock with you.'

I didn't possess a party frock, but with my new life, I could see there might be some use in acquiring one.

'Will you help me choose?' I said. 'Only I don't think I'd be much good at that sort of thing.'

'You haven't got no party frock? No cocktail dress? I'll choose it and I'll even buy it for you. I'd like to think I bought your first nice dress.'

So the following day, we met early and rambled along Oxford Street, looking in windows. Finally Mae saw something that caught her eye and she hustled me into a shop. It was a very pretty dress – well, perhaps 'glamorous' is more the word – and I tried it on. It didn't suit me at all. Mae scrutinised me carefully.

'Yes, that's it,' she said at last. 'But the underskirt's too baggy; it'll have to be taken in.' The shop assistant was instantly down on her knees with a mouthful of pins. 'And it's got to be ready to wear tonight.'

'Yes, madam, it will be ready,' she answered, briskly pinning away.

Next I was whisked away in a cab to a shop that specialised in kinky footwear and I was bought my first pair of really high-heeled shoes: black, patent leather, with heels four inches high. There were no half measures with Mae, and she rushed me from shop to shop, treating me:

'What's your favourite scent? ... That handbag doesn't go with anything; let's see what they've got in here ... That dress'll need an accessory ... Are you going to keep your hair like that?'

While Mae was dressing that evening, I took Mimi and Fifi with me to collect the dress, and hurried back with it full of excitement.

I unzipped it down the length of the back and gingerly stepped inside. The material was a black brocade, woven all over with tiny sprigs of silver roses; it had a high collar that plunged to a low V-neck; there were no sleeves to speak of and the main feature was a sort of overskirt in the same fabric, which was caught up in a bunch of formal pleats on one hip. After Mae zipped me up again, I slipped into my patent-leather stilts and practised walking about the room. Enjoying my pleasure, Mae kept one eye on me while the other concentrated on her make-up. She was wearing a floating blue chiffon affair and looked positively ravishing. She turned to me with one hand on her hip and gave an exaggerated flutter of her false eyelashes. She then bullied and cajoled me in her supervision of my own make-up, although I drew the line at false eyelashes.

'You don't look at all bad,' Mae said, standing back to survey the results.

As I walked down the stairs, I felt like a princess, but it was slightly different when I got into the street, where the combination of high heels and tight skirt necessitated a mincing walk: I felt more like a geisha girl than royalty. I was thankful when we got to the main road and Mae hailed a cab.

'Get in, then,' she called impatiently from inside. I made a futile attempt.

'I can't. My skirt's too tight.'

'Well hoist it up.'

'I can't do that either; it's too tight. All I can do is take it off, and I'm not doing that.'

'Got a newspaper, mate?' Mae asked the driver. He handed one through the sliding glass partition and she spread it on the floor of the cab.

'Now,' she said. 'Turn around and sit on it. That's right. Now shuffle backwards on your bum.'

I wriggled till my feet were in. The grinning cabby came round and slammed the door shut, and I was about to shove an arm on the seat in readiness for hoisting myself up, but Mae stopped me.

'There's no point in you getting on the seat, is there? You'll only have to shuffle out the same way.'

All this had brought on a fine fit of giggles, and we were almost hysterical when we reached our destination. This wasn't the done way to approach such a snazzy place, and the commissionaire was surprised to open the cab door and find a woman sitting on a newspaper on the floor. We tried to establish some sort of decorum, and very nearly succeeded as Mae walked and I teetered inside.

We crossed the foyer and stood in the curtained archway leading to the restaurant, Mae scanning the room.

'Look, there he is: over there. And he's just seen us.'

The head waiter approached.

'I want to sit at one of that waiter's tables, please,' she told him sweetly. She pointed at Alphonse, who did a very good impression of having been turned to stone.

Once we were seated, she clicked her fingers. 'Waiter,' she called melodiously. I turned scarlet under my make-up as he came shuffling over with his head down in a most un-waiter-like manner. He was a tall, rather good-looking man, and in my view a much nicer type than Tony.

'He looks just like a penguin, doesn't he?' Mae giggled – just as he came into earshot. 'Well, my man, where's the menu?'

Then she took us through all the courses. She was allegedly dissatisfied with each and threatened to complain to the management about the service. First she said the soup was cold and must be sent back; then she criticised the state of the cutlery and glassware and demanded replacements. I could see that Alphonse wished he could put either to violent use. However, he gritted his teeth and found admirable self-control. He was betrayed only by his trembling hands: a calamity while serving the peas was his only disaster.

When we came to the sweet course, Mae turned dia-bolical. She slammed down the menu and announced, 'We'll have crêpes Suzette, waiter.'

Purple-faced, he trundled over to us with the trolley and proceeded to go through all the complicated business necessary for the highly overrated little pancakes. Mae stopped talking completely so she could watch every part of the process. Under this scrutiny, Alphonse knocked over bottles and slopped things everywhere. After several attempts, he succeeded in getting the crêpes to go up in flames, and Mae let out a piercing shriek that made him nearly drop the lot. It all felt like a malicious charade and I marvelled that Alphonse didn't tell the head waiter he had an awkward customer – as I feared he might.

At last we ordered coffee – after Mae had conspicuously dusted the cups with her napkin – and then called for the bill. She checked it meticulously and finally opened her handbag, which was crammed so full of money it nearly erupted. She extracted a few notes and disdainfully let them flutter to the plate. Thankful to be nearing the end of his ordeal, Alphonse scuttled off and returned with her change. She picked it up in its entirety then, almost as an afterthought, dropped a shilling back on to the plate.

'There you are, my man, that's for you – although I can't really say you earned it.'

Alphonse bowed his head – partly because the head waiter was watching and partly to hide the murderous look in his eyes. Mae collected her belongings and sailed out, queenly and arrogant. I made my escape close on her heels.

Inside the ladies', she collapsed into helpless fits of laughter, leaning against the wall for support and clutching on to the roller towel.

'Oh, what a scream! What a laugh! I thought I'd die! Did you see his face?' Then she had a sudden thought. 'Hey! What if we turned up here again tomorrow?' She exploded again. 'I reckon he'd give in his notice!'

Blinkered by my loyalty to Mae, I disingenuously told myself that Alphonse must have done something to deserve this despicable treatment, but there was still a glimmer of sympathy left in my heart for him.

'Oh, Mae, you couldn't! That poor chap!'

'Perhaps not,' she said. 'I reckon he's had enough.' Then, to my amazement, she said, 'Come on then, let's get back to work.'

Twelve

~

With Tony now firmly part of her life, Mae developed a greater desire for fun and frivolity, and, being constantly at hand, I was a convenient playmate.

After my interlude with the police, she appreciated how different I was from the run-of-the-mill maid, and how innocent I was. She was tickled that the police were worried she might corrupt me, and decided to show me what corruption was.

At first she confined herself to anecdotes, enjoying my incredulity; when the fun of this palled, the practical demonstrations began. She was so inured to the ordinary sex act that she didn't think it possible I'd be interested in that, but she considered anything offbeat to be essential for my education. I, the Soho debutante, was about to be 'brought out'.

The 'geezers' known previously only as characters in Mae's tales became living personalities as, one by one, they came back and I was called in to witness their particular penchants. This course of instruction took months to unfold and I never baulked at it. I was Alice in a depraved Wonderland.

Widening my horizons was a good distraction for Mae. She was finding it difficult to settle down to work. With a new boyfriend, a new maid, a newly spring-cleaned flat and two new dogs, she couldn't keep her mind on the mundane business of ordinary work for long. She began by taking me for walks – with the dogs in tow – so I could meet her friends in the area.

Many times these field trips were abortive, as more often than not she would meet one of her regulars halfway along the alley and back to the flat we would all have to trot, with the dogs looking most perplexed. Then there would either be a rush of customers to prevent us sallying forth again, or Mae's mood would have changed and she wouldn't feel like going out after all. Occasionally, however, we managed to break past the client barrier and tread new ground.

On one such occasion, Mae grabbed my arm and whispered, 'This you got to see. That's Benzy Nell over there. You watch: she's always doped up to the eyebrows.'

She indicated a middle-aged woman on the opposite side of the road who was striding along as though she had seven-league boots on. She was tall, slim and plain, with short mousy hair and clothes that looked as though they'd been thrown on in a hurry. She was on her 'beat', which she had preordained to be about ten yards long. She tackled this like a fast-marching sentry, executing a skilful 'left, about turn' at each end.

Mae grabbed my arm again and towed me across the street, doubling the length of our strides. We managed to fall into step alongside Benzy Nell. She was singing quietly to herself as we caught up with her, but when she saw Mae, she broke into rapid speech, not pausing for anything.

We marched backwards and forwards with her until we were out of breath, though not from talking – Mae couldn't get a word in edgeways. Then suddenly Nell spied an old client and doubled her pace to get to him. We let her go and crossed the street again, where we turned to watch. The man had replaced us at her side and he too was marching up and down.

'I hope she gets him inside while he's still got some energy left,' Mae said.

The same thought must have occurred to the man, because suddenly, steering her by leaning his weight against her shoulder, he executed a most beautiful right turn and they both disappeared through an open doorway.

Over time, Mae took me to visit quite a number of other working girls, and I discovered that our flat was a palace compared with most. They were all much dirtier than hers had been when I first arrived, and many were far smaller – like the girl who had only one room and the maid sat behind a screen in the corner. Another place was boarded up on the outside, devoid of electricity – the stairs were lit by candles placed on every landing – water or drainage, and seemed to be teetering on the brink of falling down. No doubt it was condemned and had been pressed into service by an enterprising agent who had skeleton keys. Here, the maid sat in the corner of a room that was so small there was only space for her chair and an enormous galvanised water tank filled with a dark, evil-smelling liquid. At my reaction to the noxious odour, a hoarse cackle came from the maid's dim corner. Mae's friend waved her hand in the direction of the tank; the turbid contents gleamed unctuously in the candlelight.

'Our pisspot,' she told me. 'We'll have to start bailing soon.'

Our next trip led us up to an eyrie where, sitting on the stairs, we came across a fat lady who seemed to be sound asleep. Mae, who was leading, stooped down to give her a gentle shake. This had no effect, so she squeezed past her, explaining to me that the woman had epileptic fits and had to sit down when she felt one coming on. Up another flight, and a brunette, known as Fiona, looked over the banisters to see who was coming. She was wearing a French corset with the bosom so padded she was nearly falling out of the top of it.

'Sure, and if it isn't Mae,' she greeted us in a thick Irish brogue. 'It must be you heard me putting the kettle on. Hello to you too,' she said to me. 'Would you be seeing anything of me maid at all? I sent her for milk and sugar an hour past and I've not clapped eyes on her since.'

Mae told her that we'd passed her on the stairs. The girl laughed.

A client trudged up the stairs and Fiona went into the hall, drawing a tatty curtain across a slack length of string to screen us from view.

'It will be two pound to you – sorry,' we heard her say.

Judging by the sudden bumping against the wall dividing us, he must have acquiesced

'Hear that?' Mae said.

'How could I not?'

'Yeah, two pounds and not a murmur. I'd like to know what she's doing for it,' she mused with pursed lips.

When we finally left, I asked Mae if Fiona existed solely on regulars. She replied scathingly:

'Her? No! She's got a good passing trade; all she has to do is hang her tits out of the window and whistle.'

On another excursion, Mae steered me towards a café known as The Little Cabin. It was basically a large shed or small warehouse and had been erected with some haste in the middle of a bomb site. It was constructed from all sorts of oddments and had a corrugated-iron roof.

Inside, no effort had been made to make it any cosier. It was uncompromisingly stark. The tables and chairs were the most leprous assortment imaginable; having no windows, it was lit at irregular intervals by harsh electric bulbs in white enamel shades; the floor consisted of dirty bare boards resting on beams, through which the wind whistled from underneath.

At the far end, a serving counter covered with worn American cloth ran the full width. On this stood a tea urn and several glass cases full of snacks. The only other home comforts in the place were a jukebox and a couple of pinball tables that didn't work. The whole effect seemed calculated to put as many customers off as possible. It was cold, strident and cheerless; yet it was packed with people.

The proprietors, sweaty and complacent with success, had no need to play the happy hosts. They slammed cheese rolls on to plates, cups on to saucers, fat fingers on to the till and gave not the slightest hint of recognition to any of the customers.

The clientele were too involved in their own affairs to notice, let alone feel slighted. Nearly all of them were thieves, mobsters, self-appointed car-parking attendants and racketeers of all types. These were people who lived by their wits and relied on seizing chances as they arose. They were alternately flush with money or dead broke. Those who were in the steady rackets never patronised The Little Cabin as, having mostly graduated from its ranks, they would be expected to lend a sympathetic ear, which might in turn lead to their being obliged to lend cash. Mae was an exception to this rule. She was no snob and liked to recall her humble beginnings; she was never ungenerous to anyone in need.

Half the crimes in the Metropolitan area were conceived over cups of tea in The Little Cabin. If the police had ever raided it, they would have netted an impressive catch of criminals. It would, however, have been a hollow victory: fake alibis would have been conjured on the spot.

As we sailed through that sea – or rather backwater – of

people, everyone called out greetings to Mae. Despite my being in her company, this cordiality was not extended to me: they eyed me curiously, almost suspiciously. This was definitely a 'members only club'. I realised that Mae had done a most unusual thing in choosing an outsider for a maid. I was an enigma, excused only by the fact that Mae, being who and what she was, was able to get away with anything and was expected to do mad things now and again.

The twilight characters of Soho were an extremely clannish lot and resented interlopers and snoopers. Here at last my upbringing came in useful, for I had been taught to be 'seen and not heard'. I was under Mae's patronage, and because she was respected and admired, I was accepted temporarily on condition I didn't ask any questions. And it paid off: eventually I was able to elicit from them everything I wanted to know precisely because of my seeming indifference.

We took a seat and people gravitated towards our table to chat and exchange scandal. Several men at adjoining tables slewed their chairs round to face us. They flirted with Mae and even attempted to include me in the badinage. They knew that a maid – especially Mae's maid – earned enough to keep a small-time crook in modest luxury.

All of them were well dressed and their outfits seemed out of place among the cracked, chipped cups they drank from, the rickety chairs and the scarred, ugly tables. But clothes were important to this lot, intended as proof of their success and cleverness. To be seen in a frayed suit or grubby shirt was noticed immediately and taken as a sign of a decline in fortune.

Actually, it took months for me to recognise these things, but this first time, sitting amongst these affable and friendly people, I saw no further than the smiling faces, I heard no more than the jokes and I understood nothing except that Mae – all sparkling eyes and bouncing curls as she held court – was in her element.

Having been taken to The Little Cabin, I started to feel like I was really at home in Soho. The final seal on my acceptance came one evening after dark, when Mae and I were walking along Old Compton Street on our way back to the flat after visiting one of her friends. A group of men were walking towards us. Mae, who had been holding my arm, quickly dropped it and gave an apprehensive gasp.

'It's Vince! He's going to want to have a look at you: he always likes to get new people sized up. Mind your Ps and Qs, for goodness' sake!'

I had heard of Vince before; everybody who read the Sunday papers had heard of him and his notorious brother. He was the overlord of Soho, at the top of the league and always several jumps ahead of the law. He could afford very smart, struck-off solicitors, and although it was known he was the brains and organiser of every big Soho racket – and much that went on further afield – nothing was ever provable.

The approaching group consisted of six men. As they came close, they spread out across the pavement and halted, facing us. Five of them formed a semicircle round Vince. All six were utterly devoid of expression. They all wore dinner jackets and boiled shirts, and Vince had a gardenia in his buttonhole. He said something quietly to the man on his right, who then turned to Mae.

'Who's she?' he demanded.

Mae told him who I was and he in turn told Vince, who must have heard Mae's answer but, like some Eastern potentate, preferred to have no direct communication with his subjects. A few more questions about my background followed; all the while Vince remained completely impassive and said not a word.

I was puzzled as to why an important man like this should bother with someone so far down the ladder. He had probably heard that I was an oddity, and about my interview with the police.

After the interrogation was over, there was absolute silence, during which he stared at me for a full five minutes while his bodyguard gazed over our heads and beyond. Then instinct seemed to tell me he was waiting for a sign of submission on my part, and much as I detested the idea, I thought I'd better comply – so I lowered my eyes humbly. For perhaps thirty seconds more, I felt his continued gaze. Then, still without a word, they closed ranks and we stepped aside for them to pass.

'Phew! I'm glad that's over,' said Mae. 'Scares me stiff, that man.'

I felt more annoyed than scared after having this silly psychology practised on me, but I realised Vince was not a man to be angered.

Not all the Soho characters were so daunting. Every so often a character called Matilda would come round to Mae's. She was a thin, elderly lady, and the moment I first met her took me straight back to something I'd learnt in art school. She was somehow in the Perpendicular Gothic style. Everything about her ran in straight vertical lines, except round the mouth, where the flesh of her face was gathered into little pleats like the drawn-up opening of a handbag. This and her glasses gave her a prim and disapproving expression – like some impoverished gentlewoman who found her surroundings impossibly sordid and distasteful. She was shabby, but very neat, and she always brought with her her Pekinese, who, strangely enough, was also Perpendicular Gothic.

Matilda would perch on the edge of a hard chair, very upright, with the Peke sitting beside her, also bolt upright, with its lead still attached to her like a flying buttress. At her other side, as though to keep the symmetry of the Gothic image going, she would place the two ancient cretonne carrier-bags she always brought with her.

Automatically I would give her a cup of tea, and while clients came and went and Mae ran around wearing practically nothing, she would sit genteelly sipping it, her gloved little finger extended, looking for all the world as though she were taking tea at the Savoy. I feel sure everything she wore, especially her hats, had worked its way through at least six rummage sales on the journey towards her skinny frame.

The Peke would sit staring fixedly at the uncouth antics of our two poodles, who, after a period of anxiousness, would retire, unnerved, to the safety of a chair and pretend to sleep. Every now and again, one would open an eye, look at the Peke, shiver slightly and close it again.

When Matilda had finished her tea, she would readjust her crumpled little eye-veil and, if Mae were free, clear her throat delicately and say faintly, 'I have a few little things which just might interest you, dear.'

Mae, far less timid than her poodles, would say, 'Right. What you got, Till? Let's have a dekko.'

Then the contents of the cretonne bags would be carefully unpacked with a show of great ceremony. Never was such rubbish so carefully wrapped: a yard of tissue paper and several rubber bands enclosing a cheap glass necklace, brown paper and string wrapping an old scarf. One parcel was opened with a flourish to reveal a fox fur that Matilda shook to show its lustre, filling the kitchen with flying hairs.

Mae invariably bought some of this tat. The prices were

in keeping with Matilda's delusion, though Mae and I always wondered if she really was a dotty old lady or whether it was a con trick: as with most of the con tricks in Soho, you could never be quite sure. Mae could never bear to think of the Peke going hungry and would frequently fork out three pounds for an almost-new hot-water-bottle cover or twelve inches of moulting marabou.

'Chuck it in the dustbin,' she would say after Matilda's departure. 'Half an hour with a punter will pay for it.'

There was a continuous stream of people who saw fit to lift Mae's hard-earned cash from her – and even some of mine. Apart from the straight 'Lend us a nicker, love', there were other women who, for example, offered to clean the stairs for a couple of quid. After doing two steps, they would come up for their money, claiming they were hungry and needed a meal to get their strength up to do the rest. We wouldn't see them again until several weeks later, when they'd return seeking a re-engagement. Their excuses would be many and varied but usually dramatic:

'I got taken off with acute appendicitis.'

'I tripped over the bucket and broke my ankle.'

'On my baby's life – my father came round to tell me my mother had just died.'

'On my baby's life' was an oft-repeated assurance. At first I thought that no one would make such a solemn affirmation and not mean it, but I soon discovered that while at least half of them had never had a baby to swear about, the other half had got rid of so many they'd lost count.

And it wasn't just the women who were on the make. There were plenty of gay men about who would pop up to see if there were any odd jobs to be done. Even the smallest errand would warrant at least a pound in payment. There was one gorgeous boy, known as Angel, who did charring as a speciality. He was beautiful, with long curly hair – not at all the thing for men in those days. He wore jangling earrings, bracelets and flimsy Hungarian blouses. Unlike the queens who haunted many of the Soho cafés, he wore no make-up – but then he didn't have to: he had a face to match his name.

There was a little Greek shoemaker too, who would come around taking orders. Unusually, he was conscientious and earned his money. I think he lived close by, because I only ever saw him in shirtsleeves; he wore an extremely dirty trilby and his skin was like the old worn-in leather he worked with. Mae had tiny feet and took only a size one shoe. She was very proud of her shoes and spent a lot of money enhancing them. The shoemaker's name was Nick, and every time he came, he brought the pair of shoes from the last order and went away with a list of instructions for the next. His shoes cost about sixteen pounds a pair: at that time, a small fortune to spend.

Mae invented platform heels – or rather, in her case, platform soles– long before they became popular in the seventies. She maintained that increased length below the knee made for a more elegant leg. I recognised the technique from a trick that artists used in fashion drawing. It certainly had the right effect, and it impressed the other girls so much that they began to have platforms heels made as well. This offended Mae's sense of individuality, so when everyone else was eventually wearing a single platform, Mae ordered a double; when the rest of the girls cottoned on to that, Mae ordered trebles. And so it might have gone had not Mae been the only one who could walk in a quadruple.

Oddly enough, I don't recall that I ever heard the shoemaker speak. Even when asked how much he wanted for his finished work, he would merely indicate the price by holding up the appropriate number of fingers. When Mae roughly pencilled out new ideas for her next pair of shoes, he would become strangely moved, his dark eyes snapping, his fingers curling round invisible pieces of leather and his skinny little body a-tremble with eagerness, but still he never uttered a word. To me, he was an unsung genius.

Then there were the men who came round selling pornographic photographs – just like the ones I'd found in Mae's room when I first started. These pictures, usually in sets of eight, were quite necessary equipment for anyone on the game. Not only did they make a girl's work much easier by exciting the clients to the point of no return, but they were essential erectile aids for a great number of men. Whenever the photograph vendors came, Mae would flip through their wares with the cool, appraising air of a woman glancing through a fashion magazine. Now and again she would remark, 'Pity you haven't got any of queers', or 'I saw most of these last time. Haven't you got any with two fellas and a girl?' She always bought some; she needed to, because her stock was always mysteriously dwindling.

Our various essentials were not all brought so obligingly to the flat, and I had to get some things from neighbouring shops. The most regular errands were for tissues and condoms, which I got from a little place known as the 'cut-price shop', where the counters were always loaded with all sorts of products. On one side were expensive perfumes, false eyelashes and a fantastic range of cosmetics, and, on the other, an equivalent range of men's toiletries. Behind the counter was shelf upon shelf of every kind of hair preparation, skin lotion and cream, as well as hormone and vitamin pills and vitality tonics. There was a professional hair bleach amongst the hair preparations with special appeal to Mae: 'as used by hairdressers – not available to the general public'.

Here, Durex (all condoms in those days were made by Durex) were sold to the 'trade' for one pound per gross box, and we needed a fresh box every few days. The first time I was sent, I walked past the shop half a dozen times trying to pluck up enough courage to go in. Although it was to become a frequent errand, I never felt comfortable with it.

The shop was run by two pleasant middle-aged men: one short, dapper and slim and the other short, dapper and stocky. That first time, as on every subsequent one, as I reached over the counter to take my plainly wrapped parcel, a great blast of perfume caught me full in the face. This 'gift' was both complimentary and obligatory and was intended to secure my loyalty. The ladies' magazines maintained that a refined girl perfumed herself so discreetly as to be almost unnoticeable and heavy scent was the sign of a woman of easy virtue. I would walk back to the flat trailing great clouds of sickly perfume behind me and hoping I wouldn't be knocked down and have the contents of my parcel revealed.

I soon learnt from Mae that all girls who were safe to go with would take care of the rubber for the client. Although this had a titillating effect, in reality it was done for two quite different reasons. One was to make sure that it was *her* rubber and not one that had been sabotaged with holes; the other was that it gave her an opportunity for a quick but knowledgeable examination of the man for any signs of disease. It was Mae's rare negligence in this that once resulted in my being sent on yet another embarrassing mission.

'Here, Babs. Ever seen crabs before?' she called out from the bedroom.

I was puzzled, wondering what had brought this on. 'Well of course I have,' I called back.

'I bet you haven't seen these sort. Come here.'

I went in and found her sitting on the edge of the bed, nearly bent double.

'That dirty bugger I just had. I had me suspicions when I first saw him and then forgot to look when I got him up here. Just you look.'

I got down on my hands and knees and peered.

'You'll have to get closer than that, mate,' she said.

'Charming,' I said.

'I don't know what people would say if they could see us now,' she chortled, and we both went into fits of giggles. 'No, seriously, though,' she said eventually, 'have a look, 'cos I hope you won't have the chance to see them again.'

I peered hard and eventually saw little creatures exactly the shape of normal crabs and scuttling sideways.

'Good heavens! Fascinating!' I exclaimed, glued to the spot. 'Never seen anything like it before. What are you going to do about it?'

'Well it's what you've got to do first,' she said. 'And that's to go round to the chemist's and get me some Blue Unction. Of course, you can use camphorated oil if you're careful not to burn yourself, but you smell to high heaven of the stuff afterwards.'

So off I went to the chemist, getting more nervous with every step. I presumed that Blue Unction existed solely for the treatment of crabs; I wasn't aware that lice could crop up on the head as well and, in any case, could be caught by means other than sex. To my horror, I found the shop brimful with customers. When it was my turn to be served, I held back, letting several people go ahead of me. More kept coming in and the shop showed no sign of emptying.

I knew I daren't be away from Mae for too long, so I forced myself towards the counter.

'May I have some Blue Unction, please?' I said, as near to a whisper as I thought I could get away with.

'What's that you say?' said the chemist, cupping an ear with his hand and leaning over the counter towards me.

Feeling myself going hot with embarrassment, I repeated it a little louder.

'Oh, Blue Unction!' he boomed and went off to get it from the back of the shop.

For the short while he was gone, I felt sure every eye in the place was upon me. I could hardly count out the money when he returned to plonk the pot on the counter with uncalled-for abandon. I departed, head down like a charging bison, through what now seemed to be a vast, goggling crowd.

At least when I got back I was pleased to see the stuff actually worked. In fact it was an instant success, for, as Mae explained:

'The little buggers haven't had time to get a hold.'

Mae was extra cautious afterwards, but that didn't mean I was off the hook: unusual requests from clients often meant I had to buy all sorts of odds and ends. I might still have been naïve, but I was no longer the complete innocent who had met Mae that day in The Mousehole.

Thirteen

~

I hadn't been with Mae for very long before other girls – who hadn't dared to come when Rabbits was there – began dropping in and adding to the general chaos.

Strictly speaking, visiting was taboo, as according to the law, more than one convicted prostitute on the same premises constituted a brothel, which was illegal; and anyone watching the place could easily think that clients coming up were taking their pick from the girls. If the police decided to swoop, it was possible that the maid would be convicted as a brothel-keeper, and the premises closed down – though the girls themselves were in the clear. This could be one reason why Rabbits had forbidden Mae's friends to call. At this point of my 'maidhood', I was as blissfully ignorant of this risk as I had been about everything else; and by the time one of the other maids did think to warn me, the rot had set in, and Mae's friends were treating the place like a Women's Institute. By then, I hadn't the guts to put my foot down, or the heart to spoil their fun; and philosophically comforted myself with the thought that if I landed up in prison, it would be yet another experience to learn by.

Mae would greet each visitor with crows of delight and call for tea all round. Soon the floor and the bed would be littered with practically everything she possessed, cupboards and drawers would be gaping open, and Mae would be holding up a skirt and declaring:

'Here it is: this is my lucky one – I always make a bomb when I'm wearing this! Don't I, Babs?'

It was very often a garment I'd never seen her wear before, but she wouldn't be waiting for answers.

'Borrow it if you like ... but bring it back. Here, this blouse goes nice with it. Put 'em on. Let's see what they look like on you.'

I still have her 'really lucky' skirt. It was grey worsted, pencil-line, with a slit on one side. She decided one day that it wasn't quite so lucky any more and gave it to me. Even now, I wouldn't part with it for the world. The sight of that skirt with Mae's bottom inside it has stirred so many emotions and caused so much money to change hands that I have come to regard it as of historical importance: like the Black Prince's armour. This – and a pair of the hand-made shoes in which she walked so many miles – still helps to clutter my home.

The other girl's clothes would promptly be shed and added to the pile on the floor, and Mae's skirt and blouse would be donned in their place. Then Mae would eye her friend up and down in a critical manner. She would give a tweak here and there and perhaps add a necklace or a patent-leather belt to the ensemble. At last, satisfied, she would say, 'Fucking lovely. You'll make a bomb in that.' Then, amongst all the debris, we would sit, drink our tea and exchange the latest gossip.

In the middle of this, a client, tired of waiting outside for Mae to emerge, would creep up the stairs. His arrival would cause Mae to sweep the bed clear while the other girl and I would snatch up our cups and migrate to the kitchen. Eventually, the girl or girls – there was often more than one – would leave and I would be left to clear up the mess at breakneck speed before someone else came up.

The most frequent of these visitors was a girl called Rita. She and Mae were as close to being real friends as was possible under the circumstances.

Rita had very fair skin, jet-black hair, vivid blue eyes and a fascinatingly large bosom. On first sight, she was icily beautiful, but the effect was altered by her strident cockney accent. There were two things I found disconcerting about her: one was the fact that her eyes had a hard, insolent stare and the other was the scar that ran down the length of her face. It wasn't unsightly, just a raised white seam; in fact in a strange sort of way it added to her good looks. It turned out that the stare was caused by extreme short-sightedness; while the scar was the work of another girl and a razor, not long after Rita had started on the game.

'Nasty it was, for a long time,' she told me. 'It went right through me cheek. But I was a lairy little bastard; I asked for it and it taught me a lesson.'

She stared for a while into space, reliving the moment and the lesson it had taught her, but said no more about it.

On the first occasion she came round, she had not been seen for several years after having disappeared suddenly. Everyone had supposed the absence to be one of her periodic retirements – which in a way it was – until word got round that she'd married one of the bigger racketeers. She'd had a daughter by him and they'd recently divorced. She was now living with a burglar and was hustling again to raise money so they could get a nice home together.

'It didn't work out with Billy,' she said. ''Cos really, I only like thieves.' (Or *feeves*, as she pronounced it.)

All her feeves had been English; the Maltese never bothered with her because her preferences were well known, and more so because she was forever 'resting' rather than out earning them some money.

Early one Saturday afternoon, accompanied by her new feef, she brought her little girl to visit. The child was about three years old. They were about to go to a cartoon cinema, after which the daughter would be put to bed and Rita would go off to work. I felt sorry for the little tot. She sat demurely on a kitchen chair, wearing the working-class notion of a rich child's apparel: leggings under a coat and bonnet of thick velour. Rita and Mae, at their ease in normal sweaters and skirts, sat and chatted for an hour or so while this plain, pale child, encased in her thick finery, sat fidgeting slightly, solemnly watching her mother and new 'auntie' talking. Over the following years she was to observe the arrival and departure of three legitimate stepfathers, a host of temporary 'uncles' – all feeves, of course – and the arrival of two half-sisters and a brother. Bewildered and largely neglected in favour of the newcomers, she was to run away from home many times.

Rita and Mae had both started on the game at the age of eighteen ('I was a real little dolly then,' Rita said) and had kept in touch with one another ever since. They told me how at first, for a long while, they had no flats to work in and had to use taxis instead, and how between them they scared off any little 'mysteries' who hung about their pitch. They giggled a lot over their various escapades and had me in fits of laughter too. They described how, twelve years earlier, they had made a striking pair, standing together outside Lyon's Corner House in Coventry Street with a couple of co-operating taxicabs parked at the ready.

I was puzzled as I pictured the scene. I'd thought Mae was, at the most, only in her mid-twenties.

'You didn't tell me you were so elderly,' I said. 'No

wonder you're always on at me to swap places with you: you're past it, aren't you?'

She told me to hush my lip and said she'd had her last birthday about ten years ago.

'I'm never going to get old,' she said. They would prove to be tragically prophetic words.

Other characters crowd into my mind. There was Jessie, who was always in financial trouble but never particularly upset by the fact. She had a profusion of cloudy dark hair, Algerian features and more than a little of the *Mona Lisa* about her expression. I found her quite fascinating (and was later to paint her portrait). Her problem was that she had five children boarded in various convent schools. It seemed a complicated business and I couldn't quite understand it, but the gist seemed to be that she was only able to afford the fees for four of them and so always had one at home. Care and food for the homebound child was, of course, also expensive for a working mother, regardless of the work she did. Jessie came and went, always untroubled by her predicaments and often amused by them. All she asked of Mae and me was a friendly ear; she never requested financial help. She was known to love her work, and because of this, literally sold herself short.

Penny was another mother, and a relatively good one, but she only saw her two sons for half of Saturdays and all day on Sundays. During the week they were off to school before she got up and, of course, she was working when they returned. She would phone them as soon as they were home and again every hour all through the evening, giving them instructions. It wasn't a perfect system; her twelve-year-old took to stealing, and much as she punished him, he continued to do so. In keeping with the parenting methods of that time and place, she resolved to knock it out of him in the end, 'even if I have to half kill him!'

I winced at the thought, remembering my own childhood.

Hilda was well over fifty and looked even more. She was also caught in a vicious circle. Because she was old and couldn't earn very much, she drank; the more she drank, the less she earned. The problem was simple enough to understand, but its solution was elusive. She was always fighting desperately to get her rent together, and the more desperate she became, the drunker she got. Whenever I saw her, she was staggering slightly and clutching at the men she accosted, as much for support as anything else.

One evening she came up at about eight o'clock, almost sober so she was obviously skint. There was a client in the kitchen, so she sat down with me in the waiting room. Great fat tears were rolling down her cheeks.

'What's the matter, Hilda?' I asked.

'Haven't got off once all bloody day,' she sobbed. 'And I've been out since two.'

'Oh that's terrible,' I said. 'Poor old Hilda; you must be fed up.'

The tears continued to flow. She was silent for a while, then burst out: 'It's not so much the money, you know – though Gawd knows I could do with it – but it makes you feel so low when nobody fancies you any more.'

She gave a great gulping sob and the tears fell faster than ever. Lying nobly, I told her that it had been a bit quiet for everyone that day. While I racked my brains to think what could be done to comfort her, she gazed at me mistily through her tears, sniffling every now and again. She looked a mess and it suddenly occurred to me that the only make-up she ever wore was smudged lipstick.

Inspiration struck: 'Well, we can't have all this; we've got to do something.'

I popped into the bedroom to see Mae, who'd just said goodbye to her client. I explained that poor old Hilda hadn't 'got off' all day and asked if I could use Mae's make-up.

'She's been crying,' I said sotto voce. 'You have to admit, she does look a bit haggard, one way and another.'

Without a word, Mae pulled out the complete drawer of make-up. 'Give her the whole works – even these,' she said. She fished out a pair of false eyelashes, then turned and clattered off downstairs into the street again.

'The works' was exactly what Hilda got – from cleansing cream onwards. Doing this I had a queasy premonition of things to come. It struck me vividly that one day my own face would have this loose, crêpe-like texture. I carried on applying the make-up, pulling Hilda's skin to get it taut enough for the eye pencil to make a straight line, then letting go and finding it crooked. Eventually the eyelashes were stuck on and I did her hair – putting on a bandeau and coaxing a wispy fringe forward to cover the wrinkles on her forehead – then stood back to survey my handiwork. I complimented myself enough to say that she looked quite nice – at least she'd been groomed; in street lighting, she would probably look quite good. She had sat all the way through the renovations with an eager docility, expecting magic to be wrought; I was thankful that when finally I gave her the mirror, she was thrilled.

'Who'd have thought it? You've made a new woman of me!'

With growing confidence, she examined herself from different angles. Remembering some of Mae's psychology, I fished about in my handbag and gave her a broken key ring shaped like a palette.

'Here, take this. It's lucky – you'll see. Now, you pop off and make some money.'

She made her exit wearing a beatific smile and holding herself as though she were balancing books on her head.

Mae, coming up with another client, had passed her in the street. 'Looks much better, don't she?' she said as she passed. Then she stopped and added absent-mindedly, 'Poor old cow.'

Half an hour later, Hilda hurried up the stairs again, all smiles and good cheer.

'I got off! That was so good of you, dear. I won't forget it; you're an angel! But right now, I'm going to have a drink to celebrate!'

Eleven o'clock was Pearl's calling time. She was a very beautiful black girl who was extremely haughty. She would sit drumming her fingers impatiently until Mae was free, then go with her into the bedroom, departing after only two minutes. She didn't speak – even to Mae – beyond a few syllables. After her first visit, when I'd realised her preference for silence, I just said hello when she arrived and carried on with whatever I was doing. I asked Mae to explain.

'There's this lovely queer I know,' she said. 'He's got this pretty bed-sitter near Goodge Street. He's a night valet at a hotel, so, 'course, he doesn't use his room in the evening. Pearl had got nowhere to work so I told her about Rodney. He jumped at the extra cash but he doesn't want to get done for poncing, so . . .'

. . . So he'd added the condition that he should never see the girl and that Mae must collect the rent nightly and get it to him somehow. With the addition of a screen for the maid to sit behind, this worked out very nicely; hence Pearl's nightly appearance at our place for several weeks. The arrangement lasted until Rodney's alleged nervousness of 'the law' caused him to see police officers in every dark doorway and he called a halt to it. But we heard later that on learning of the big money involved, he'd chucked his hotel job to become Pearl's maid himself.

Mae just grinned at the news and said, 'What a sod!'

All the girls that Mae and I visited repaid the compliment. As well as French-corseted Fiona and Benzy Nell (when she could force her feet further than the groove she'd made in her own bit of pavement), there was aristocratic Anne, Cindy, a lanky Scottish girl who I grew very fond of, and Meg, a short and plump Scottish girl, who I was not so fond of. There was also the fiery and nigh-on psychopathic Tina and the sadistic Sadie, who was making a fortune.

There were a number of other girls who merely rushed in and out once or twice, and an even greater number of maids, who came to borrow or return items of clothing, bits of jewellery or small sums of money. The most common call was for condoms, because 'the cut-price shop is closed and we've had a rush on'. In the fug of cigarette smoke that shrouded us, there was a sisterhood and a knowledge that we would sink or swim together. Even clients were not allowed to interrupt a particularly juicy bit of scandal; I would be sent to banish them. It was huge fun.

When I took up with Mae, I had made the first true friend of my life, and it was in Soho and through Soho that I first came to feel a sense of belonging to a broader circle, a group of friends who included me among their number. I was still an outcast, perhaps, but if so, I was an outcast among outcasts, an exile among her fellows. It was as though life had begun anew for me; or more accurately, as though life had begun properly for the first time. In my crummy room and in Mae's chaotic flat, I had found freedom. Freedom, friends and happiness.

Fourteen

~

Although being sisters in sin welded these girls together, there was also a tremendous amount of cattiness between them, and this became apparent as I listened to their gossiping. According to them, every girl in Soho – present company always excepted – earned her money by 'not using rubbers', 'taking it in the mouth' or 'going with chocolate' (at that time such racism was accepted without question).

The other standard indictment was that a girl handed over all her earnings to her ponce to do just what he liked with. None of the girls ever recognised their own boyfriend as a ponce; rather, *he* was a man with ambitions that she was helping him attain. In the beginning, it had been Mae alone who introduced me to Soho's underworld, but after a while I found I could place more reliance on what the other maids told me. They gave me straight facts and – almost – unbiased views. They weren't so personally involved as their mistresses, and although no paragons of virtue, they were not as scatty. The prostitutes were inclined to embroider their stories or recount things differently according to their mood.

And so it was from the maids that I first learned of this creature: the 'ponce'. This was the 'business man' behind practically every 'business girl' and, as I came to realise, it was the job Tony had successfully applied for.

Many people may think that 'ponce' is synonymous with 'pimp', but in those days a pimp was a go-between who prowled the streets on the lookout for wandering customers. As such, he actually earned his living, which was something no self-respecting ponce would have dreamt of doing. But in Soho, where the girls introduced themselves to potential customers direct, there was no scope whatever for the pimp, and in fact that very word was unknown in West End jargon.

I had quickly learned that there were several distinct areas of prostitution in the West End. There was Mayfair, with its focus in Shepherd Market, which was considered the classy area, and which the more wealthy and elite men patronised. This select group of flats in Mayfair, where the best pickings were to be had, was controlled by a powerful Mafia-like syndicate who specialised in organised prostitution, and they used strong-arm methods whenever necessary, and without hesitation. They were themselves the landlords of these flats, and they financed the girls, setting them up with smart clothes and the like. As far as I could gather, they specialised in bringing over French girls; obtaining British nationality for them by paying a hundred pounds to anyone willing to marry them and disappear off the scene. These were truly business girls, and reckoned to work hard for two years, then return to France as respectable women and set themselves up in business there.

There was a northward sprawl of professional flats from Mayfair too, and other isolated but very small pockets of prostitution, run discreetly in various parts of the West End, which depended on carefully worded, ambiguous cards on display in newsagents' windows, with just a phone number to ring. These girls were the vanguard of what came to be generally known as 'call girls'.

There was also a parade of girls along the Bayswater Road, from Marble Arch down as far as Queensway. They'd walk the pavement where the railings ran along the northern end of Hyde Park, and get picked up by passing drivers. Some took these clients back to flats around the nearby Lancaster Gate area, and further afield as far as Paddington; but most had only bed-sits and couldn't take clients back with them. Instead, the girls would be taken back to the punter's own flat or some accommodating hotel, or, most often, to some quieter spot for action in the car.

Quite a lot of girls also stood along the Broad Walk which ran through Hyde Park, alongside the bright lights of Park Lane, from Speakers' Corner at Marble Arch down to Hyde Park Corner. These girls came from everywhere, and generally worked in dark corners of the park on the grass under the trees.

Then there were the 'mysteries', who surreptitiously used the same beats as the established prostitutes – which led to many a fracas. Once they had hooked their man, they let him pay the cab fare to where their homes were situated, sometimes miles away. As often as not, these women were ordinary housewives who only worked when they were a bit short of money. They were known as mysteries simply because so little was known about them.

There were local centres in all the other London boroughs, but they were negligible; and of the major centres mentioned, our little patch of Soho was the most concentrated and best known. After all, wasn't the statue of Eros our cornerstone?

Here in Soho proper, the prostitutes were the real, genuine, well-known thing: reasonably priced, clean and honest, and their overall earnings were enormous. In the cheaper districts, the girls couldn't afford to look glamorous, and so didn't feel or act it. In the more dignified districts, they had to appear to be sedate and normal ladies, or their high-status clients wouldn't dare to be seen in their company; so those girls, too, didn't act enticingly. No, for real whoopee, most people preferred Soho.

But behind the bonhomie of the women was the pernicious influence of their men. I was sad when I learned from the other maids that, beyond any doubt, Tony was a ponce. Sad that my suspicions of him had been confirmed; and sadder still to realise that there was nothing at all I could do about it. You cannot tell a woman that the man she's in love with is only after her money – she wouldn't believe you anyway. I felt that all I could do was to be around for Mae when she needed me, as I felt sure she would in time.

The ponces had perfected the art of luring and trapping the girls. They'd choose a target: a prostitute already set up in a flat and working, but without a regular boyfriend. Then a bribed maid or friend would begin the process by telling the chosen victim about a handsome young man who is pining away with love for her but too shy to make himself known. The girl would be moved by the fact that in spite of her profession, someone has put her on a pedestal. A meeting would be engineered – and the whole thing beautifully staged. In fact, no expense would be spared to show her that the very last thing he needs from her is her money. As the relationship develops, he will buy her presents, but she will buy him many more, and her gifts to him will be of a far more costly nature. Apart from wishing to please him, it gives her the opportunity to show her world how well she is doing. So the girl will deck out her ponce in expensive suits and all the trimmings, and buy him the most expensive car she can afford.

Then, the requests for money start. A gambling debt,

perhaps, or something to keep the police quiet. The ponce now has a regular income. The habit of giving is gradually acquired by the girl; and before she becomes aware of it, she is giving him all she earns. The ultimate argument of the ponce is that he, as a businessman, should be the one to take charge of all the cash, in order to save and invest it and procure an early and comfortable retirement for them both. The tables are now turned, and she is the one waiting for handouts and pocket money.

Up to this point, Mae and Tony were still in the honeymoon period of their relationship – the time of enchantment when, like a snake, he was drawing her closer into his coils. He was asking her not to work so hard, and she, taking him at his word, indulged in her flitting around the streets of Soho with me. But it was destined to be short-lived.

Mae was not the only girl falling into the trap. The ponces were evil men, hard and often dangerous. One girl, Treesa, was owned – and I do mean owned – by a monster called Dino whose vices were not counterbalanced by a single virtue.

Treesa was a big, doll-like woman with an oval olive face and long dark hair cut in a straight fringe. She had a gentle and tractable nature and her maid – a nice woman named Connie – was so heartbroken on Treesa's behalf that she was permanently on tranquillisers. When I first knew Treesa, she was going home to Dino one night every week. She said it was because the police were keeping a particularly strict watch on him and he daren't take risks. She loved Dino with a desperation I've seldom seen equalled and she lived for that one night when she could be with him. In gratitude for it, she spent half of the next day cleaning their love nest – until it was time to go to work. As time passed, even this minuscule joy was prohibited:

according to Dino, it had become too dangerous. Thence-forth, for weeks at a time, Treesa's only link with him was when he chose to ring her.

Connie was given the job of calling on him on her way home every night. Dino took the wad of notes that represented the day's earnings and shucked off the pound note that was all Treesa was to be left with. Treesa put up with all this, believing in the fantasy of a growing retirement fund for them both. It was fortunate she actually liked buns and buttered rolls, because along with the bits and pieces Connie brought in from home, that was mostly what she lived on. Connie was a true friend, and knowing Treesa could never resist taking anything left lying about, she would 'forgetfully' leave small sums of money in the kitchen so Treesa could afford an occasional cheese or ham roll.

Then Treesa found a lump in her armpit and another in one of her breasts. She showed them to all the girls she knew, but none of them said what was in their minds. Instead, they urged her to see a doctor.

'Oh, I can't take the time off just yet,' she said. 'I'll be retiring soon and then there'll be plenty of time.'

The other girls nodded in agreement, but they knew that Dino would never allow her to retire. They also knew the reason that Dino never let her go home was because she would find there the glamorous and bright sixteen-year-old he was buttering up. It was policy to say nothing and that was how it would have been had not someone let it slip one day. Treesa was frantic enough to confront Dino. and with an amazing bit of quick thinking, he admitted it – sort of.

His story was that, although he was indeed 'messing' with someone, he had been hoping to keep it as a surprise for Treesa and she was wrong to be cross with him. Far from being a young girl, the 'someone' was a woman in her mid-thirties who had an enormous bank account. It was all in aid of Treesa's early retirement. Once the woman's savings had gone, so would the rival be. Treesa was instantly reassured and went around happily telling everyone of Dino's clever plot. Everybody pretended to accept it.

Dino couldn't be certain that Treesa had no suspicions left, so he and his brother sent the brother's girl, Pam, to stay with Treesa every night, claiming it would be company for her. In this way, each girl would keep an eye on the other. It couldn't have been much fun for Treesa, who only had a single bed and was not, of course, provided with another. Unusually amongst the girls, Pam's standard of bodily hygiene was terrible. Every time she reached a point where she was unbearable to live with, her maid would have to positively drag her to the bath and scrub her.

Although everybody agreed that Treesa must be as gullible as a child, we felt that surely, some day, the scales would fall from her eyes. We almost made bets about what would happen when they did. The general opinion was that she had two choices, either to shop Dino to the police or to commit suicide. Eventually she confounded us all by doing both. For the first time in her life, she had used logic and decided there wasn't much point in doing one without the other.

The more I heard these stories, the less I liked Mae's alliance with Tony. These women were now my life. I was happy and becoming very good at my job. Mae's world had become my world and it was one I embraced with eagerness. The subtleties of my role took time to seep into my consciousness, but my three main functions were clear from the start: I was companion, bodyguard and housekeeper (this last trailing far behind the other two in order of importance). From the companionship angle, the need was great and I found it touchingly so. The life of a prostitute was not a frivolous one where every night was a party, awash with champagne. On the contrary, the ponces ensured that the conveyer-belt process of making money continued. I was slow to understand just how calculating these ponces were, but had I been swifter on the uptake, I would have been even more wary of Tony. He certainly remained wary of me. I was too devoted to Mae and her happiness for his peace of mind. If I'd had purely financial motives, I would have had his interests at heart. I would have kept him informed how much Mae earned, how much she 'weeded', who she talked to, what she said and whether she worked conscientiously enough. I couldn't have been more different from his ideal, or more determined to be so.

For the moment, however, I was in a position of strength. Tony was still fairly new on the scene. Mae was still in love, or thought she was, and at the same time I was her friend, her confidante, the person in whose company she spent nearly every waking hour. Tony couldn't move against me yet, and I had not thought of moving against him. Even if I had, I would probably have failed, given the weight of Mae's wilful naïvety. All the same, and even if I was largely unaware of them, the battle lines had been drawn and would become dangerously clear before too long.

Fifteen

~

All the girls had a similar routine. They rose late in the morning, drank a few cups of tea or coffee, travelled to their flats in Soho, worked until about midnight, then returned home to their bed-sitters in Paddington, Brixton or Notting Hill. For some, where the ponce wanted to keep closer control by actually living with the girl, home could be as far out as Romford or Slough, where their arrangements were less likely to be noticed. And so, after what might be a considerable journey from the West End, the girls would arrive home, have a bath, eat – the cohabitees having to cook for their men – and finally fall into bed at about four in the morning. Without much time for other friends, the maid, therefore, became the surrogate best friend, confidante and mother figure. Maids were mostly too canny to have sponging boyfriends and so could be better off than the women they worked for. They would often provide the only real home comforts the girls ever had.

Companionship aside, the major function of the maid's role gave me a real sense of unease. Being the only tenants in the house, we were very vulnerable and, after the shops closed, extremely isolated. As bodyguards go, I was small, and in any case, I flinched from any form of violence. In readiness for any 'happenings', Mae flanked her dressing table mirror with two reproduction Staffordshire cats. These, she explained, made admirable weapons if grasped round their elongated necks. She said they were as good as bottles but more ornamental. Apart from this main purpose, they also served as stress levellers when the irritations of the job got to Mae: if a client changed his mind at the last minute, the unfortunate cats would be dropped from the upper window as he left the front door. She always aimed to miss him by an inch or two and was generally successful. While I was with Mae, I swept up no end of defunct cats; fortunately, the supplier was nearby and was always well stocked with replacements.

Taking a leaf out of Mae's book, I kept the hammer with the broken shaft concealed but handy. It was a far more lethal weapon than a Staffordshire cat, though I had no intention of actually using it; I just hoped that the sight of it in my hand would daunt any passing maniac. My only other aid to the quelling of riots was the few bits of judo I'd picked up from Fred – Mae's rejected suitor – but I couldn't be sure of an assailant being obliging enough to fall into the right position to enable me to use those.

So there I was, talking to the strange men I had been warned about, laughing and joking my way through days and nights of sin and scandal. The flippancy disguised an ever-present, real fear that each client might be the last. Every prostitute, every maid, knew this all too well; the newspapers frequently told of prostitutes murdered in or on their beds. All the customers who came up those stairs would see our self-confident front but would rarely appreciate the isolation and danger we also felt. We would joke and flirt but all the time keeping one eye on the cash and the other on where our weapons lay. And remembering never to turn our backs on them.

As the one who dealt with the money, the maid was, in

some ways, a more valuable target than the girl. I met several really neurotic maids who were clearly terrified of the job they were doing, and were always taking tranquillisers to keep their nerves under control. These I considered a terrible danger too, as men are a bit like horses, I think, and smell fear and uncertainty; and if the maid was nervous, then the girl usually became nervous too.

One girl had a maid who was well over eighty. She was frail and wizened, and as the girl said: 'The poor old sod can't doing nothing but make the tea, and then most of it ends up in the bleeding saucer. If ever I get any bother, I don't think she's even strong enough to open the window to shout for help.'

Just as useless was the near-narcoleptic Italian woman whose girl was obliged to serve her cup after cup of black coffee and poke her with a loud 'Wakey, wakey!' The Italian would drink the coffee, fold her arms over her ample bosom and nod off again. 'She goes with the flat,' said the girl gloomily, nodding towards the sleeping form. 'I s'pose they couldn't keep her awake long enough to get her out of it after the last girl left.'

There were motherly maids who were always cooking and serving up meals: wholesome shepherd's pies, stews and thick soups. They would see the clients as obstacles to proper digestion. One of these considerate souls combined her culinary obsession with a running commentary on her hot flushes. She claimed she couldn't bear a bra on account of her heat and was happy to discuss the matter further with everyone – including the clients – if given half a chance in between stirring the gravy.

Older maids were often of a different calibre from the girls they worked for. They would read books in between chores, show an interest in world affairs; they would embroider, make lace and tackle a crossword puzzle.

Generally, younger maids seemed to be sullen, moody creatures, married to small-time crooks who always seemed to be 'inside'. The older type were more usual, and many of them could play 'Mum', some even having the credentials of a wholesome background and a husband in a well-paid, responsible job. In these cases, maiding was just to provide the 'bunce' to give their children a good schooling.

But not all the maids were quite so maternal. Others were tough customers who squeezed their girls for ever-larger tips. They would want paying for everything they contributed, however small an item. Despite – or maybe because of – this penny-pinching, some of the girls really needed them around.

One might have thought that maids were often prostitutes who had become too old for the game, but this was hardly ever the case. It occasionally happened in dire emergencies, but only for minimal periods; however old a convicted prostitute was, in the eyes of the law she was still considered capable of prostitution, and therefore the two of them together could constitute a brothel. I knew only one maid who was an ex-pro; she, being French, had received her convictions in France, and so all was well.

One maid stands out above all the others as worth her weight in gold. The aptly named Prudence knew all the laws concerning prostitution – and knew them as well as any lawyer. She was polite, smart, tactful and a great psychologist. She knew every quirky aberration in existence and how it should be handled, and could quickly calculate the correct rate for the job. She could prepare light, appetising snacks and could converse on practically anything. When she trusted a person, she was warm-hearted and kind; when she did not, she was as cold as ice. Only once did she ever work for a girl who was worthy of her. That particular person listened and learned and retired a very wealthy woman.

I often wondered how Mae and Rabbits had got along with each other for as long as they had. But in the end a girl and her maid were working towards the same end.

I remember one incident, round at one of the other girls' flats. The ponce had been sent for – an almost unheard-of occurrence – as a result of the maid being threatened by some thug with a knife. She had promptly handed over twenty-five pounds – too promptly, the girl was arguing. The ponce remained in the background, moodily chewing his nails. When I arrived, the maid was making a big show of collecting her belongings and getting her coat on. But within half an hour we were all – minus the ponce, who had left – sitting down amicably to the usual pot of tea. The scene had been engineered so the girl could prove to her boyfriend that she had a legitimate excuse for taking home less than usual that evening.

Everyone generously conceded that it was harder work being Mae's maid than anyone else's. We, the maids, were a little clique of our own – 'partners in persecution'. One day, I met a maid in the street who was breathing fire because her girl had been counting the used rubbers to check the number against the maid's written total.

'After all the time I've been with her, she starts not trusting me! But I've got even with her, haven't I? Now, every night I go in and whip a few out of the bin before she counts 'em.' Then, with typical loyal protectiveness, she added, ''Course, I don't really blame her – *he* must have put her up to it.'

And so the weeks went on and my expertise increased. It was autumn now. Cold winds blew down those inhospitable alleys, bringing tides of brown leaves, which were caught in puddles of water, there to rot down into a black mat, lethal to the unwary foot.

I thought less and less of my previous life, much as I expect angels have little reason to think of their time on earth once they've passed through the Pearly Gates to the life beyond. Even if I had thought of my former life, what would I have done with the memories? My grandmother had cursed me and was hardly a woman to let go of a grudge. My mother had been fast enough to flee when I was a child, and would be no more delighted to see me now that I was an independent adult. The only school friend with whom I'd enjoyed a real bond had moved off to South Africa, half a world away.

My little bed-sit, with its gas fire burning in its nest of fireclay, and its other small comforts, was still my home. Although sometimes when I got home I recalled uneasily how I'd arrived there vowing to become an artist. I'd had visions, once, of earning enough money to buy art materials with which to practise relentlessly at my craft, in the hope one day of painting that perfect painting.

Foolish hopes! My artistic ambitions had been entirely mute since meeting Mae. For six days a week I was simply too busy to lift a paintbrush. On the seventh, I had my domestic chores to attend to. I was tired – and besides, my attention had strayed. I was now fast becoming a Soho expert and a genuine Soho native. The police officers' concerns were confirmed: I had become inured to depravity and no longer saw it as anything other than normal life. As the old Rabbits Regime fell into almost total decay, the corruption – and the sheer pace of life – increased to a level I could never have guessed at in my old, sheltered existence.

Sixteen

❧

Pandemonium was both the hardest thing to get used to and the only constant that I could rely on to define a day as 'average'.

Mae would arrive, propelling a client before her. As she passed, she would break off chatting to him to say, 'Hello, love, make us a cup of tea, will you?' And with that, battle commenced. I continued to begin work an hour earlier than Mae in the mistaken belief that if I got everything under control before she arrived, I could deal coolly and efficiently with whatever ensued. The reality was that within half an hour of that first cup of tea, the day would rapidly scuttle into tragedy or farce. Like a boulder crashing down a mountainside, Mae had a momentum that left havoc in its wake.

To arrive with one customer was, perhaps, understandable, but it was not unknown for her to kick-start the day with as many as five men at once. On one such occasion, these were visitors to London who, with a little persuasion from Mae, had decided to all have a go. Handling these groups was a speciality of hers, and she managed to round them all up with the added encumbrances of the two dogs and – as was quite usual – a large bunch of flowers. With a grin and a wink, she passed the dogs' leads over to me, piled the flowers into my arms and, leaving brief instructions to give the waiting men tea, feed the dogs and put the flowers in water, swept into the bedroom with the first of the friends.

With the dogs yapping round my feet, the flowers in my face and the remaining men standing self-consciously on the landing, I was helpless for a few moments. I deftly shut the dogs and flowers in the kitchen before ushering the men into the waiting room. I had enough experience to stand in the doorway in the pretence of chatting to them. Our division of labour was clear enough: Mae had caught them and I must prevent their escape: so early, so sober, they might easily have changed their minds. It was all rather tricky, because I also had to be ready outside her door when her hand came through with the money. I could do this and be back, blocking the waiting room door, before anyone realised I'd moved.

Another client wended his way up the stairs. On being shown into the waiting room, he bucked like a frightened horse at the sight of so many other faces. I decided to put him in the kitchen with the dogs and the flowers; if he liked dogs he would be kept amused, and if he didn't, he'd be too scared to move.

At first, performing as cloakroom attendant, gracious host, prison wardress, dog minder and tea lady nearly drove me demented. As time went by, I realised that 'give everyone tea' needn't be taken literally, and if I cocked a deaf ear – as the local parlance had it – life became less difficult.

Once the first influx was dispensed with – always remarkably quickly – I could draw a breath, untangle the dogs and put the flowers (or whatever else Mae had lighted on that day) in a vase. Then Mae would fish for other men and I would be presented with her unpredictable catches.

One afternoon, some months after I had started, business

was a bit too quiet for Mae's liking and she declared she would be out longer than usual. When she returned, she galloped up the stairs calling triumphantly, 'I've got it! I've got it!'

I went to the landing and found her brandishing a square foot of striped mirror.

'I've been trying to get this for ages. Look, you can see through it.'

She held it up to the light, and what had appeared to be dark stripes showed as plain glass.

'What I want now is a hole in this wall about here.' She thumped a spot on the kitchen wall that divided it from her bedroom. 'Do you think you can do that for me, love?'

Some of the other flats had spyholes so the maid could check on the girl; the mirror was evidently a refinement so the client wouldn't know he was being watched. I tapped the wall for myself and it sounded hollow.

'You're in luck – or rather *I* am. What do you suddenly want this for? Are you going to start lumbering back with villains and desperadoes so I've got to keep a constant eye on you?'

'Not at all, lovey! This is for the geezers to look through. A pal of mine's got one and she makes a bomb out of it. But apart from that,' and her voice became more serious, 'it *is* a bit safer for me if you've got a way of seeing I'm all right. After all, you heard about Millicent last week, didn't you?'

I'd never heard of Millicent before, but I looked as though I understood.

'It sounds a good idea,' I said. 'But you do realise the hole will have to be covered so the kitchen light doesn't shine through all the time. In fact, the light will have to be switched out when anyone's peeping at you.'

I still hadn't bought many tools but I'd kept the miscellaneous selection I'd inherited. I said I would do it the following day when I could buy something more appropriate for the job. Her face fell with disappointment.

'I so wanted to see it done tonight,' she said in that crestfallen way she always used to such advantage.

'But I need a drill,' I protested.

'You'll think of something,' she said. 'I'm off.'

And with that, she was gone. To show willing, I could at least mark the place where the hole should be made. I chose a spot on the kitchen wall at *my* eye level – to hell with the clients; they came in all shapes and sizes anyway.

After her next client, Mae asked if I'd thought of something yet. I told her I'd chosen the place for it and she examined my pencil mark studiously.

'It doesn't have to be a round hole, you know. Bollocks to that when you're in a hurry! Where's your tools, love?'

I showed her the motley bag of odds and ends and she picked out the bent screwdriver and placed the point against the mark. 'Sure it's the right place?'

I nodded, and she walloped the palm of her other hand against the butt of the screwdriver, and lo, we had a hole (although the plaster on the other side of the hollow wall was still intact). She was about to repeat the performance but I stopped her.

'What's up?' she asked. 'You said this was the right place.'

'Yes,' I replied, 'but the other hole has got to be more precise, so you're looking downwards at the bed, otherwise we'll only see the curtains opposite.'

She handed me the screwdriver and said, 'Well, work out where that's got to be and we'll have another bash next time I'm up.' She disappeared down the stairs, chattering merrily to herself: 'It's all bash, bash, bash! Out on the bash, in on the bash – bash, bash, bash . . . !'

Calculating the correct angle was quite a problem, and

it was two clients later before I'd found the spot for the other hole. I decided to make it myself, so I went round to the bedroom and began the attempt using Mae's method. I only succeeded in hurting my hand, so I brought the half-a-hammer into use. I placed a handkerchief in the centre of the bed to represent the centre of interest for the viewer, and on testing it from the kitchen side, found my calculations had been perfectly accurate. The opening still needed to be widened, but success was within reach. Mae came into the kitchen after the next client had gone to find me quietly jubilant.

'I've done the other hole,' I announced triumphantly, 'but all I can see through it is my handkerchief.'

'Was that *your* handkerchief on the bed?' she asked. 'My last one wiped his you-know-what on it.'

She had a look through the hole but at first saw nothing at all because I'd temporarily plugged the other side with a twist of newspaper. I rushed in and removed it.

'We've got to have a bit more of the bedroom wall out,' she called. 'Get bashing!'

I soon got the hang of the bashing, hitting the screwdriver over a tiny area to flake away the plaster, and then knocking bits off the comparatively soft plasterboard into the recess. The chips of hard plaster were flying everywhere, so I asked Mae if she would help me pull the dressing table over the messiest part of the floor to hide the worst of it. First, she wanted to lie on the bed and get a report on how much of her could be seen at that stage.

'If you shove up a bit, I'll be able to see your hips,' I called out.

She wriggled herself accommodatingly but the wrong way.

'So they'll get a good view of me, will they?'

We got the dressing table into position and cleared up

the existing mess. Mae departed and I got cracking on the wall again. The frequent interruptions were annoying, as they meant humping the end of the dressing table back into place each time. Though it successfully screened the actual area of demolition, it didn't hide much mess, because stupid little white chips kept ricocheting all over the place. Eventually I smoothed off the jagged edges with the bread knife and disguised the kitchen side of the hole with a teacloth before taking a break.

'Have you done it, then?' Mae asked excitedly next time we were alone. 'Let's have a look.'

We went out to the kitchen; I removed the cloth and she peered through.

'Ah, that's better! Fabulous! You can see the lot now. Well done, old girl.' She was beaming happily. 'Let's go in and see what it looks like from the other side.'

We went in, but I'd forgotten to replace the cloth and a circle of light burst through, looking like the midday sun. I rushed back to hang the tea towel on its nail. Mae decided we should use a picture instead; she knew just where to get one, but the shop was shut. Next time back, she wanted to know why the mirror wasn't up on the wall.

'What do I stick it up there with?' I asked wearily. 'Lipstick?'

She just waved her hand airily. 'I'll get some glue.'

I called out down the stairs at her retreating figure: 'It'll have to be quick-setting stuff.'

She waved acknowledgement. On her way past the kitchen with the very next client, she handed me half a tube of glue.

When the client had gone I said, 'You'll have to stop bringing them up until I've fixed this in place; otherwise it'll fall off and frighten the life out of them.'

While the kettle boiled, I fixed the mirror to the wall.

We took it in turns to hold it as we drank our tea, then cautiously took our hands away to see if the glue had held.

It had, and with it, one of the main pillars of the Rabbits Regime had crumbled silently into dust. The spyhole meant we could now cater for voyeurs. Mae was delighted; according to her, Rabbits had gradually discouraged all her kinky clients, whose appetites were many and various.

'She used to take the piss, so in the end they stopped coming. I like kinks about the place. They liven things up a bit . . . Think I'll try and get 'em back.'

Slowly, but in ever-increasing numbers, like sheep to the fold, her kinky clientele began returning.

Mae planned their reintroduction with some consideration for what remained of my naïvety. It would not have suited her plans if I had jibbed – and I almost certainly would have done – had she brought the more extreme ones back too early in the campaign. My compliance was needed, not just for administrative purposes, but also because many of them required an audience, and thus I was promoted from backstage to chorus.

In the vanguard of the returning clients was an extremely pleasant and cultured Greek restaurateur known to us as 'Vera'. Vera was in 'her' late forties, with receding hair and fairly nondescript features. In his other life, he was Victor, a married man with two absorbing passions, one being a motorbike and sidecar and the other the woman he could only be within the confines of our flat. I liked him right from the beginning, and as time went by began to look forward to his visits and was always pleased to see him appear at our doorway.

He viewed being Vera with a sprinkling of self-deprecating humour, and this eased my rite of passage into the world of 'drag bags', falsies and square-jawed femininity. My initial impression was of a children's picture book in which the pages had been cut into sections, enabling one to put all sorts of unlikely heads on to equally unlikely bodies. However, it wasn't long before Vera looked no more remarkable to me than anyone else.

She knew far more about make-up than I did and must have studied the women's magazines minutely for all the little tricks. For instance, she had a whole battery of eye shadows and knew just where to put them to make her eyes seem larger and wider apart. She also knew how to apply rouge to make her face look thinner and could tell me all about moisturisers. She would apply her eyelashes with two deft flips before donning the *pièce de résistance* – the wig. After a little backcombing, the gorgeous six-foot Vera was ready.

'Lovely,' I'd say, as she stood and smoothed down her skirt.

Vera would then tie a little frilly white apron round her waist and begin her chores. This was no leisured drag queen, nor was she an S&M slave; Vera delighted in the daily round of ordinary household jobs. Out would come her rubber gloves, and she would fill a bucket with hot soapy water and start scrubbing the floors and staircase. Looking back, I think she would probably have enjoyed playing hostess at a select tea party. In those days of firmly divided gender roles in the home, I often thought how much housework Victor could have saved his wife if only he'd been able to introduce her to Vera.

One evening, just as Vera had almost scrubbed her way down as far as our landing and I was hanging over the banister rail talking to her, Mae emerged, leaving her client behind.

'That twit in there' – a jerk of her thumb indicated the twit in question – 'only had ten bob, so I told him he could toss himself off in the corner. He should be out any minute.'

Here she raised her voice and shouted back towards the room, 'Hurry up about it – I haven't got all night, you know.'

She looked sharply at Vera, whose face was red with suppressed laughter.

Trying hard not to laugh herself, she said, 'And you can stop grinning and listening to everything I say, you silly cow. I want them stairs clean enough to eat off when I come back.'

Then, delivering a smart and none too gentle kick to Vera's behind, she clattered off down the stairs, leaving us spluttering. Just then the do-it-yourself client came scurrying out of the bedroom with a face the colour of lipstick and sped past us down the stairs as fast as his legs could carry him. He never became a regular.

One evening, when I had a day off, Victor took me out to dinner with some of his friends. Occasionally he met my quizzical gaze and I saw mischief dancing in his eyes. This situation offered him at least the semblance of risk, and he was enjoying seeing Vera's ghost hovering round us in the presence of his straight friends.

On the evenings he was at the flat, he would drive me home in his sidecar. It was after one of these rides that he asked if Vera could sometimes do the housework at my home. Though the prospect was tempting, my bed-sitter was no place to hide a transvestite maid and my neighbours lacked the benefit of my gradually broadening mind.

'It's too small a place,' I said. 'And besides, the landlord might make a pass at you and then where would you be?'

Vera/Victor represented the palatable face of kinkiness, and by degrees I learnt to accept less genteel manifestations. There was one middle-aged man who had a mother and baby fetish; I found it disturbing but somehow touching.

He would take all his clothes off and then, while he sat

cross-legged on the bed, Mae would dress him in a large baby's bib and bonnet that he brought with him. In the role of his nanny, she would then get to work until the moment when he would shriek out, 'Mummy!' That was my cue to rush in and catch them red-handed at what he saw as the most degrading moment.

Even if, as I supposed, this fantasy had been caused by a mother's actions (whether too much or too little love I don't know), I still baulk at it. I didn't feel the revulsion that many of my 'respectable' compatriots would, but a kind of sadness swept over me and I felt how important it was that accommodating people like Mae should exist to cater for such needs.

When I first met Mae, I had been so taken with her warmth, immediacy and sheer charisma that I had been unable to see anything dark in her. Whether it was the dazzle fading or whether she did indeed change personality a little as the kinks returned to her welcoming fold, I did start to see more of that side of her that had been in evidence on the evening we went to torment poor Alphonse.

There was, for example, a very pleasant little regular – complacent and gentle – who without fail visited Mae once a week. He was short and plump, with black patent-leather hair and an affable smile. He wore a ring on his little finger, which Mae coveted for Tony. If Mae wanted something, she got it. She campaigned for the ring every time he visited: she wheedled for it; she was petulant; she was pleading . . .

One day she called me in to look at it. He stuck his hand out to show me and I obediently admired it. It was a heavy gold signet ring with a fair-sized diamond and it was embedded in the plump flesh of his finger.

He was gazing at his own hand in admiration when Mae

148

suddenly declared, 'You come up here giving me a measly few quid and all the time you tell me you love me! I don't believe you. You'd better not come any more.'

He looked from one to the other of us, trying to detect if Mae was joking. She turned her back on him, her shoulders heaving, and put her hands to her eyes. He knew what would be required to prove his affection to be genuine.

'Look, Mae,' he began desperately, 'I never wanted to hurt your feelings but I couldn't give it to you even if I wanted to; it won't come off. If I could get it off, you could have it.'

This polite excuse was obvious for what it was, but Mae whirled round instantly.

'I'll get it off,' she said.

I took pity on the man, whose only crime was to gamble on Mae's sense of decorum.

'But Mae,' I said. 'He's right. It's bitten right into the flesh. I don't suppose it's been off for years.'

'I can get that ring off,' she said firmly.

She promptly sat on the bed and pulled the hapless client down beside her.

'Soap!' she ordered imperiously.

When I returned, she had his finger in her mouth and was sucking at it furiously. Whatever had been the precursor to this had brought back his usual placid expression.

She sucked and soaped; she pulled and twisted until the little man began to yelp with pain. After about ten minutes they gave simultaneous shouts: his of agony, hers of triumph. She leapt up from the bed, brandishing her prize, and danced round the room holding the ring at arm's length and twisting it about so the diamond flashed and sparkled. Then she turned to him and crowed jubilantly, 'Well, you told me I could have it if I could get it off. Didn't think I could, did you?'

'No, I didn't,' he admitted weakly.

He was clasping his finger tightly; I went over to him and took his hand. The flesh was churned, torn and bleeding. Horrified, I looked across the room at Mae, who was still crooning joyously over her acquisition.

I think I would have found these proceedings sickening had I not thought of Mae as a beautiful animal perfectly suited to its environment. Her cruelty was part of her, as forgivable as that of a cat who could torture a bird before curling, soft and loving, into one's lap and purring itself into sleep.

I didn't think we'd see the little man again, but he confounded expectations by continuing to turn up every week. It was much later that I discovered him to be one of the kinks; as Mae put it, 'He'd plenty more rings in other places.'

She spoke only the truth. The fact was, the flat was becoming gradually cluttered with chains, ropes, bits of electrical flex, adhesive tape and all kinds of other impedimenta. Rather than carry them backwards and forwards, clients would leave them there ready for the next time they called. I tried to keep them in some sort of order, but it was quite hopeless. Mae would borrow from them and other clients would try them out; they never found their way back to where they belonged. However, as each regular could recognise his own toys, I soon stopped bothering. Besides, I was kept busy enough without all that; the peephole in the kitchen wall was creating its own complications. My apprenticeship as maid had much further still to travel.

Seventeen

~

In one respect, the peephole proved to be a tremendous success. The number of Mae's regulars swelled as she introduced straight clients to voyeurism as an hors d'oeuvre before taking their place in the bedchamber. Strangely enough, these amateur Peeping Toms never seemed to mind that they would be part of the subsequent show. Maybe it didn't occur to them; maybe they had confidence in their abilities; maybe the thrill of voyeurism turned into the thrill of exhibitionism.

During the early days, Mae pushed the would-be watchers into the kitchen without taking their money first, relying on my restraining presence. This, of course, required a metaphorical hands-on approach from me. As I stood guard, listening to the hoarse, ecstatic whispers, I was still innocent enough to be embarrassed.

'Crikey! What a whopper! Oh, my – that is good! Oh, well done, old man! That's it: harder – harder! Go on, give her what for.'

Sometimes they'd be more graphic. The more gentlemanly of them might remember I could hear them and apologise, but they were in the minority. It was all a bit much, especially as, being in darkness, I couldn't pretend to be engrossed in some chore or other so as not to notice their remarks. All I could do was stand with my back to the sink and peer into the gloom, coughing slightly if they got too worked up.

The last straw was when a spate of the more enthusiastic peephole aficionados decided, one after the other, to include me in their sport. After the first hand came groping, tarantula-like, towards me, I armed myself with a large, heavy spoon with which I rapped the next over the knuckles. After the fourth man had been sent yelping away, I told Mae she'd have to take their money before putting them into the kitchen; I was strictly front-of-house and wished to remain so.

Establishing a 'cash before delivery' system proved to be no problem, and money poured into Mae's coffers like coins in a What the Butler Saw at high season. She would gauge exactly how long any particular man needed to look through the hole before she took him into the bedroom (some she'd let watch several programmes). By the time she had her client in front of her, he was so excited that her time and effort were halved. True to form, instead of relaxing, she doubled the number of clients. Henry Ford would have been proud of her.

'Jolly good job you made of that mirror,' she said at the end of the first week. 'I don't know how I managed without it.'

'It's all very well for you,' I complained, 'but it's put years on me.'

She took my face between her hands, kissed me on the forehead and scurried down into the street once more. In the twenty-one years I had spent on earth before arriving in Soho, I had never encountered such a kiss as I did then.

Straight clients in my charge were difficult enough, needing a great deal of tact and observance to keep them on the simmer without allowing them to either boil over or cool off. My conversation being often misunderstood, I had to be very careful what I said. In my early days, it was not unusual for a man to adopt a shifty expression and edge nearer, saying, 'Don't you do it too?'

I liked to get waiting clients seated so the distance between us could not be surreptitiously diminished. I had learned that a seated man gave indications of when his thoughts were bringing him to a dangerous level of excitement. I also discovered the knack of conversing in such a way as to keep a man's ardour alive but static. The weather was a good subject, in that it left a large enough chunk of his brain free to anticipate sex but not sufficient to make him a trial to me.

With the 'cash first' plan working admirably, I supposed I'd be free to sit in the waiting room whenever the kitchen was occupied, which was most of the time. The difficulties came along with the increasing number of 'slaves' arriving every weekday (Saturdays were reserved for straight in-and-outers because of the fast trade they provided). Monday to Friday saw the place littered with trussed-up naked men. There was always one in the waiting room, one on the stairs, one in the kitchen . . . Once, when putting a garment away in Mae's wardrobe, I found one in there too. I was so surprised I said, 'Oh, I beg your pardon' and shut the door hurriedly. For a moment, I wondered if I should have knocked. The situation continued to develop until it became necessary to hunt all over every night, prior to going home, in case she'd forgotten to release one or two of her prisoners.

One chap asked to be tied up, covered with a blanket and left in the bedroom while Mae carried on working. This caused no problem for three or four customers, but then one arrived who objected to the inert, breathing lump in the corner of the room.

'I know he can't see anything,' he explained patiently. 'But I don't like eavesdroppers.'

So between us, Mae and I carried the unwanted bundle into the kitchen and dumped it next to the man who was then currently at the peephole.

When having to share the waiting room with any of these roped, handcuffed or fettered figures, I would try to read or do a crossword puzzle, but it was very difficult to concentrate. Sometimes I recited to myself the bracing words of Kipling's 'If', but to no avail. One of the things I didn't like about them was the baleful way they stared at me. I found the whole thing so silly; after all, they had brought the ropes, they had paid to lie bound on my waiting room floor or hang crucified in the doorway, and yet as soon as they had achieved their heart's desire, they seemed to be blaming me for their predicament – at least, those of them who retained a spirit of aggression in their degradation, as distinct from the small minority of out-and-out masochists.

Ever the artist, I recall studying one of our victim's contours, wondering if I might one day paint a heroic picture full of roped prisoners. Suddenly I realised, with a twinge of excitement, that no painter I'd seen had ever depicted a tied-up man truthfully. They hadn't caught the correct colours of the hands and feet – ours were always blue. I was so thrilled with my discovery, I wanted to share it with someone there and then. Naïvely, I was about to tell the man himself, though since he was strung up to a hook in the ceiling, maybe a chat about art was not paramount in his mind. As I looked up eagerly to his face, he spat at me. What he wanted, of course, was that I should leap across the room and belt him one, but he was wasting his saliva.

I wiped myself clean and pondered. I was here in a

prostitute's waiting room, contemplating the colour of a masochist's trussed feet. Would I ever stay true to my vocation and return to art, or had I truly forfeited all of that by my choice of lifestyle? This was not, or not yet, a question about whether I would stay in Soho. I would; I knew I would. I would no sooner abandon Mae and Rita and Benzy Nell and the ever-capable Prudence and the cross-dressing Vera and all the rest of that colourful crew than I would choose to go and live on the moon.

I went home that night in quiet and reflective mood.

Eighteen

~

The autumn nights deepened. It was dark by seven, a boon to women like Hilda, but none of the girls looked forward to the cold, dark, dangerous months ahead: especially those who were not so quickly 'in and out' as Mae was. With the first frosts expected soon, true to form, Mae took the dogs to be clipped. They had sweltered all through the summer under their thick curly coats, and now they shivered resentfully. By way of consolation, Mae bought them smart polo-necked doggy sweaters.

The advance of autumn brought good omens with it. Mae's two most redoubtable kinks, Daisy and Houdini, were back in the fold, and she was already, optimistically, beginning to tell her regulars what she would like for Christmas.

In the meantime, something was afoot for the shop below us. Over the weeks, we watched its metamorphosis with interest. While the work proceeded, there were piles of rubble outside, lit at night by red hurricane lamps, to warn pedestrians. Mae heartily approved of those and occasionally moved one to the side of our front door. She had taken to chatting to the man who had leased the shop, and had learned it was going to be a high-class snack bar.

'I told him,' she said later, 'he'd better not make it too high-class 'cos it's not the district for it. But he's a toffee-nosed, know-it-all sod, so what can you do?' She mimicked him: '"Oh, I don't know. We'll see." We'll see all right! It'll be one big flop; you mark my words.'

From then on, on her sallies into the street, she noted every item of progress in the ill-fated venture below and regaled me with snippets of news:

'Putting in the first mosaics on the wall' ... 'Fixing the spotlights' ... 'Edging the counter with stainless steel' ... 'Fixing a row of bamboo poles along one side' ...

I got numerous reports every day and was so well genned up that I didn't need to look at it myself until the day she told me the fascia had gone up.

'This you gotta see,' she said. And she took me downstairs.

'Toffee-nose' was dancing about in a state of acute excitement and gazing up delightedly at the name of his shop – stainless-steel letters superimposed on black: *La Milano*.

'Isn't it gorgeous?' he said rapturously when he saw us. 'When I open, you two must be my first customers.'

When we left him, Mae said, 'Poor sod, what a waste of bloody money!'

By the following week, the final touches had been made: indoor plants had been forcibly trained up the bamboo poles, red leather stools with chrome legs were placed in front of the counter, two neatly trimmed potted bay trees were set at each side of the entrance – 'They won't last five minutes,' Mae had remarked gloomily – and the window was garnished with a large, beautifully roasted turkey, nestling in a bed of lettuce and tomatoes, flanked by two lobsters and surrounded by parsley.

The day it opened, Mae and I went down and indulged ourselves in a chicken sandwich, a rum baba and a cup of mocha coffee, which we consumed to the soft accompaniment of recorded mandolins playing 'Come Back to Sorrento'.

'Poor bastard!' Mae said, licking her fingers. 'It'll never pay.'

This was not the only change to our little world. In order to produce a charge of 'living on immoral earnings', the police had to prove a ponce was living with a girl for a certain number of consecutive nights. To safeguard Tony, Mae had been staying at the flat for as many as two nights a week, and because of this, the bedlam had increased. Presumably she must have spent some hours sleeping, but that didn't decrease the amount of havoc she could wreak in the night. It was a relief, then, when she told me that Tony had found a furnished house for them 'out in the sticks' at Rickmansworth – that being outside the Metropolitan Police area.

As her new route practically passed my front door, I was offered a lift home each night in their car. Predictably, this turned out to be something of a drama. To keep the police in the dark about the new address, Tony waited in a different part of central London and we took a cab to meet him. As soon as we left the flat, Mae began to peer through the rear window to see if we were being followed. Then, when we reached the prearranged spot, she waited for the cab to disappear before we were allowed to approach the waiting car. To me, unused as I was to private cars, it was all deliciously luxurious. The soft glow of Tony's cigar and the dance music issuing from the radio added to the atmosphere as Tony glanced at Mae briefly:

'All right?'

An equally brief nod from Mae:

'Yes, love.'

And off we drove, Mae singing quietly to the music, her scent drowning slowly in his sandalwood perfume intermingled with cigar smoke. There was little conversation between them but nor was there anything to indicate strife. The more I knew of Tony, the less I liked him, and I have no doubt at all that the feeling was heartily reciprocated. Nevertheless, these encounters took place so late and I was so tired that I had no energy to indulge in duelling with this spiteful little man, nor would I have dared to do so in any case. I sat in the back, watching the red glow of Tony's cigar butt and letting the music prepare me for bed. I allowed myself to think that, as ponces went, Tony was as good as any.

That happy delusion was quick to disappear. One day, near the end of October, Mae 'ran into something in the dark' and arrived sporting a large black eye. Perhaps 'sporting' is the wrong word, as it was lurking behind a pair of dark glasses. She later referred to Tony as 'that bastard' and I knew the honeymoon was over at last.

During that day, her mood alternated between darkly sombre and gaily frivolous. She couldn't concentrate on her work at all; she said she didn't feel like it, and spent a lot of time cuddling the dogs and sifting through her clothes. I suggested it might do her good to take the rest of the day off, spend a quiet evening at home and have an early night.

'What. And get another of these?' she burst out, jerking her hand up to her eye.

'Oh Mae,' I said. 'I am so sorry!'

By evening, the takings were lower than I had ever known them to be. Mae was only dealing with regulars; she was not going out at all. Besides feeling too truculent and depressed, she didn't want to advertise her 'accident'.

Suddenly there came the sound of feet on the stairs – too decisive and quick to be a client. I felt alarmed: Tony must either have been told or, worse, seen that she had remained indoors all day. The same thought had crossed Mae's mind too, and she was clearly anxious. I went out to meet him, hoping to at least act as a sort of mediating force. A huge bunch of red roses rounded the bend in the staircase, followed by a complete stranger. He muttered, 'From Tony', thrust the flowers into my hands, turned on his heels and departed as hurriedly as he'd arrived.

When I took them in to Mae, she went into paroxysms of joy and relief. She sniffed the flowers and admired them ardently. Several times she started to count them before giving up the task with a happy sigh. To me, Tony's gesture seemed like that of a poultry farmer who reassures a chicken by stroking it prior to wringing its neck.

Soon we had arranged the treacherous gift in two vases and put them on the dressing table so the blooms were multiplied by their reflection in the mirror. Then Mae turned to me, as if she'd had a sudden revelation. In great excitement, she instructed me to call on a certain Betty Kelly – I didn't know this woman – and ask her to pop round as soon as possible.

'I'll be all right on my own for a while,' she said. 'I'll shut the door and only let in regulars.' She gave me her old grin and a playful tap on the nose with one finger. 'Don't look so worried! Off you go!'

I tramped out into the cold Soho air and found the market area she'd indicated. After passing through several streets where fish and chip papers drifted dismally among other fresh rubbish of the day, I came to the place I was looking for. Here, the litter was predominantly orange boxes and the debris of a daily market. The last few barrows were being trundled away for the night and the familiar smell of rotting fruit prevailed. Scavenging cats were appearing alongside the incoming tide of Soho's tattered human flotsam, who slouched around, stooping here and there amongst the little piles of discarded merchandise.

I located the building I wanted. It was a sombre Victorian block, comprising shops with tenements above. There was a cluster of bell pushes outside, but as the street door was ajar, I went in. I walked up several flights of stone steps, looking on all the doors for the name Mae had mentioned. It was difficult, as most of the plates were encrusted with grime and the low-wattage lighting, high on the ceiling, soaked into the parchment-coloured walls.

The flat I wanted was on the fourth floor. My knock brought shuffling and creaking sounds from within before the door opened. A very large elderly woman stood there. The lighting inside was only infinitesimally stronger than that on the staircase, but I could see that she had dark, watchful eyes and iron-grey hair clamped tight to her head. She wore a voluminous old cardigan and skirt and her bulk in the doorway blocked my view of her rooms, but they looked pretty basic and meagre from what I could see: a cheap lampshade and a shabby old armchair in front of a depressingly low fire.

'Yes? What d'you want?' she said in a tone that most people reserved for the bailiff.

'Are you Betty Kelly?' I asked and she affirmed with a curt nod. 'Mae sent me,' I said. 'She says, would you come round to see her as soon as you can?'

'Blonde Mae?' she asked.

I said yes, and started to tell her the address.

'Yes, I know,' she interrupted, and taking a step back into her room, she shut the door, narrowly missing my nose. I stood there for a second or two, a little stunned by the brevity of this exchange; then, shrugging to myself, I picked my way back down the dingy stairs.

Later that night, Betty Kelly laboriously picked her way up our stairs. Knowing her to be a woman of few words,

161

I said nothing and showed her in to Mae. She stayed no longer than a few minutes.

When she'd left, Mae leapt into the kitchen, full of chirpiness. She stuffed a wad of notes into my hand.

'I borrowed a hundred quid from her,' she crowed jubilantly. 'Put fifty in with today's takings, take a fiver for yourself and keep the rest somewhere safe for another day. I'll show that bastard . . .' she said it in a loving way, 'that I'm still the best! I can still earn more than anyone else, even when I stay in all day. I bet he thinks I've only taken about twenty quid. I can't wait to see his fucking face when I give him that lot!'

Prancing like a skittish pony, she started back to the bedroom. She paused halfway and called out, 'Oh, by the way, what's today?'

'Tuesday,' I answered.

'Well remind me, love, won't you, early every Tuesday? Betty will be up for her money and she'll want paying twenty-five a week for five weeks. Don't forget, will you?'

I pointed out she would have to work harder than ever to pay that and to keep the takings up to the same amount as usual, but she wasn't to be deflated.

'Don't matter – I can do it, no trouble at all.'

She went to have another peep at the progress of her black eye. 'Cor, what a shiner! The bastard!'

'Bastard' was now an official term of endearment; she giggled again.

'Mae, you'll be the death of me,' I said, bringing in our tea and hurling myself down on the bed. 'Funny, though,' I added reflectively, 'the way that Betty lives and dresses, it doesn't look as though she's got a bean.'

Mae lovingly prodded her eye and gazed into the mirror.

'She's rolling in it,' she said. 'Richest woman around, I should think – and it's not bleeding surprising with the interest she charges.' Her giggles consumed her like spontaneous combustion.

'We're in the wrong game, mate!' she declared.

Despite her new gaiety, I felt sure she was right.

Nineteen

~

From that day onwards, a subtle change in the atmosphere took place: one that probably wouldn't have been sensed by anyone less close than myself. A slight cloud seemed to hover over the flat, and Mae's natural high spirits were replaced by a more forced and strident quality. I noticed, too, that there was more intensity in the way she worked and more enquiries as to how we were doing financially. She gradually began to see Tony for what he was, and realised that the affection she could expect from him as a ponce was directly related to her earning power. But it was too late to leave him and admit to everyone she'd been wrong. Nor was it just the humiliation of the climbdown stopping her. There was Tony himself. Had he not displaced Alphonse by playing with his evil little flick knife as an open threat? And if he was happy to use his fists on Mae after a day or two's low takings, then what might he not do if his milch-cow sought to abandon him altogether? These were thoughts that neither of us put into words, but they were present in us both, I am certain.

In the meantime, life – and my eccentric education – continued. Mae, never one to be picky about the company she kept, would sometimes entertain the local beat policemen. Their excuse was concern for our welfare, but they didn't seem to be able to make their enquiries without having a cigarette and a cup of tea. To be fair to them, I did wonder if it was me they were keeping an eye on: checking I wasn't progressing further down the Primrose Path than was advisable.

This type of uniform in the kitchen would, of course, be enough to cool the passions of the most ardent customer, so I had to make sure the door was shut tight. I learnt this lesson after a client once crept up without my hearing him. He peeped through the gap in the door and alerted us to his presence with a sudden intake of breath. By the time we'd turned, he was scampering down the stairs at break-neck speed. The friendly bobby gave a snort of amusement.

'If he was better acquainted with the law, he'd know that what he was about is quite legal.' The front door slammed very loudly and he added, 'I suppose I could book him for disturbing the peace.'

The police had a tolerant attitude towards the girls, whom they regarded as necessary evils. Over the years an agreement had been reached whereby it was understood that arrests must be made (because it was the done thing), but not too often (because that wasn't kind). It wasn't particularly warranted, because those girls who did break the law by soliciting on the street seldom got desperate enough to actually accost a man; they hardly ever blocked the pavement, stripped in public or hurled abuse after men who weren't interested. A girl could advertise herself simply by doing nothing more than twirling her keys. Likely men were sometimes asked if they were looking for a good time – even then a cliché – or sometimes, more candidly, a short time.

Mae's old friend Rita was one exception to this code of conduct. I was on an errand when I was treated to the sight of her making a most ladylike approach to a passing man. After he'd given her a short brush-off, she persisted,

walking beside him a little way, making sweet bland-
ishments in a wee, demure voice. The man told her to get
off the pavement, and in an instant Miss Sweetness turned
into a shrieking banshee.

'Get off the pavement? I'm not fucking getting off the
fucking pavement, you fat sod!'

Assault and battery followed, using her handbag to
emphasise her point. I don't think she normally went that
far and I wondered if the violence had been provoked by
her embarrassment at my having seen her being refused.

Every now and again a newspaper, short on lucrative
horrors, would 'discover' that Soho was full of prostitutes.
This revelation would necessitate some Member of Par-
liament or other proclaiming that something must be done.
Senior police officers would be told to do it – whatever it
was – and then everybody could forget about it again.
Everybody, that is, apart from the police rank and file, who
had their orders and must be seen to be carrying them out.
They endeavoured to do this without allowing the scandal
sheets, the MPs and their own superiors to do any real
damage. Being on the game therefore meant knowing the
rules and occasionally landing on 'Go directly to jail
without passing Go'.

Naturally, some kind of balance had to be reached. Just
as the police didn't want to hang around all day waiting
for a catch, the girls didn't want them there, frightening
off the customers.

To solve this problem, a sort of rota system developed
whereby every two or three weeks – depending on age,
circumstance and convenience – a girl was expected to
more or less deliver herself up for arrest. The procedure
was that, in a perfectly friendly fashion, the policeman
would approach the girl and say, 'It's about time we took
you in, you know.' The girl then had to accompany him to

Bow Street police station for a charge to be made out. She had the choice of walking with him all the way along Long Acre, gauntleted by the curious glances of passers-by, or paying for a taxi to take them there. Mae occasionally came rushing up from the street saying, 'Quick, give us some money. I've just been nicked.' I would hand her a couple of pounds from the takings and off she would hurry. About an hour later she would be back with her bail slip – and another client.

Paradoxical though it may seem, the arresting officer would be quite sympathetic to the excuse that there were far too many men about to waste time going to the police station to be charged with prostitution. Accommodating this would mean the girl was morally obliged to be caught in the act the following day. This respectable arrangement kept both sides happy until one or the other party attempted to cheat.

Mae often came close to risking the wrath of the local police, especially now she'd started borrowing from Betty Kelly and had to work solidly. If she knew her arrest time was due and the expectant officer was hovering about, she would avoid him by walking in the opposite direction. Sometimes she would only go out as far as the front door and entice men in from there – or even from the window on some occasions. However, these were simply delaying techniques, and she would take her turn at Bow Street as soon as she could fit it into her busy schedule. Younger and newer girls, who perhaps didn't appreciate the beauty of the system and avoided arrest indefinitely, found them-selves taken in as often as twice a week until such time as they learned.

From the girls' point of view, the drawback of getting nicked was not the stigma of the public seeing how they earned a living, nor was it having to fork out for a fine or even the taxi fare to the police station: it was having to get up early to appear at the magistrates' court. It must be said that even in this, the Law might have been thought reasonable, but ten o'clock – the usual appointed time – was the middle of the night to these women, and lack of sleep would seriously affect their work. A man is not likely to choose a prostitute who propositions him with a yawn.

At court, notwithstanding the unsociable hour, the girls chatted away together cosily while they waited for their names to be called. Their real names, bellowed from the mouth of a burly sergeant-usher, were distinctly less colourful than their professional ones. This was, essentially, their 'backstage', and they didn't bother to wear make-up or to pout prettily at a magistrate who had seen it all before so many times. (In fact, very few prostitutes ever bothered to wear make-up outside of business hours.) Appearing after the drunks, they would exchange news and catch up with each other's gossip before enduring the ten seconds or so it took to put their crimes to them and decide on suitable punishment (usually a two-pound fine with the alternative of a week in jail if they preferred). Exactly what public good it all did is hard to say, but it seemed to keep everyone happy.

First offenders could be a bit of nuisance, for in deference to the older, more experienced members of the sisterhood, the Law found it necessary to point out their status. As an apprentice, the fine was reduced to ten shillings, after which it became one pound, only reaching the full two pounds at the third 'offence'. Very occasionally, the conga-like procession was disrupted by a girl being pedantic enough to plead not guilty. This foolishness, of course, led to the need for evidence and cross-examination. True, as there were never any independent witnesses – especially a curious absence of the men who were supposed to have been annoyed – it was likely that the accused would be vindicated. However, the arresting officer was robbed of the notch on his truncheon, the court's coffers were denied their two pounds and the magistrate was annoyed at the waste of the court's time. Again, repeated arrests over the next few weeks generally persuaded the miscreant that pleading guilty from time to time was the right and proper thing to do.

After court, everyone had time to kill; it was not worth going back home and it was too early to start work. Mae would usually arrange for me to meet her at the hairdresser's – Gaby's in Shaftesbury Avenue. It was where all the girls went; in fact, I never saw anyone 'straight' there: just girls and their maids. As it was in a basement, passersby probably didn't even know it was there.

Gaby's had none of the glamour one associates with beauty parlours. It was strictly a 'three-sink, two-dryer' sort of place. No two towels were alike; the two laconic women who made up the staff wore different overalls and wouldn't so much as knock the ash from their fags for you – but they were friendly enough. A newcomer might have supposed that no staff were in attendance at all and a roster system had propelled these two into their role for the day. It wasn't unusual to find one of them with her own hair in curlers. Perhaps because of this, the place had a cosy, kitchen feel about it, especially as there were always cups of tea on the go, made on the spot by anyone who felt like bothering. The girls sometimes sent their maids to get sandwiches from a little café nearby. Two or three hours spent in Gaby's was a happy time – a sort of return to the cradle. Tired after rising before midday, we would drowse in the steamy warmth, sprawling amongst the clutter of damp towels, basins, bowls and kicked-off shoes.

The lazy, random conversations that took place in

Gaby's never aimed beyond the mundane but occasionally rose above it. One day, a girl who was in the tedious process of having her hair 'pinned up' and was making a half-hearted onslaught on her fingernails addressed the room in general:

'I had some geezer the other day who brought his wife up with him – only wanted her to watch him perform with me! I told him, "I should bloody cocoa!" Some people just haven't got any morals.'

All the girls fully agreed with her sentiments and most brought forward other examples of this type of debauchery. They fell to musing on what made couples want to do such a disgusting thing. One girl said that a pair came to her once who were an engaged couple. The man wanted to show his allegedly virginal fiancée what would be involved once they were married. All the girls were terribly shocked at this story; they tut-tutted and gasped their disapproval.

From that, the conversation veered to men who brought their womenfolk to Soho – usually at weekends – just to point out the girls to them. On Sundays, the streets had apparently become so cluttered with these nuisances that the working girls preferred to stay inside and rely on clients calling.

'Like we was on show at Madame Tussaud's!' one girl said.

It would be easy to see these protestations as comic, but in truth the girls had their own dignity and knew when it was being insulted. I never heard any of them tell rude jokes. Perhaps, I thought at the time, it's because their whole life is really like one big rude joke and telling one would be rather like talking shop – or perhaps the jokes were too close to the truth to seem funny.

It was at Gaby's that I had my first hairdo, facial and professional manicure, and later, during a mad moment, it was there that Mae persuaded me to go blonde.

'Go on – it'll give you confidence,' she said.

My not replying was taken as assent, and in a flash, my head was smothered with what seemed to be runny plaster of Paris that was left on for about an hour, making ominous crackling and popping noises in my hair. When it was washed off, I arose like Venus from the foam, a dazzling platinum blonde. I could hardly believe my eyes.

The other girls admired the results enthusiastically, and Mae was so pleased with the change it made to my whole appearance that, later, she put me in one of her strapless, long-skirted dresses and made me pose for a photograph. She was, of course, quite right: it did give me more confidence. Unfortunately, it also meant that as well as wearing an apron at work, I now had to wear a headscarf as well to make sure no punters confused me with Mae.

I have been blonde ever since, and often think it appropriate how Mae should have made her mark on me physically, the way she had already done emotionally. I was a new woman now, in more ways than one.

Twenty

~

For all Mae's careful instructions to her clients with regard to the Christmas presents she wanted, she wasn't around to see if any of them bore fruit, because when Christmas came, she was in hospital.

For a while she had complained of sharp pains in her stomach. Then, quite suddenly one night, she had woken in agony and been rushed into Casualty. It was found that she had an ectopic pregnancy that had ruptured.

The phone woke me at six that morning with an agitated Tony at the other end to give me the news. I had no doubt he was responsible for her condition. I felt furious at him, and resented the whining way in which he implored me to go and visit her to 'help keep her spirits up'. But of course, I took the necessary particulars of where she was and the visiting times.

I went to see her that same evening and was shocked by her waxy face and listlessness. She had tubes running into her from all directions, and was evidently extremely ill. But Tony's greatest worry was that the flat would be eating rent without producing anything in return. I was not surprised, therefore – though still appalled – when he telephoned me to say he'd found another girl and maid who would be glad to take it over for the month Mae was going to be away. As an afterthought he added, 'But what about you? Do you want I should find a girl without a maid?'

He sounded so anxious that I shouldn't upset his speedy arrangements that I toyed with the idea of breaking his heart by saying yes. On second thoughts, I contemplated time off and getting back to my painting: this was my chance. As our replacements were to move in that same afternoon, I raced over to put all Mae's personal things into the waiting room and lock it. After that, I stayed on in town to get myself a canvas and a few bits of art material. It felt strange to be buying these things from my old life and old ambitions. The empty canvas felt both extraordinarily inviting – a New World of its own, an undiscovered territory waiting for me to map it – and also alien. What had it, after all, to do with the life I led now?

When I got home, I was deciding whether I should try my hand at a naked captive with blue feet or a bowl of grapes when the phone rang. I lifted the receiver to my ear and hurriedly moved it six inches away as Rita's brazen voice shattered the space between us. After I'd told her how Mae was, she proposed an idea that had obviously been thought out prior to her ringing.

'My maid keeps on about having time off for Christmas and says she hasn't had a holiday in years. What d'you say I give her a month off, and you come to me till Mae's back?'

Thoughts of the exciting *Blue Extremities* and the relaxing *Nature Morte Avec une Grappe de Raisin* tugged at me for a moment but weren't strong enough to resist Rita's call to arms. I looked hopelessly at the unmarked canvas, which stared back at me unblinkingly, and weakly submitted without a fight.

'Right,' she shouted. 'I'll tell Toots the good news and I'll expect you here tomorrow about four.'

I turned the canvas to the wall, so at least I didn't have

to endure its unspoken reproach. The other materials I placed in the drawer where the slice of toasted cheese had once held lonely court. A maid I was, and a maid it seemed I would remain.

Rita's flat was in Berwick Street – at least the approach to it was. Playing safe with the law, the astute landlord had effectively made two separate premises from the one. An inside passage led through a shop building to a back door and a cobbled yard. At the far side of this was a lean-to shed that accommodated Rita's kitchen and the entrance hall. At the back of the entrance hall was the bedroom, housed inside the back of another building. A stone staircase rose out of this room, blocked off at the top by a brick wall. The occasional sound of feminine footsteps pattering above the ceiling betrayed the fact that there was another girl operating there.

Rita's decorating tastes were stark and colourful, as personified by the linoleum – hard, cold and bright. Her room was enormous: about four times the size of Mae's, and as hygienic as an operating theatre. The only furnishings were a single divan, a side table – on which was a lamp and a box of Durex – a rubbish bin and a cane-bottomed chair. There were no windows, therefore no curtains, and the only luxurious touch of softness was a satin bedspread on the divan with a pillow covered to match. On the foot of the bed was the usual folded travelling rug to prevent the bedspread getting ragged and dirty – the baggy trousers of those days could be jettisoned without removing shoes.

The kitchen, where I was to spend my time, was small, but not as small as Mae's. There was no running water in the flat – you had to get that from a standpipe in the yard – and so no toilet, apart from a bucket in the kitchen that was emptied down a manhole in the yard. The bedroom was heated by an electric fire; the kitchen had an oil stove:

the cylindrical sort that throws pretty patterns of light on to the ceiling but would eventually blacken it with smoke.

Like the flat, Rita's attitude to her work was purely functional. She supplied the barest minimum and not a tittle more. She gave no endearments, no kind words, not even a smile. There was not a single cane, rope or even a dirty photo in the place.

'Oh, I can't be bothered with all that messing about,' she said.

On the cobblestones just outside the lean-to was the only light between there and the dimly lit Berwick Street: a hurricane lamp. I watched Rita take this to find her way through the long passageway; she left it just behind the door to the main street, ready for lighting her way when she returned with a client. Once outside, she went to her particular spot and stood gazing into space with those hard, short-sighted eyes. When, eventually, a man came past, she asked him if he wanted a nice time in exactly the same tone that a bus conductress would have said, 'Tickets, please.'

Surprisingly, although it took as much as quarter of an hour, Rita did manage to hook clients. To her advantage, she had striking good looks, enhanced by a pronounced bosom that she displayed to full advantage. She wore jerseys with stripes that undulated like tracks on the big dipper and, weather permitting, a plunging neckline that revealed the Grand Canyon.

She rushed her catch back without a word. As soon as the door was shut, she asked briskly for his money. She shoved this through the bedroom door to me and there was complete silence for about five minutes; then the door opened again and the client, having had his 'nice time', silently departed. On the occasions that a client required longer than five minutes, I heard the clonk of her high heels against the floor as she sprang from the bed.

'Do you think I've nothing better to do than hang around waiting for you? Shove off!'

There was a murmur of protest from the man, who presumably *did* think she had nothing better to do. Protesting was not going to work.

'I can't stand here talking to you all night! Sod off!'

Most clients saw reason and slunk off, but some had the temerity to demand their money back; a few went berserk, but this was as fruitful as arguing with an iceberg. True, there were a *very* few – those who threatened violence – who *would* get their money back, thrown at them along with a stream of invective. Rita had very few regulars.

Rita's approach exemplified the term 'hustling'. She jockeyed the men into the flat through sheer force of will while they were still trying to make up their mind. This, of course, could account for their tardiness once inside, although Rita never did anything to foster an amorous mood. She had never quite got over the days when she worked in taxis; to her, a flat was just a big cab with facilities for making tea.

She arrived every day immaculately turned out, spotlessly clean and brightly burnished, and that was how she still was at the end of the day: not a hair out of place. This meant I had no constant sorting of her clothes, and as she didn't want snacks and cups of tea every five minutes, life with her was like a rest cure in comparison with Mae's ménage. I was even able to do a bit of reading, though when Rita saw this, she became most concerned about my wasting my time when I could be knitting something. It transpired she was a fanatical knitter herself.

'I'd do a lot more too,' she said peevishly, 'if it wasn't for having to keep coming here to kow-tow to sex maniacs.'

When she learnt I couldn't knit, she insisted on teaching

me. I was glad enough of a change to help fill the long hours and it appealed to my creative instinct. She was fabulous and fast. She confided that she had learnt at reform school and practised in prison, where, unlike the other inmates, she had actually taken to it wholeheartedly. She could also make beautiful silk lampshades and she cooked like a dream. She informed me, almost reverently, that if she'd never gone inside, she'd have missed half the pleasures of life.

Rita was known by all to be tactless and outspoken. A very difficult girl to know, to like or to get close to, she made enemies everywhere. I had grown much bolder, and after one clash early on – when I'd told her that she could save her nasty ways for her clients – we began to enjoy one another's company and have quite a good time together. We took to meeting at about four o'clock in the afternoon and having a meal, over which we would sit and chat for about an hour. That was when we indulged ourselves in a little hilarity and exchanged confidences. It was then that she revealed her understanding of the ponce racket and why she would have no truck with them.

'I can't stand their greasy, lying mugs. They're bone idle too! And if they ever went to school at all, they certainly never learnt nothing. I'll stick to my feeves. A feef's got to use his loaf and know what's what. They're clean, upstanding men.'

I'd also hear about the progress of her latest romance. They never lasted long. Rita was a lone wolf and her own mistress. She was living comfortably in her own house in London, and if a boyfriend wanted to risk living in it with her, then that was up to him. Men couldn't pick her; she picked them.

Generally she disliked men and wasn't thrilled at having the unwanted attentions of amorous clients round her. She confessed to me one day that the only way in which she could get any sexual pleasure at all was if a man 'went down' on her. At one time this would have shocked me, but now I took it in my stride. I realised that the only regulars she had were men who liked oral sex and were good at it. These men always stayed a lot longer than five minutes. Their arrival was marked by laughing and talking all the way to the bedroom – though she never forgot to take their money. When they left, she was positively cordial with her farewells.

After these sessions, she pranced into the kitchen saying, 'Put the kettle on, mate,' and plonked herself down to wait for a celebratory cup of tea, chattering very animatedly all the while. As I began to recognise these clients and to understand the signs, I put the kettle on unbidden so that it was boiling by the time she emerged. Seeing it ready, she giggled, blushed and called me 'cheeky sod'. She took to pre-empting me, 'Put the kettle on' ringing out through the yard as soon as she arrived with a client who was going to do things her way.

The toilet bucket was next to the oil stove, so that our exposed flesh wouldn't get too chilled. One day, coming out from the bedroom, voluble after one of these nice regulars, Rita pulled her knickers down in something of a hurry to plonk herself on the bucket. Partly because her mind was elsewhere and partly because of her short-sightedness, she sat on the oil stove instead, then immediately shot up into the air like a rocket, shrieking, 'Oh, me bum! Oh my Gawd!'

As she was in no position to do it herself, I investigated this delicate situation and found that the perforations in the top of the stove had burnt pretty red daisies all over her behind. As I reported on the condition of her nether region, I couldn't suppress a stifled choke in my voice. Her shouts of pain mingled with tears of laughter and she rolled around yelling, 'Oh Gawd! My poor bum!' One hand was clutching her buttocks and the other holding her stomach, which was aching with laughter; her knickers were round her ankles and her legs were crossed because she still hadn't used the bucket.

I applied ointment to the damage, followed by a whole boxful of sticking plasters – which came in all shapes and sizes; her bottom looked like a patchwork quilt. At last we calmed down and I made tea. Giggles broke out when Rita had to lie on her stomach to drink it, with the red and white pointillism of her backside uppermost.

All that month I continued to visit Mae whenever I could, avoiding times when I thought Tony might be there. Mae forced herself to be cheerful of course, but the thing that must have occupied her mind most of all – the fact that she was in the grip of a ponce whose capacity for violence could not be underestimated – was territory that both of us were forbidden to talk about.

I still loved Mae, of course – I still do – but I could also feel my feelings changing. To start with, she had been my only friend, my tutor, the impish, unpredictable spirit who had made me a member and co-conspirator in her riotous underworld. As time had moved on, however, the balance of things had changed. I had other friends now, for one thing. Rita was Rita and would never be Mae, but I was no longer lonely and crying out for friendship. For another thing, I realised that I was becoming maternal towards Mae. I felt sorry for her in some ways. I wanted to take care of her, and knew the limits of what I could do for her. It wasn't that she and I were less close than before, but it was not the same kind of closeness. She knew it and so did I.

As if to mark the change in my relationships, it was Rita who invited me to her home when Christmas came round. She said she wouldn't take no for an answer. The thought of spending Christmas on my own wasn't particularly appealing, and I was glad to accept.

On Christmas morning, Bert, Rita's current feef, was sent to collect me in his car. All Rita's boyfriends were of the hearty, back-slapping variety. True to form, Bert brought both hands together in a loud clap and followed this with a booming, 'Well, 'ow's it going, then?'

Rita's house was in the East End. It was Edwardian, tall, dilapidated and stacked to the roof with lodgers – all feeves – whose weekly contributions paid her expenses. What she earned on the game was really pin money.

When I arrived on this festive day, the smell of cooking was overpowering and I swam through it to join Rita in the kitchen. She was dressed in a shimmering, wine-coloured cocktail dress and an apron and was absolutely surrounded by food. In the enormous double oven was a goose, a giant turkey and a large leg of pork.

'Well, we're not likely to starve, at any rate, mate,' said Bert, giving her a playful slap on the rump.

'Do you mind?' said Rita, straightening up and giving him a withering look. 'We've got guests. Don't be so bleeding common.'

I gave Rita her Christmas present, which was a little sexy nightie – it was my year for buying flirty nighties; I'd also bought two for Mae and one for myself. When Bert saw it, his 'Cor!' received another look from Rita and an enquiry as to whether he'd had too much to drink.

'Instead of standing round acting bloody stupid,' she said, 'take Babs inter the other room, and introduce her to me bruvver – and give her a gin.'

Now that I was a blonde, I had decided it was high time

I learned to like alcohol, to go with my new image, and so was slowly learning to enjoy gin. I took my glass happily and met the rest of the crowd. Rita's brother was a thin, bellicose man named John, who came in tandem with an uneasy-looking wife. Then there was Rita's little girl, sitting on the thick carpet, bewildered by the piles of new toys surrounding her. I sat down on the floor next to her and added to the bewilderment by giving her the doll I'd brought.

Everything in the room was opulent and lush, and it all looked brand new: heavy brocade curtains, silk flock wallpaper, deep velvet armchairs and a very ornate bar stocked to bursting point. John, the brother, was gazing around him as though he bitterly disapproved of every item.

'Must have cost her a pretty penny, this little lot,' he said to his wife. I went back to the kitchen to help Rita, who had a spare bottle of gin tucked away in there. By the time the meal was ready, both of us were slightly tipsy, dropping baked potatoes on to laps and enjoying ourselves enormously. It was a jolly, plentiful meal, and despite our inebriation, it was cooked to a turn. Although John enquired about the cost of the turkey, I noticed that he partook of it with gusto.

After dinner, Rita remembered her present for me: a silver cigarette lighter, with an intaglio of Siamese dancers. It was the most beautiful thing I'd ever owned.

I stayed overnight and through Boxing Day. I was so grateful to Rita, and touched that she had included me in her family at that time of the year. It was a Christmas that stays in my memory to this day; a perfect opposite to the VE Day that had once come and gone, unremarked and uncelebrated, in my grandmother's uncharitable home.

Twenty-One

~

I greeted the end of that month with mixed feelings. Working with Rita was far less nerve-racking than working with Mae. On the other hand, I'd developed a taste for the excitement, strange sights and hurly-burly with which Mae surrounded herself, and to my surprise, I really wanted to jump on the merry-go-round again and get back to Mae's mad one-girl brothel.

In addition to my various hospital visits, we'd enjoyed a lot of late-night, bed-to-bed telephone conversations when Mae was back home convalescing. When she was finally on her feet again, we'd met in town for a meal or two and she'd even visited me in Rita's flat, where she'd snorted in amusement at the sight of my knitting and made disparaging remarks about Rita's working methods – which I tacitly agreed with.

Of course, Mae was raring to go, long before her month was up. She would have gone straight back to work had it not been for the other girl in her flat. When we at last started work again in the New Year, she was positively straining at the leash.

In this, she was destined for disappointment. Although the streets were full of men wistfully eyeing the means of breaking their fast, Christmas had left them without the funds to do it. Mae had reason to be impatient: her loan from Betty Kelly had not been anywhere near paid off when she had been taken ill. With the interest that had accrued in her absence, the debt was nearly back to the amount she'd first borrowed. She was also keen to replenish Tony's coffers, because she was touched by the way he'd stuck by her through her hospitalisation and worried because he'd announced that he was 'in debt up to the eyebrows' because of it. I hated her gullibility – assuming that she was truly still that gullible – but there was nothing to be done. In the meantime, she fretted.

'I know those bastards out there have got it tucked away somewhere,' she grumbled. 'All I need to do is squeeze it out of them somehow.'

As day followed day without a real breakthrough, her mood grew increasingly gloomy and a trifle waspish. She eventually decided that one particular day was going to be it, 'boom or bust'!

The first hour augured more towards the latter. She changed her clothes and jewellery, hoping that something would turn out to be her Aladdin's lamp. Nothing did, and there was no sign of any boom. By nine o'clock in the evening, she had earned only forty pounds; then Betty called and turned it into fifteen pounds.

Mae muttered something, braced herself and, tight-lipped and grim, clattered down the stairs. She came back five minutes later – on her own – and sailed past the kitchen door without a word. I waited for the hysterical outburst, but none came. Instead, she called out – quite cheerily – asking for a cup of tea.

I made two cups and carried them in. She was waving a Benzedrine inhaler at me, and informed me that the 'boom or bust' promise was still on.

'I didn't know you had a cold,' I said.

A mock-puzzled look spread over her face, then, as if for

the first time, she read out the print on the tube, '"Breathe easier!" or "Take the lot to make a lot," I say.' She shrugged. 'Well, Nell says it'll do the trick,' she said. 'She says this is what drummers take when they want to play their drums really fast.'

'You don't take it; you sniff it,' I said. 'And surely not the whole lot.'

Mae wrinkled her nose speculatively for a while, before saying, 'Time's getting on and I need fast results.'

I asked her if she needed water to take it with, but she ignored me. She placed the tube on the floor and brought her heel down hard on it. There was a tightly wound, pungent stick of wadding amongst the broken pieces. She pulled this apart and, bit by bit, dropped the whole lot into her tea. I watched, appalled, as she stirred it into a thick, brownish porridge, exuding a strong scent of lavender, which gradually filled the room.

'*Ugh!*' she said. 'It doesn't look very nice, does it?'

I wasn't very optimistic about it. I watched, fascinated, as she lifted the cup to her mouth and, holding her nose with her other hand, drained the nasty concoction to its bitter dregs.

'Oh Gawd!' she gasped. 'Get me some water, quick – it's bloody horrible!'

She gulped the water down, lit a cigarette and lay back on the bed, saying, 'I might as well take it easy for a few minutes, while I've got the chance; if this works like that girl says, you won't see me for dust.'

It hit her ten minutes later, halfway through her next cigarette. Her eyes became brilliant and enormous and she suddenly leaned up on one elbow and turned them on me at full beam. Her voice was breathy and long-distance.

'Babs, it's wonderful! I feel like I'm queen of everything. I'm ready to take on every man in London.'

She rose slowly and voluptuously, quivering all over. She was like a powerful machine that had just been switched on and was throbbing with suppressed energy. Suddenly something threw the 'start' lever, and she became frenetically animated and could not stop talking. She chattered her way down the stairs, her voice dipping out and then in again as she chattered her way back up, hustling clients before her. The only respite I was to get from this incessant prattling was during the brief intervals when she was down in the street. I thought she might give it a rest while she was in the bedroom, but she didn't. One after the other, dazed men found themselves in her room without quite knowing how they had agreed to it.

She was ruthless and she was rapid. Man after man was chewed up and spat into the street without stopping. She was seized by a drug-induced recklessness, grabbing anyone and everyone – among them a protesting, venerable old gentleman, who quavered, 'You've gone to all this trouble, my dear, but I don't know if it will be any good.' It seemed like only seconds later that his faltering step had regained its spring and his face had somehow achieved a delicious grin.

She made a bomb all right – and more, because she couldn't stop working when midnight came. In fact, she kept on throughout the night. At some godforsaken hour of the morning I did manage to squeeze in a few words to ask what time she was going home, and was told she would be staying at the flat until she'd restored the family fortunes.

The West End of London settles down to sleep with one eye open for opportunity, but even so, there comes a time when men are too drunk, too tired and too few to be divested of their hard-earned cash. Mae's need to talk supplanted her need to work. Long before dawn broke, my bed seemed like a lost paradise to which I would never return. I felt my eyes burning, my mouth turn into a desert and my body tremble with sleep deprivation. During the ever-longer intervals between men, Mae talked and talked and talked. She even carried on lengthy monologues concerning things she knew nothing about, including a long treatise on the cracks in the wall.

The stupendous, crackling energy that raced around inside her carried on through the morning to midday, then through the afternoon to the evening, by which time I was almost asleep on my feet. I was hot and feverish, but Mae was still bouncing around like a spring lamb. When we were nearing the second midnight, I put my foot down.

'Mae, I have got to get some sleep and you must go home too. Perhaps, if you lie down quietly, you'll just drop off.'

Privately, I didn't hold out much hope of her ever sleeping again. Seen through my bloodshot eyes, she still had the appearance of a pre-race Grand National favourite. Nevertheless, I prevailed on her to go home by giving her the happy idea of how pleased and surprised Tony would be when he saw how much money she had. She was all a-quiver at the prospect.

'Yes! I'll cook him a marvellous meal and I'll have a lovely bath.' With some relish creeping into her voice, she added, 'And I rather fancy him tonight, too.'

I passed a clammy hand over my fevered brow and gasped. She'd had about a hundred and fifty different men in the past thirty-six hours and she still wanted him! Her poor feet!

Twenty-Two

~

Eventually I managed to get home. I collapsed on to my bed without undressing and fell asleep immediately. It seemed only moments had passed when I was woken by a banging on my door. I staggered over and groped around, feeling for the handle, opening the door with my eyes still tightly shut. I was jolted into sudden wakefulness by that eternal and chirpy voice:

'Oh, look, Tony love: she's still asleep!'

Mae was so full of beans I wanted to scream. By her side was 'Tony love', looking like the vanquished foe of a mighty army.

'S'eight o'clock, love. I thought we'd make an early start. A nice cup of coffee and you'll be as right as rain.'

Tony was eyeing me anxiously. 'Do you mind?' he whispered. For once we were allies.

I paused for a little while. Tired as I was, I wanted to make the most of the sight of Tony in defeat. Recognising the inevitable, I turned and picked up my coat and handbag from where I had dropped them and staggered after the dancing figure of Mae into the waiting car. Tony followed behind us to make sure I didn't make a run for it and leave him alone with her. By the time the car was moving fast enough to prevent my jumping out, he was his old arrogant self again.

We arrived at the flat by the usual devious means of Tony dropping us near enough to get a taxi. Mae's eyes, in the stark morning light, were still bright and enormous but her face appeared to have had more of her voice than it could take. As soon as we arrived, I had a wash and made coffee, while Mae kept on saying, 'Gawd, don't I look 'orrible!' as she made running repairs to her face with high-density make-up.

Over my second cup, I began to perk up a bit and, in spite of myself, was able to join in with Mae's boisterous frivolity. Though the blood was still pumping exuberantly around her veins and her toes tingled with a desire for action, she was becoming ill from fatigue. She was sick several times, and by the afternoon, she was bent over the sink, retching.

The drugs had given her a thirst but taken away her appetite, so she was running on innumerable cups of tea. Her talking had, at last, begun to dwindle. For one thing, her brain was running out of subject matter to talk about, but it was also becoming painful for her to speak. Despite this, she still *wanted* to talk and constantly leant against the door jamb of the kitchen saying, 'Bu . . . u . . . u . . . t . . .' This gave her time to grope around in her tired mind for something to say.

She still managed to race up and down the stairs at top speed; she still raked in the money at breakneck pace, but as the afternoon wore on, the staccato tapping of her heels on the staircase and the sight of her hand poking round the bedroom door with the cash took on a nightmarish quality. I had a welcome hunch that we were almost at a full stop.

It came the very next time she leaned against the door jamb and opened her mouth to say something. Instead, she doubled up, retching and heaving in paroxysms – painful even to watch. She straightened up at last, with black mascaraed tears streaming down her face, and I took the bull by the horns.

'Right,' I said sternly. 'I'm taking you to hospital. I can't stand any more of this, even if you can.'

To my surprise, she grinned weakly and said, 'All right, love – just to please you.'

Ten minutes later, we were sitting side by side in the casualty department of St Thomas's. It was just forty-eight hours since she'd drunk that awful cup of tea, but it seemed like weeks ago to me. There were several rows of chairs in which people were dotted about; I gently pushed Mae into one in the front row, instructing her to stay there while I went and spoke to the nurse in charge.

'All right, Mum!'

She grinned at me. Her new soubriquet for me might have been meant as a joke, but it seemed accurate all the same. The dark hollows of her eyes showed clearly now through the make-up, but she still tapped out a rhythm on the floor with her heels and drummed her fingers on the vacant chair next to her.

I gave a few slightly vague particulars to the nurse, who nodded, looked over my shoulder towards Mae and wrote some notes on a card. She told me to sit down; she'd get someone to see us, so I returned to Mae and collapsed into the chair beside her, relieved that she had stayed put.

The tapping and drumming continued, broken by the occasional 'Bu ... u ... t ...' Suddenly she leaned forward, craning her neck to look past me. Then she gave one of her deep, infectious chuckles and clutched my arm.

'Just look who's coming,' she gurgled.

She pointed towards one end of the vast room. Approaching us was a consultant, followed by a gaggle of students hanging on his every word. With white coat fluttering, he was making his awe-inspiring progress along the length of the department; his acolytes walked reverently behind him with hands clasped behind their backs. He had one on each side of him: favourites, no doubt, whose job it was to nod their heads gravely whilst keeping to his exact pace.

'Recognise who it is?' Mae chortled, as he came nearer – the procession was soon about to pass right in front of us.

I did indeed. The great man was one of Mae's regular clients. And only three days earlier, he had presented a ludicrously different image. He had wanted a witness – me, of course – and my memory of this majestic creature was his bare bottom bent over the end of Mae's bed. He was a pretty experienced masochist and I knew his behind to be a complex road map of scars. Halfway through the session, Mae had thrust the knotted whip into my hands and instructed me to have a go because she was getting tired. The thought of touching those terrible lacerations with anything harsher than cotton wool had defeated me, and I had whispered, 'Honestly, I couldn't, Mae.' She'd snatched the whip back – scornful of my concerns – and proceeded to lay it on with renewed zest in an effort to get the job over with more quickly. A particularly vicious blow proved to be the crowning glory of the session.

'Oh, that's wonderful!' he'd said gratefully.

And now here he was: the high priest in his temple. The moment, he caught sight of Mae's bouncing blonde curls, her grinning face and my incredulous expression, he turned brick-red and his head attempted to collapse into the safety of his white collar. Had Mae not still been as high as a kite, she doubtless would not have let on that she knew him, but she *was* as high as a kite and it was all great fun.

As he was about to draw level, she gave me a hefty dig

in the ribs with her elbow. The red face was now an ugly purple and his waistcoat button appeared to have become the most interesting thing in the whole world.

'Oh, if only his trousers would fall down and let those young chaps see his arse!' Mae announced.

At last we were called into a cubicle with a doctor who was, happily, unknown to us. I told him the story of the inhaler. Mae lounged voluptuously in the doorway, ogling him and rolling her hips gently. He blinked at her uncertainly and, transferring his gaze to me, said, 'You say a whole inhaler?'

'S'right, love,' said Mae, smiling provocatively.

'Do you realise that it's a wonder you're not dead by now?'

'Can't kill me; I'm as strong as a bleeding horse.'

'You must be,' he muttered.

Between us we persuaded her to sit down while he took her blood pressure and sounded her heart. He was the perfect fall guy for her lewdness, and she managed to get him blushing furiously as he hurriedly gave her an injection and declared that he was 'all done now'.

It was with extreme thankfulness that I unloaded her on to Tony, who collected her now snoring corpse and took it home to bed.

Twenty-Three

~

All round Mae's beat there were quaint little shops selling antiques, jewellery and second-hand goods. Here, you could buy a diamond ring, a Georgian washstand, a rusty flat iron or a mouldering top hat. When Mae was bored with walking or standing about, she would browse these displays. This was not, as it might have seemed, a purely idle pursuit; from time to time she did make purchases on the premise that it was good policy: as a fairly regular customer, the shopkeepers would be less inclined to complain about her.

Nevertheless, she had a keen nose for a bargain and an unerring eye for quality. When the same object attracted both nose and eye, she pounced. She could never 'pass up a snip', whether she wanted it or not, and because of this – and the fact that she didn't like Tony to know how much money she was spending – a lot of her 'finds' got passed on to me. All sorts of strange objects would nonchalantly be tossed to me with the one word:

'Present!'

Among these treasures were exquisite items of jewellery, pretty bits of china and glass, a Chinese peasant carved from ivory, a mirror in the shape of an artist's palette held by a serpent stand ... The *pièce de résistance* arrived at the tail of a little procession led by a client, followed by Mae, with the shopkeeper bringing up the rear. He was carrying something large, covered with snowy tissue paper. Even on this occasion, Mae didn't pause on her journey to the bedroom, but with a grin and a backward jerk of her head said:

'Your birthday present – hope you like it.'

The shopkeeper insisted on staying and unwrapping it, saying proudly, 'I've never seen anything like this before, you know. I should think it's unique.'

When he took the last wrapping off, I gasped at the glitter of porcelain, silver and cut glass. It was a tray: but what a tray! All the paraphernalia for breakfast in bed nestled between silver railings; the little cup was cut glass, resting on a silver saucer, and the silver eggcup was perched on a silver bridge, above a cut-glass dish.

As well as giving me many of her barely worn clothes, Mae also bought garments especially for me – luxurious ones that I would never have dreamed of buying for myself – and several cuddly toy animals with musical boxes hidden within their anatomy. Also, she had clients who travelled in cosmetics and, via them, often received bottles of perfume, many of which she passed on to me. (Contrary to the popular myth, the scent that prostitutes admittedly were smothered in was certainly not cheap.)

All her suits and coats were bought from Kravetz, an expensive, wonderful ladies' tailor in Wardour Street. She had them make a beautiful coat of chestnut-brown velour to her own design. I fell in love with this coat instantly. It was the first time I'd actually coveted anything; I was wild for it and would have lived on scraps for a month to possess it.

'Please, Mae,' I begged her. 'Promise me when you're fed up with it – even if it's threadbare by then – you'll let me buy it from you.'

She laughed and pirouetted, making it flair out even more. "Course, love. I won't forget.'

But despite her usual largesse, she was unpredictable, and only a few months later, she gave it away to someone else. I don't recount this out of any pettishness, but to illustrate the sort of inconsistencies that were common among all the girls: strange, incomprehensible quirks that would lie in wait for your assumptions and trip them up. Conventions like punctuality and keeping promises were ignored; lies and excuses tripped off the tongue with the ease and lightness of birdsong. Life in Soho had different rules.

These facts were to be accepted and that was that. The best you could do was look after yourself. I always arranged to meet friends in a café rather than the street, so that their lateness – or, as like as not, non-appearance – didn't matter so much. Excuses were always heartfelt, profuse and totally untrue, but the golden rule was to accept them courteously. Any other reaction led to the bother of being marched round to a third person, who would happily vouch for the truth of the lie, without having the vaguest idea of what it was all about.

Following the maxim of keeping in with the local shop-keepers, Mae and myself were almost literally keeping 'Toffee-nose' – the café proprietor below – in business.

Having predicted the failure of his venture, Mae took a morbid interest in seeing herself proved right. The succulent turkey in the window had given way to a chicken, and the lobsters had been replaced by two small dishes of prawns. Before summer came, these meagre offerings were in their turn to give way to a few long-lasting salami sausages. There was now no sign of the bay trees: passing merry-makers had broken the hardier one of the two, even though, unlike its neighbour, it had managed to survive being used as a urinal.

Soon, though, the sounds of activity on the floor immediately below us took our minds off Toffee-nose and his problems. There were stepladders, pots of paint, all sorts of tools and a couple of men hammering, banging and sawing like mad.

We were both eaten up with curiosity, and in the end, Mae cornered one of them and asked what was going on. The answer was that it was going to be opened as a private drinking club. It was an exciting idea, and henceforth we enjoyed all the noisy sounds of construction going on beneath us.

The future proprietor and her husband came up to introduce themselves. He was a grey-haired little man, who almost never spoke, was constantly chewing his nails and looked uncomfortable. The woman was big, florid and very theatrical, always saying 'my *deah*' and calling everyone 'darling' and 'lovey'.

All her remarks were carried to the limit of probability. If asked if there was enough sugar in her tea, she would answer:

'Oh, my *deah*, it's absolutely perfect, really heavenly – a quite, quite wonderful cup of tea!'

They were rather a sickening couple.

Eventually, the club was finished – all concealed lights, illuminated brocade, bows and potted plants vying for space around a domineering bar in a clubroom that could never be accused of spaciousness. On the other side of the landing – and directly under our waiting room – was the toilet (which until now had been ours alone) and a storeroom.

A visitor to the clubroom had to find his way along a newly painted corridor, where embossed hearts and coronets attempted to lend the walls a regal, romantic air and the red lino on the floor was at least easily cleanable. This last went a little way towards appeasing Toffee-nose, the café owner, who had noted every occasion when one of our clients had spent a surreptitious penny in our passage. This was understandable, since it had gone straight through the bare floorboards and on to his electrics below, fusing all his lights.

On the afternoon of the club's opening, there was a continual procession of bouquets and telegrams, and then, as the day turned to night, a plethora of guests began arriving. Above all this, like children allowed up late, Mae and I hung over the banister rail, drinking in glimpses of the spectacle and neglecting poor old Houdini, who was tied up in the waiting room.

Accompanied by the music of Nat King Cole, Peggy Lee and Ella Fitzgerald, amorphous pleasantries grew briefly louder as the door opened and closed on yet another . . .

'*Da-a-a-arling!* How wonderful you could come to our little *thingummy*!'

Mae and I were not invited to the little *thingummy* – although I seem to recall that a glass of something was sent up to us. Each time that door shut us out, Mae expressed her displeasure by walloping Houdini.

It was, perhaps, unfortunate that this gathering was the club's one and only moment of glory – and *Schadenfreude* aside, Mae was probably right in suspecting that it only achieved that much by serving free drinks. During the week that followed, we continued to hear Nat, Peggy and Ella, but without the accompaniment of 'voices off'. Most of the footsteps we heard on the stairs continued on past the club door and came up to us.

Actually, the club being there helped our business enormously, as it erased any embarrassment that might have been felt at the front door. The few people who actually did go into the club were mainly chorus boys and other tired theatricals. *'Da-a-a-arling!'* rang out like infrequent door chimes every time a newcomer arrived.

Mrs *Da-a-a-arling* must have drunk all the profits herself. Around nine thirty every evening this caused her to become cantankerous, and her husband was an easy, obvious and perhaps justifiable target.

The reason for his nervous nail-biting became clear. When she became nasty – and she *did* become nasty – he had to ease her out to the landing so she could swear at him and hit him without disturbing the clientele. When she had verbally and physically abused him for about ten minutes, she was perfectly all right again and business continued as usual. By the end of the evening, when she was pretty far gone again, she was too tired to bother with a repeat performance.

After the customers had gone, he washed the glasses while she slumped in a corner, ranting at him in a slurred monotone that came to us via the fug of cigarette smoke wafting out through the open door. Some of her comments were fairly stock ones, not taxing her imagination too much but nevertheless satisfying her vitriolic mood:

'You're a filthy, rotten, stinking little bastard. You know that, don't you?'

'Yes, dear.'

Others were marginally more poetic:

'You're a smelly, snivelling little snail, a crawling, lousy little worm ... a moronic coward who should have been stamped on at birth. Aren't you?'

Whatever the accusation, when his cue came, the answer was always the same:

'Yes, dear.'

If it was claimed the enterprise went gradually downhill from the opening night, it would be more accurate to say it was pushed off a cliff. After-hours drinks briefly provided a parachute, but not for long. Some six months after that first '*Da-a-a-arling!*' graced our ears, the police raided the club and took away their licence. We quite missed them, really, but on the whole, agreed that our life was hectic enough without them.

Soon after the club had shut, some men came to remove the jukebox. It became wedged halfway along the passage, where the wall bellied out and narrowed the passageway that vital inch. The two removal men were sweating and swearing. They were only six feet from victory, but no amount of pushing or heaving would budge it. Mae needed to get out to provide something for a peephole punter to be voyeuristic about. Annoyed at being blocked in to the corridor, she surveyed the scene and gave helpful advice.

'You'll never get it out that way; the chaps who brought it pulled it up through the window on ropes.'

'*Now* she tells us,' said one of the men, wiping a streaming brow.

'Well I'm not your bleeding guv'nor,' said Mae. 'How long's the damn thing going to be stuck here?'

After a short conference, the two men decided that the only thing to be done was to break the jukebox down into smaller pieces. The man on the door side was the obvious choice to go and fetch a big hammer.

'God knows where from!' he muttered as he went.

Mae came and conveyed all this news to me and the expectant voyeur in the kitchen. Seeing his forlorn expression, the ever-resourceful Mae went down and chatted up the marooned removal man as a convenient stand-in.

So Mae got herself another client, the peephole functioned again and everyone was happy, except the owner of the jukebox – although it hadn't done the hearts and coronets on the wall much good either.

Twenty-Four

~

Mae always spent her Sundays at home, washing her hair and her undies and lying around reading the *News of the World* and the *People* – newspapers that served the underworld as trade papers. She often arrived on Mondays, flapping a copy and chortling over how the doings of someone she knew had been reported before giving me the real story. I think Sundays bored her; she had no hobbies or real interests and Tony wasn't the most exhilarating of companions. She lived for her work and looked on time off as an irritating interruption to her life.

Most of the girls felt that way and a lot of them preferred not to take time off at all. Because I was known to live alone, my Sundays were treated as 'on call' time; I was often asked to deputise for those maids who had deserted their posts in favour of their families. Actually, I found these one-day stands quite pleasant; Sundays were very quiet for business in Soho; there was no real work involved and plenty of time to chat. Besides, having a pretext to leave my room was welcome to me. I still hadn't so much as opened a tube of paint, or drawn a line on my single precious canvas. If I was being fiercely honest with myself, any thoughts I'd once had of becoming a painter had become mere delusions. Being able to leave my room, lock my door, and go out to work at least provided me with a tangible reason for not touching paint or canvas that day.

Unlike my weekdays with Mae, my 'Sunday girls' didn't tend to hustle on the street. Maybe the shadow of religion prevented them or, more likely, they were very obvious in the quiet streets and they resented being viewed as a tourist attraction. Working on my day off, I at least allowed myself the indulgence of being particular about my employers. Some, I found, were not to my taste.

The angelic-looking Lou, for example: I went to her once and once only. As the only nymphomaniac on the game that I ever met, she would spend at least an hour with each client, which left very little socialising time and made the day drag for me. As if this wasn't dull enough, she expended so much energy on sex that in the time between, she was in a state of permanent lethargy.

Like most of the girls, Lou was quite happy to regard herself as bisexual, but she was predatory with it. I had first-hand experience of this. After all, I had no boyfriend, so what was I? She would regard me coyly and invitingly through fluttering curled eyelashes, but to no avail. After my Sunday stint with her, she phoned to say she'd got a rich male all-nighter who wanted an orgy with two girls; Mae accepted the job and Lou asked if I'd like to tag along as referee. I thanked her kindly and said no.

It was some time later that Lou's voracious appetite for sex was to save the day for us. I found Mae counselling a genteel woman, looking distinctly nervous, who had made her way up to the flat after extreme hesitation. She halt-ingly told us that her husband, whom she'd adored, had died two years earlier. The loneliness was terrible, but she'd coped with that, up to a point, by taking up work in charitable organisations. We waited patiently while she told us all this. Perhaps Mae had already guessed what she was leading to. The woman had, she said, always been a very passionate person, and had reached a point where she could no longer abstain from sex. To practise it alone was abhorrent to her, and the prospect of sex with another man still felt like a betrayal. Lamely, and with some embarrassment, she concluded that perhaps she could find a woman she could visit from time to time.

'It might just work out for me,' she said. 'I don't know what else to do.'

We restored her with a cup of tea, and Mae stopped everything, took her round and introduced her to Lou.

Sadie the Sadist was another of my Sunday stand-ins. She was dark and slim, with a certain natural aggressiveness about her that must have come in useful. Her flat was a veritable temple to 'Chastisement, Punishment and Correction'. Had the Spanish Inquisition employed women, Sadie would have been first past the selection panel. There were manacles fixed to the walls; there were stocks and pillories – one to take the head and wrists between two planks and one that fastened the prisoner to a vertical stake with rings; there was a rack, a cage and an enormous, sombre black oak cross that she frequently threatened to nail men to.

As well as these items of furniture, she kept whips of every description – tawses, cats-o'-nine-tails, birches and a range of canes. The first time I saw Sadie's flat, I marvelled at the things men would pay for. But if you like that sort of thing, I had to admit that it was a beautiful set-up.

The Sundays I spent with sweet, innocent Cindy were like days spent with a younger sister. She was only eighteen and Scottish, with that lovely, soft 'D'ye no ken?' sort of accent. She was coltish and pretty and I was very fond of her.

On those long, quiet Sundays, she told me many things about herself. Not so very long before, when she was a kid in Scotland, she had belonged to the Salvation Army and had to sing in the streets with them – 'Wi' one o' the bliddy bonnets on me haid.' She'd been brought up in an ordinary working-class home, but longed for the gorgeous clothes she saw in magazines. She'd come to London with the sole purpose of acquiring them by whatever means was quickest, and prostitution was exactly what she'd been looking for.

She had no regrets – none of the girls I knew had – and her ambition to own a dress shop was looking attainable. Her ponce was a real rarity: a young Maltese who was fond of her, a nice man who made sure she was happy all the time. He always left her with more than enough money and she always looked like a fashion plate. That, and her youth, ensured she had plenty of clients, without making much effort – if any at all.

In contrast to Lou, Cindy was undersexed and told me that she didn't get anything at all out of 'this sex lark'. Sometimes, when she had a young, good-looking client, she let him stay longer in the hope he might give her some sort of thrill, but it was never any good. She knew sex was supposed to be exciting, and she felt deficient. She acted her part well, the mask only slipping when those same handsome young men came again and, thinking they'd made a hit with her, expected to pay less. They were sent packing, wondering what they'd done to inspire her rage.

Her sharp temper was typical of those demure people who flare up only when necessary. I saw it in action when she bundled one client out through the bedroom door. He had arrived looking very smart but was now the stuff of Whitehall farce: he was trying to rescue his trousers from below his knees with one hand, while the other made quick, nervous snatches at the jacket she thrust at him. His crime? He had apparently 'tekked off his trews and felt ma titties' before he'd paid her. He wasn't allowed back.

There was a modesty to Cindy that I found touching. Once, there was a particularly risqué film on at one of the West End's more notorious cinemas. It caused a furore, though today it might be the stuff of Saturday-afternoon TV. I asked Cindy if she'd seen it. 'No,' she said, utterly seriously, 'my boyfriend says it's not fit for me to see.'

One late Sunday in December, business was extremely quiet. The run-up to Christmas had led men to suppose they should be spending money on their families rather than on Soho prostitutes. Cindy said that she'd like to try out the efficacy of an old whores' superstition: scatter salt, pepper and mustard on the stairs and it would magically draw customers. We each mixed half a cupful and, like flower maidens strewing petals, gleefully threw little handfuls about. To our astonishment, it worked! No sooner had we done it than we heard footsteps. We were slightly nervous about our success, but we continued to flavour our stairs till they got quite gritty and nasty – and each time we did it, it worked.

Cindy's boyfriend didn't have to spend an awful lot on her clothes. Of those she actually purchased, most were bought on impulse and usually weren't very expensive things. The really snazzy section of her wardrobe was built up in quite a different way. She got on extremely well with a contingent of gay men who, apart from adoring her, also happened to be proficient shoplifters.

She spent part of each day browsing round her beloved dress shops, noting the details of a dress here and a coat there . . . All she needed to do was describe these garments, and in virtually no time at all they would be laid at her feet. She usually gave her shoplifters a small fraction of the actual price to keep them happy, and in this way she acquired the most fabulous wardrobe

Working for so many different girls on Sundays made life even more of a variety show. I must have run the gamut of every type of girl there was and every sort of working place that had a roof over it. The next act was more suited to the Grand Guignol than cheery music hall.

Ladies and gentlemen, let me present Tearaway Tina!

If there was anyone more outrageous than Mae, it was Tina. To say she was an undesirable acquaintance is no exaggeration, but I did not know how undesirable until she had become fascinating to me and it was too late to avoid her. Every bad character trait it is possible to have — venality, mendacity, malevolence — Tina had. Any therapist trying to rehabilitate her would have had to go back a long way before he found any signs of bedrock to start building upon.

Tina seemed to be larger and taller than she really was; her figure was better in appearance than reality and her looks were deceptively attractive. Behind this impression there was nothing more than a lot of black hair and a gigantic, drug-induced personality. She loved false eyelashes to the extent that she always wore three pairs at a time. As a result, her eyelids were so heavy she had to tilt her head back to see. This gave her a challenging, aggressive appearance that was at least in keeping with her challenging, aggressive personality.

She loved wigs and hairpieces as long as they were black. Assisted by these, she built her hair into massive edifices set off with huge rococo gilt earrings. Her offstage self was disconcertingly different: in dowdy clothes, she turned into a sallow, sharp-faced, suspicion-ridden mouse to whom no one would have given a second glance. This was probably necessary, because, like Cindy's gay friends, most of her mornings were spent in shoplifting.

She came from a perfectly respectable family, and it

was from one of her sisters that I gleaned facts about her background. Tina had begun life in a large family in the north of England. Her father was immensely respected in his neighbourhood and her brothers and sisters all grew up to be solid citizens with responsible jobs. By the time I got to know Tina, her sister was the only member of her family still speaking to her. The sister was a nicely spoken, intelligent woman who regarded Tina with awed puzzlement, no doubt wondering whether it was totally wise to remain on friendly terms with her.

Pretty early on, Tina upset the domestic scene by stealing from members of her family and playing truant from school. She graduated to petty theft, terrorising her teachers and getting into trouble with boys. The theft resulted in reform school, but when she had finished her time there, she was welcomed back home with open arms.

Just for the heck of it, she took to burgling. During one of her maraudings, she was disturbed by the elderly lady who owned the house. Tina beat her up and left her unconscious. She used what she had stolen to get to London. Once there, she borrowed a bit, thieved a lot, lived with several men, produced four children – all placed in various homes – and gravitated into prostitution.

Tina made her own fantasy world up as she went along. The stories she told her clients about her past and present life were amazing. Her mother's nationality was never fixed. Sometimes she was Spanish:

'You can see where I get my looks from, can't you?' she would say, swaying and clicking imaginary castanets.

Or again:

'My mother was Mexican, you know. I take after her.' Here, she would grasp a plastic flower from a vase and place it between her teeth.

Another time:

'Would you ever guess my mother was Egyptian? You can see now, can't you?' She hurriedly pencilled her eyes into black slants to prove her point.

Though her mother's history varied, her father's was more consistent. She was, when I first knew her, the illegitimate daughter of a duke. Though his title varied from day to day, he always remained true blue-blooded English.

By the time I met her, she was in her late thirties and had been on the game for a number of years. In time, she was to tell me she trusted and loved me as she had never trusted or loved anyone. I replied that I would just as soon befriend a viper. Her good opinion of me remained undiminished. Had I allowed it, she would have overwhelmed me with stolen gifts, and my principled refusal puzzled her. When she finally realised it was genuine, she said, 'Ah well, I suppose I admire you really.' Others were not so chary about receiving her 'shopping', and she was able to walk out of a store concealing anything from coats to cosmetics. She didn't necessarily limit herself to things she wanted or needed – she had the largest collection of sunglasses I have ever seen.

Once, she gave away a jumper that she'd nicked and made the mistake of telling her friend which shop she'd taken it from. Finding that she could do with a size larger, the 'daft cow' – as the friend in question was later described – took it back to change it. Tina's name was mentioned and the police turned up. Somehow, in a flat crammed with ill-gotten gains and confronted with damning evidence and a witness statement, Tina managed to emerge from the interview without charge. She was unrepentant and took her friend's betrayal in her stride, though she admitted it was 'a bloody close thing'.

Tina worked from a house containing two 'gaffs', and

she had the better one on the second floor. She made the life of the girl above a perpetual misery, and the house was a permanent battleground, with the laurels mostly going to Tina. She was never really happy unless someone was annoying her. She was forever running upstairs to accuse the cowering occupant of some domestic misdemeanour or hurling verbal abuse up at her from below.

Her vocabulary and turn of phrase were quite fantastic – and not something I'd be brave enough to repeat here!

The other girl alleged – probably justifiably – that Tina was intercepting some of her regular clients on their way up and stealing their custom. The accusations continued as private grumbles until, at last, a client said he was willing to state that Tina had tried to ensnare him.

Still in a state of undress from her latest client, Tina clenched her fists and shrieked something to the effect that the man was a 'fucking liar' and demanded to know where he was so she could 'get my fucking hands on him'. She hurled herself up the stairs like a troop of commandos. I managed to get out a few words, but Tina wasn't taking any notice. Fascinated, I listened to the sounds coming from above. Finally Tina reappeared on the landing, clutching one hand to her bosom.

'I think I've done my fist in!' she said. 'I'd just got him propped up nice when the little bastard ducked and I hit the wall instead.'

Her hand was a ghastly sight, swelling like a purple melon. I hated to think what would have happened to the man's face if he hadn't ducked. Needless to say, the girl upstairs ceased to press her client-rights after that.

Tina had no real need to steal other people's clients; she could pick them up herself when she needed to and would work hard if she had to. Her ponce was called Paul, a mild, nice, long-suffering man who was virtually on the retired list.

'My old man makes me die,' she told me once. 'Do you know, yesterday I had forty quickies – forty! By the time I got home I was fit to drop. I told my old man what the take was – 'cos I was ever so pleased with myself – and collapsed into bed. Then bugger me, he got in, all pleased with me too, and by heck, he starts getting randy! I told him to give over and let me get some sleep. Do you know what the stupid bugger said?'

'No,' I said. 'What?'

'He gets up on one elbow and switches the light on. Then he stares at me and says, "What's the matter? Have you got another fella, then?"'

Tina's uninhibited way of hustling was to go into a café or milk bar, position herself next to a likely man at the counter, touch him up for long enough to hook him and then simply walk away. The men never failed to follow.

It wasn't always plain-sailing, though. Tina's second-floor flat was one room converted into two: the bedroom and a kitchen-cum-sitting-room. The bedroom door had a lock for which there was only one key, and Tina was always locking herself out. When she came back one day with a punter called Edward, she realised she was shut out. After a few minutes of effing and blinding about it, she was struck by sudden inspiration. In a gesture worthy of church hall dramatics, she banged her forehead with the heel of her hand and exclaimed, '*Madonna mia!*'

Edward was led to the kitchen window. Tina pointed out a 'good ledge' connecting them to the bedroom window. Edward saw a very narrow strip of ornamental corbelling and vehemently refused to have anything to do with it. He began to back off, but Tina took his hand and led him back to the window.

'Oh, love, not even for me?' she cooed. Her hand strayed caressingly over his framework. 'If you do that, you and me could have such a lovely time in there.'

His continued protestations might have been more convincing had he removed himself from the questing hand. He didn't, and she knew she'd already won. She brought her other hand into play and nibbled his ear, winking at me over his shoulder.

Once Edward was performing his acrobatic feat and was out of earshot, Tina turned to me and said:

'He must be mad. Don't forget, if he falls, we've never seen him before in our lives.'

She had quite a big S&M clientele and relished her role as a dominatrix. There was, for instance, a headmaster who, ironically, visited during the school holidays to allow enough time for the weals on his hands to fade. There was also a fair sprinkling of judo and wrestling devotees whose punishments caused the floor to shudder with bangs and crashes.

Hidden amongst Tina's toughness, brutality and general indifference, there were tender spots – if you could find them. She was very upset about a girlfriend of hers who had committed suicide. It was a sad but not unfamiliar story. The girl had married one of her wealthy regulars and then fallen for his cook. The cook – happily married himself – had rejected her, and unable to deal with her feelings, she had taken a massive quantity of sleeping pills.

Tina could also weep buckets over her absent children and over the plight of the poor, old or sick. These were not crocodile tears; she would help where she could. There was one old man who used to visit her who needed a lot of help to reach her room, let alone an orgasm. She never charged him, but as if to lessen his obligation, he always brought his own rubber, carefully enclosed in his wallet.

'I have to help him on me and I have to help him off me,' she said. 'And I'm dead scared all the time he's going to peg out on the job, but you can't let him go without it, can you?'

For all her sharp-tongued comments and quick wits, it came as no surprise for me to discover me that Tina was illiterate, though she thought no one would ever suspect.

'I don't mind telling *you*,' she said darkly. 'Because I know you'll not take advantage of me. But there's a lot as would.'

From then on, she took to bringing me documents and letters that had hitherto gone unread, and I was able to sort out a few of her problems. She was, like all the girls, keen to start a bank account, but had not known how to go about it. She didn't want to look silly at the bank, but neither did she want to ask any of her friends to help her.

'I don't want them to know where my hoard is,' she said. 'It'd be nice to know I've got something behind me for a rainy day, though, and anyway, having a bank account sounds posh.'

So I went with her and helped her open an account with the ten pounds she had to spare at that moment.

'I wonder how long that'll stay in there,' I said to her.

She was adamant:

'Oh, it's going to stay there, and I'll add to it all the time, you'll see.'

Having joined the ranks of the banking classes, she was as pleased as Punch. She kept flapping her new chequebook around, riffling through its pages from time to time. After that, she often showed me a bank statement to prove she'd kept her word and never drawn the ten pounds out. I also noticed that she'd never put any more in.

'It's lovely to have someone I can really trust,' she told me.

I didn't pay much heed to this–I knew she would stab me in the back at any given moment if it suited her. However, in my way, I loved her, because I understood her. After all, there are not many people you can know that well and who are so open about their darker nature: nastiness is usually snuggled under a thick eiderdown of culture and politeness. If nothing else, Tina was always herself.

She was – but was I? In the early months of 1949, I was a very different being from the one who had left my grandmother's house with her curses reddening the air behind me, a very different being from the one who had taken up with Mae on that fateful evening in The Mousehole that third summer after the war. I had a job, I had friends, I had money. But my sense of vocation had dwindled into invisibility and the Soho that had liberated me was now, in some ways, also a prison. I could leave it at any time, of course, but showed no sign of doing so. It was as though I had become a working girl and Soho had become my ponce. I was drifting on a tide, and somewhere deep inside, I wasn't sure if I liked where it was taking me.

Twenty-Five

~

It was late spring, 1949. Mae was still working too hard, still borrowing money, still experimenting, off and on, with the Benzedrine. The Rabbits Regime was long gone, and life was the same glorious confusion I had come to expect and require.

Mae's clothes were generally sexy and figure-hugging; one day, though, she felt like having something different. On impulse, she bought a frilly silk dress with a nipped-in waist and little puffed sleeves. It was the epitome of fresh innocence and she had no idea when she would wear it, though she was desperately anxious to do so. It hung in immaculate glory from the picture rail and we would sit gazing at it during spare moments, wondering where she could give it an airing. Then Mae suddenly remembered the Kursaal at Southend.

'Smashing place,' she told me, seeing my mystified expression. 'It's a great big funfair. Haven't you been? I thought everyone had been to the Kursaal. Point is, we must go on a Saturday – Saturdays are really crowded at the Kursaal.'

'Point is,' I reminded her, 'Saturdays are really crowded here as well. Tony will never agree to it.' (By this time, Tony's financial interest was no longer a secret and we spoke openly about it – she indulgently, and even with amusement.)

'Well, it's jolly well got to be a Saturday,' she said with a scowl. 'Southend's nothing without lots of people.'

I wondered why she always had to make life so difficult for herself. I knew that if she lost her Saturday income, she would have to work like a maniac the following week to make up for it – she'd be very likely to borrow more money as well. She was still taking Benzedrine, together with Dexedrene tablets, and from her actions and manner recently, I suspected that she had been increasing the dose.

'I'll manage it,' she continued. 'Don't you worry. I'll work the next two Sundays. And I'll tell Tony I've already invited you to come with us. He won't like to say no, then.'

She must have spent the next few days selling the idea to Tony. He finally cracked and the outing was arranged for the following Saturday.

It was a sunny morning when they arrived to pick me up. Mae was sitting bolt upright in the middle of the back seat of the car, with her dress spread out carefully around her. I slid in beside Tony. I could see at a glance that he wasn't exactly falling about with pleasure at the prospect of our little jaunt to the seaside – but then I'd never seen Tony fall about with pleasure over anything.

He worked hard to exude the aura of a Chicago mobster. Tony's god was Al Capone, a man who talked in monosyllables and who never smiled except when pulling the trigger. When describing the latest gangster film, he would become animated and childishly enthusiastic till he remembered he was supposed to be morose and abruptly fall silent again just in time to preserve the image. Now he gazed murderously at the traffic, whilst chewing savagely on an unlit cigar. I noticed, with spiteful satisfaction, that his double chin was progressing nicely.

Attempting to bring a little festivity into the atmosphere, I remarked on the beautiful day but met with no response from Tony. Mae, however, began to chatter: I supposed her last tablet was beginning to take effect. Throughout the forty-three-mile drive, Tony's contribution to the conversation was an occasional grunt or burp and a frequent clashing of gears. At least he showed a mild interest when I pointed out a spot known as Gallows Corner, and he actually came quite near to merriment when he narrowly missed running over a dog.

At last the sea hove into view, which thrilled me, as I'd only seen it two or three times before in my life. I would have loved to go paddling along the strand, examining seaweed and looking for shells. But that wasn't the point of the exercise: it was the Kursaal that had brought us, said Mae, not all that 'soppy' water.

By the time we got in – with Mae about four steps ahead, fluttering in her bouffant silk like a giant butterfly looking for a flower – it was obvious from Tony's expression that whatever misgivings he'd had about the outing, he was now in the process of trebling them. Mae was positively sparkling; she had already swept the car park attendant off his feet and flustered the man we bought our tickets from. If she'd had 'Whore of Babylon' stamped on her forehead in fluorescent ink, it couldn't have been more obvious what she was. To my shame, I shared a little of Tony's embarrassment. I don't think either of us were worried she would use bad language, but she had spent so many years ogling men, it had become more or less habitual. Her only concession to being respectable was to refrain from actually winking at them – although from some of the startled expressions I saw, I'm not so sure she always managed that.

Tony was convinced that every West End plain-clothes policeman had decided to visit Southend that day, and kept trying to maintain a discreet distance between himself and Mae's conspicuous flamboyance. He stiffened with

alarm whenever she disappeared into the crowd after something that had attracted her attention. She then had to trot
after him in her four-inch heels in order to catch him and
cling on to him affectionately.

'Oh, Tony, look – candyfloss,' she said with a squeal of
joy. 'I must get some.' And off she swooped.

'*Ma – don – na!*' he muttered, staring gloomily after her.

We walked along with our candyfloss, Mae eating one
and carrying Tony's, as he refused to take any part in this
exhibitionism. At least while she had both hands full, she
couldn't clutch at his arm.

Whilst she was working her way through the second
cocoon of sticky pink cotton wool, we came upon a merry-
go-round.

'Come on, both of you, let's have a go,' she said as she
shot forward. I looked enquiringly at Tony, but he stood
his ground.

'*Mella!*' he growled.

I don't suppose Al Capone went on roundabouts any
more than he would eat candyfloss. Tony would have been
relieved to be standing on his own, watching the two of
us, had Mae not taken it into her head to warble out '*Tonee!*'
every time our horses passed him.

We rolled pennies, went on the Ferris wheel, the roller
coaster, the Whip and the Cakewalk, with Tony '*Mella*-
ing' and '*Madonna*-ing' at every new suggestion. In an
attempt to restore his mood to normal, Mae looked around
for a rifle range.

'He'll love that,' she whispered to me. 'He likes guns.'

When we found one, she paid for a rifle and, beaming,
offered it to him, looking for the warm twinkle in his eye.
There was none. He glared and muttered, '*Ostja!*' – another
good old Maltese expression.

'Oh well,' she said with a shrug, and turning to point

the gun at the targets, proceeded to make a spectacle of herself once more.

Having done her bit towards placating Tony, Mae made a beeline for the dodgem cars. There, she succeeded in banging us into everything in sight, until going into a slow gyration in the middle of the arena. This, of course, necessitated the attendant's aid, and she rewarded him with dazzling smiles and a few provocative words, during which I stole a glance to where we had left Tony and saw him turn away with a murderous scowl.

After that, we giggled our way through the Tunnel of Love, got ourselves thrown around in the Giant Caterpillar and exhibited our underwear to greater-than-ever advantage on the chair-o-planes. Meantime, we managed to eat all the things one should eat at a fair: ice creams, hot doughnuts, saveloys, bags of crisps and peanuts, whelks and jellied eels.

Eventually we actually achieved the impossible: we got Tony into the hall of mirrors, which had an economical admission charge, no call upon one's skill, no risk to life and limb and no chance of him making a spectacle of himself. He was not amused, however. In fact, he didn't even look at any of his reflections, though they were making Mae and me hysterical. So when we chanced upon the haunted house, we didn't press him, but just accepted his snarled '*Mella!*' and left him outside.

Halfway round this, after encountering clanking skeletons, fabricated cobwebs, corpses in coffins revealed by lightning flashes – all to the accompaniment of blood-curdling screams – we stepped on the inevitable grating, which blew a fierce gust of wind up our dresses. We were reduced to howls of laughter when Mae's yards of skirt flew almost over her head, making her look like a parachutist going the wrong way.

When we emerged from the darkness into the sunlight, still giggling, we couldn't see Tony anywhere. At last Mae caught sight of him skulking about a hundred yards away. We walked towards him, still chuckling. I could hardly miss the fact that he was wearing his most diabolical glare to date. Apparently he had stationed himself directly outside a window at the precise spot where Mae's skirt had blown over her head.

'And,' he hissed, 'you've got a great big hole in your drawers – and everybody saw it.'

This set us off laughing again, which didn't improve his temper at all, and we left the Kursaal to get a meal of fish and chips at one of the many seafront cafés. At last Tony became slightly more buoyed up, and almost smiled at Mae's dismay when she dropped a glob of tomato ketchup on to her party dress. Perhaps he hoped that might curtail her activities for the day; but he should have known her better. On the way back to the fair, she spied a small boating pond.

'Oh, we must have a go on that,' she cried. 'I haven't been in a boat for ages.'

Surprisingly, after much persuasion, we managed to get Tony into a boat with us. Although Mae and I rowed him twice around the pond, he remained unhappy, until Mae caught a crab and liberally splashed herself. She saw his grin this time and called him a sod.

When our time was up, we manoeuvred the boat – stern first – to somewhere near the landing stage. Mae thought it was time to stand up and take stock of things. Her little hysterical shrieks for help, which were intended to enhance the fun of it all, ensured us a substantial audience and the assistance of every available attendant – particularly when it came to lifting her to safety. Tony hated having to be hoisted out of that boat by two pairs of sturdy, willing hands. His face now wore the bitter expression of someone who had reached the end of their tether. He had been looking at his watch all through the afternoon – no doubt totting up what Mae could have been earning – and he now checked it again, more definitely.

'It is six o'clock,' he announced firmly. 'We must go.'

'Oh, Tony, must we?' Mae wailed. 'I wanted to go back to the Kursaal.'

'I have to meet a man on business,' he said and, added in a matter-of-fact way, 'and you can go back to work.'

'Oh well,' she acquiesced, unenthusiastically. 'All right.'

We walked along to the car park, where Mae gave a final dazzling smile to the attendant, before sinuously sliding into the car with a last lingering display of leg. She was hardly in before Tony crashed into gear and reversed with a screech of brakes. Then, giving one more '*Mella!*' to Southend in general, he lurched us off at breakneck speed. When we reached London, he dropped us at the first taxi rank he saw, then drove away looking happier than he had done all day.

When we stepped from the cab at the end of our alleyway, our Saturday men were lurking everywhere. By the time we got to the front door, they had formed into a procession behind us. I sat in my crowded waiting room while Mae picked them off one by one, with better results than she had displayed on the rifle range, regaling each with snatches from her day's adventures.

At the end of a very busy evening, I took our tea into the bedroom, where, in an exhausted state, we both sat down to drink it. The frothy dress was now lying in a discarded heap in a corner of the room. It had been shown off, honour had been paid to it, and it was now of no account. I picked it up and put it on a hanger in the wardrobe. Mae watched me thoughtfully, then said:

'I wish we could do that sort of thing more often. Don't you? It must be good for me because . . .' she lied, 'I haven't take a single Benzedrine all day.'

We sat for a while, sipping our tea in silence, then she sighed. 'Oh, Babs! Hasn't it been a lovely day?'

It wasn't easy to answer that. Had it not been for Tony, we could have had any number of such days. With him, that was all but impossible. I blamed Tony for her Benzedrines, Tony for her fits of ill-temper. But there was nothing much to be said or done about it. She was the prostitute, he was the ponce, I was the maid and we all knew our places.

Twenty-Six

~

When I began my maidship, I could see only affection and friendship in the streets of Soho, but as time went by, I realised that malice and enmity walked there too. It was a restless little world, full of undercurrents of turmoil and strife, ever poised for vicious attack or aggressive defence.

It wasn't always the ponces to blame, either. Trouble often sprang from intrusion by the girls on to one another's territories. This could be a girl new to the district trying to carve out a manor for herself; but more usually it was a girl already established on a neighbouring beat purposely setting out to settle a grievance or just feeling bloody-minded.

Mae had a generally sunny and happy nature, and left alone, she never picked quarrels; but when this sort of thing occurred, she felt she had to fight in order to save face. In these situations, if words and threats had no effect, she would ram a nail file down the middle finger of one of her gloves and go flying out like an avenging Fury. She was a trim, lithe, and amazingly strong girl, and she always made her point in the end.

Another constant source of trouble was the rent. No one ever knew who their real landlords were, as each place had been let, sublet, and underlet again. All that the girls themselves ever knew was that X was their rent, and Y the person they gave it to; the same face appeared every week, and the cash was handed over. If for any reason that face had to be changed, then the old rent collector and the new would arrive together, and the changeover would take place before our eyes, such was the continual Soho caution. If it weren't for such precautions, some slick operator would inevitably make a note of rent day, and call earlier than the legitimate collector, pretending that the usual man was ill and had asked him to collect on his behalf. If the girl *did* fall for this old trick, it was no excuse when the rightful collector called. Such slow-wittedness found no tolerance in Soho, and there would be nothing for it but for her to pay again. Generally, to avoid the possibility of a girl trying to claim any tenancy rights, and to assist in dislodging her when necessary, most landlords would never permit the girl to sleep on the premises. Then, if she refused to pay the rent, their first step was to padlock the street door, or change the lock on it during the night.

The police would often overlook these internal Soho struggles. You see, trying to clean up vice and crime in Soho was rather like trying to dig a hole in dry sand; you dig some out, but other grains slide down the sides to fill it up again. There were occasional big purges, though; I remember one in particular, where the old crime bosses were taken away and had to account for various foul deeds that their henchmen – with more brawn than brain – had committed in their names. When the bosses were removed, these henchmen, who were the really nasty fellows, snarled and fought for the spoils, and everything became chaotic. Flats that one girl had been working in happily for years now had strings of girls passing through them, until the girls didn't know whether they were coming or going. Those who dissented received harsh and violent treatment from these thugs, who imposed a reign of intimidation. The protection racket got more greedy and spiteful; there were also mysterious and seemingly pointless batterings, and even a murder or two.

When these kind of reshuffles took place, the ponces would start hunting around to find a policeman they could bung. Reckoning that a copper who was being bribed would tip them off about any lurking danger, they felt safer. But generally, a policeman could be bought only for a time, and a kind of justice would eventually prevail – a fact that the ponces never seemed to recognise.

One day near the end of August, Mae arrived for work late and in a poisonous mood because she'd had to travel by train.

'It was the middle of the bleeding night,' she told me. 'That copper that Tony's been bunging, he actually came to our house. I tell you, poor old Tony went white as a sheet. I mean, he's never told him our address and you'd think it was far enough away for us to be safe. Well, the copper makes himself comfortable in the best armchair, orders a brandy as if we were the Savoy and then starts yakking on about how he's finding it difficult to make ends meet on an inspector's pay. "Oh," he says. "You're the lucky ones, you know. At least you can afford to run a car. I'm taking the wife on holiday next week. I don't suppose I could borrow it, could I?" Well, of course, Tony's just *got* to say yes, hasn't he?

'"Oh and by the way," he goes on as soon as he's got the keys. "It'd be nice to have a bit of music in the old lodging house where we stay. Could I borrow your radio, too?" So we had to wave goodbye to that as well. He's got the car, he's got the radio, and then he looks at me and smiles as though he's sucking a lemon. "Do you know, it would make the old lady feel like a queen if she could wear Mae's fur coat while we're away." My fur coat! He dumps it in the car and then says, "Mighty nice of you. You're not in a hurry for them back, are you?"'

'He might return them all,' I said, hopefully.

'Nah,' said Mae. 'That's the last we'll see of that lot!'

She was quite right. They were never seen again – nor was the inspector, who, it transpired, had already been transferred to another district when he'd made the visit.

While Tony had a tame policeman, he had some sense of security, in the belief that, should the Law start gunning for him, he would receive ample warning. When that dubious comfort went, his peace of mind departed too. No doubt he thought London was becoming too hot for him, and sure enough, the very day after Mae told me about the loss of the car, she arrived, full of excitement, to say that she and Tony were off to Malta for a holiday. They were catching the midnight plane in two days' time.

'Just imagine,' she said, 'a whole fortnight in the sun! When you think how much it's going to cost him! Apart from the fares and things, look how much we lose by me not working for two weeks.'

She became almost dewy-eyed at his generosity. I congratulated her, trying my best not to let my own attitude to this supposed paragon of virtue creep into my voice. I suggested she take some time off to buy a couple of summer dresses and a bathing suit.

'No,' she said. 'I've got to get me skates on and earn some money for the holiday. Tony doesn't want to draw too much out of the bank; he says it might not get put back. He's sensible like that.'

She set to work with a will, determined to earn enough in the next two days to cover the entire expense of the holiday. I asked her what was going to happen about the flat, and she told me that Tony was finding a girl for it and that she hoped it would be someone I would like.

She had never been abroad before – ordinary people didn't in those days – and during that day and the next, she worked up a terrific enthusiasm about it.

'Lucky you caught me,' I would hear her say on her way up with a man. 'Another couple of days and I won't be here. I'm going abroad.' The man would ask where she was going; even if he didn't, she would tell him. Each time it was somewhere different. As always, I was fascinated by her flights of fancy: on the first evening, her trip took her as far west as New York and as far east as Egypt. Impressively, when she eventually returned from her holiday and the same clients turned up again, she remembered exactly what she had told each one and was able to continue the deception with a colourful and fanciful description of her time there.

The day before she was due to leave, I noted that she didn't appear to have any clothes ready to take with her, and even if she had, she hadn't got a case to put them in. Also, her blonde hair had a brunette parting half an inch wide. I asked if she didn't think she ought to do something about it. She told me she would be bleaching her roots when she got home that night. She wasn't catching the plane until midnight the following day; there was masses of time and I wasn't to get in a flap about it. The following day – the day of departure – she was still flaunting her brunette parting. I was aghast.

'Mae. You didn't do your hair.'

'I know, I know. Don't worry. I've brought the bleach with me.' She fished around in a carrier bag and pulled out a bag with some white powder in it and a bottle half full of peroxide. 'I'll take it with me and I'll do it when I get there.'

By eight o'clock that night, despite frequent admonitions from me, there had still been no signs of preparation, and

I was going practically frantic on Mae's behalf.

'Mae, you haven't even got a case yet.'

'All right, all right,' she groaned. 'You do carry on. Tell you what, I'll go and see if I can borrow one now. Will that please you?'

She gave me a comforting pat on the head and a reassuring smile before departing on her quest. She was gone for half an hour, and when she came back, she was bearing in triumph a battered relic of goodness knows how many moonlight flits and trips to Margate.

'See. I got one,' she crowed as she dumped it on the bed.

Having a suitcase seemed significant to her, and after staring at it for a little while, she declared that she supposed she'd better start putting things in it.

She began with the items that needed no thinking about – the bleach and peroxide – then she reached into her carrier bag and produced a hair-dryer, which she also dropped into the case. After that, she paused and thought for a bit.

'Make-up,' she announced briskly and opened the dressing-table drawer she kept it in. She rooted about and threw one or two items into the case, but seemed unable to take any positive line about how much or what type she would need. She ended up by pulling the drawer right out and tipping its entire contents into the case.

'Ah, perfume!' she said, after some reflection. With that, she swept in half a dozen bottles off the dressing table. Then she looked round at me, smiling brightly. 'We're coming on, aren't we?' she said. 'Now, I'll want some clothes.'

She fished in her carrier bag again and came out with a handful of dirty briefs.

'Didn't have time to wash them, so I'll do them when I get there. Oh, and a bra; must have a bra. There's one in this drawer somewhere – if I can find it. It's my favourite one.'

Like a mole, she burrowed her way into the tightly packed garments, throwing items of clothing all over the floor behind her.

'Ah, here it is,' she cried jubilantly, pulling out a screwed-up string of lace. 'And that's why I haven't been wearing it lately – the strap's broken. Be a dear and mend it, will you? No, don't bother. I'll do it when I get there.'

She finished off her packing by ferreting out a few jumpers, a couple of skirts, a grimy blouse and her favourite suit, which badly needed cleaning.

'I'll get it done when I get there. Oh, better take another pair of shoes.'

She sorted through the jumble of shoes and abandoned chastity cages at the bottom of the wardrobe.

'Do take your nice garden-party dress,' I said, getting it out and starting to fold it. 'You can iron it when you get there,' I added, by now thoroughly brainwashed.

She turned and looked at me quizzically, then grinned. 'S'right,' she said, and gave me an affectionate clump on the side of the head.

It was now about half past nine, two and a half hours till her flight.

She looked at her watch. 'I've just got time for a couple of more geezers,' she said, 'and then I'll be off.'

Luckily, one of the geezers was already sitting patiently in the waiting room.

'Let's be having you,' she yelled, but when he told her that he wanted a long session in captivity, she bundled him out.

Half an hour and three geezers later, the lid of the suitcase was closed for the last time, but not before a few more items had been added.

She eyed the dogs' mink lying in the corner. 'Good thing they've been sleeping on that,' she said. 'It's the only fur coat I've got left now.' She picked it up and shook it; out flew two or three of Mimi's knotted rubbers. 'Ooh, look! Buried treasure!' she giggled.

She hung it over her arm as I picked up the disreputable suitcase and we departed.

'The new girl's name is Phyllis,' she said, as we hurried down the stairs. 'I don't know what she's like – Tony got her. I expect she'll be all right.'

I was left on the pavement, feeling desolate. I realised what a bulwark against my loneliness Mae had become. Being with her was like swimming through breakers, with time only to splutter to the surface and gasp for breath before the next one hit. Irritating though she sometimes was, she possessed a gaiety and optimism that was gradually changing my own rather sombre nature into something much brighter.

Oh well, I thought, as I turned to make my way home. She'll only be away for two weeks. Then I smiled to myself as I pictured her entrance at the airport: Mae could never just walk into a place like other mortals.

Suddenly I was struck by a thought that made me stop in my tracks and grin insanely. Malta! Why, I was as gullible as the rest! It was just as likely that Mae was now on her way to Blackpool!

Twenty-Seven

~

When Phyllis arrived the following day, my heart sank.

She was about forty, large, solid and matronly, with a bosom like a bolster – and she was grandiose with it. Her attire would have done credit to the chairwoman of the parochial church council but was considerably less suitable for prostitution. She wore an ugly brown tweed suit of uncompromising cut, with a tailored blouse, thick brown brogues and a brown porkpie hat. She carried a large brown Gladstone bag. Her hair, her eyes and her thick lisle stockings were brown too. Only the blouse offered a slight gesture to whimsy – it was pale fawn.

She sailed in like a duchess, giving me a curt nod as she passed the kitchen en route to the bedroom. I followed her slowly, trying to recover from the shock of her appearance.

Lady Phyllis seated herself primly on the dressing table stool and, depositing her handbag carefully beside her, proceeded to survey the room with an expression of sour distaste written plainly on her face. I had arrived extra early, to clear away the debris of Mae's chaotic packing and to clean the place, but even so, I felt suddenly defensive and embarrassed by the shabby tawdriness of everything. Robbed of Mae's presence and under this imposing woman's sharp scrutiny, the furniture, curtains and even the little table lamps looked drab and cheap.

Eventually, her gaze, still full of aversion, anchored itself on me and dwelt there joylessly.

'You must be Barbara – the maid,' she decided at last, without a trace of enthusiasm. Her voice had a slight cockney twang, not quite concealed by her carefully cultivated accent.

I answered in as friendly a way as I could muster, but she wasn't having any of it and, still eyeing me with disfavour, told me she was ready for a cup of tea.

The first time she came back with a man, I waited outside the bedroom door for the money to be passed to me, but in vain. Phyllis had never worked from a hustling flat before and, consequently, had never had a maid. I thought I'd better give her a few tactful hints and tips.

'It would be much safer to let me look after the money, you know,' I said, as gently as I could.

She looked at me with cold suspicion. 'I keep it in my handbag and that has a lock on it. I keep the key round my neck.'

'Well let me take charge of your handbag, then,' I persisted. 'It really isn't wise to keep it with you.'

'I *prefer* to keep it with me,' she said firmly. She had decided I was showing far more interest in her cash than an honest person should. Thereafter, the handbag never left her side, even when she went to the toilet.

She didn't show any vestige of friendliness during her whole stay. Amazingly, she did quite well. Mae's regulars weren't all that keen, but the men Phyllis brought back were obviously intrigued by her buxom respectability. She even got quite a few regulars of her own.

The catastrophe I had feared happened towards the end of her second week. There was the sound of footsteps crashing past the kitchen door as a client charged out of the bedroom and raced down the stairs. This was accompanied by Phyllis's screams, intermingled with words that no respectable lady would have known. The handbag had gone.

On her remaining two days, she took the gamble of giving me her money to look after. When she finally left, she paused on her way out and, as though to the manor born, said, 'Well, goodbye, Barbara. You have done quite well.'

Afterwards, I wished I'd risen to the occasion and bobbed a curtsey, saying, 'Goodbye, ma'am. So pleased to have given satisfaction, I'm sure.'

Mae returned to work without the slightest trace of a tan, but I had been wrong in assuming she'd been in Blackpool. She said she'd spent most of the time playing cards with Tony's brother's girl, Lulu. Otherwise, she said, she would have gone mad with boredom; she wasn't surprised Tony had left the place.

'Nothing to do, and that heat! It's enough to drive you potty!'

Apart from Tony's brother, Guido, she made no mention of Tony's relatives. I concluded that he hadn't seen fit to introduce her to them.

She gave me a Maltese lace tablecloth and a bottle of duty-free Chanel No. 5 and then threw herself into work.

'I'm really going to get down to some hard graft now. Tony wants me to retire as soon as we've got enough money behind us.'

There were two events that marked Mae's return, the first of which was that the café owner below – still Toffee-nose to us – got done for receiving stolen goods.

'I always knew there was something funny about him,' said Mae. 'What a bloody cheek to act so high and mighty when he's no better than anyone else.'

A short while later, the 'bistro' was taken over and

turned into a sensible, no-nonsense caff by someone with a much more realistic eye to business, and from then on, it did a roaring trade, whilst Toffee-nose did time.

The second event – perhaps 'event' is the wrong word to use for something that began so quietly and insidiously – was that Mae began to get hooked on a mixture of amphetamines and barbiturates: pills known then as Purple Hearts. During Mae's boring holiday, Guido's Lulu had claimed that, besides making her feel lively in the same way that Benzedrine or Dexedrine did, Purple Hearts made her feel sexy. Because of them, she said, she could earn a bomb every day.

On her first day back, Mae was all impatient until Lulu arrived with a small quantity of pills for her to experiment with.

'You'll only need one at a time,' she warned her. 'They're very strong.'

'They might be for you – but not for me,' Mae boasted – and she swallowed two. 'These sort of things don't have any effect on me unless I take plenty. I swallowed a whole Benzedrine inhaler last Christmas, and even that didn't do much, did it, Babs?'

She caught sight of my face and, very sensibly, didn't wait for an answer.

She went on, 'I bet I'll have to take three or four before I feel any different.'

And with that, a new era dawned – or perhaps it would be more accurate to say that the effects of being ponced showed themselves in their true colours for the first time. It was money that bound Tony to Mae; it was drugs that Mae relied on to keep up her earning power. We were in the early stages of the endgame and I think I knew it.

In the past, I had sometimes wondered whether I could

cope with much more of Mae's hectic business extensions; I now began to look back on those days as comparatively peaceful and tranquil.

After a month, she was eating Purple Hearts like sweets. Long before that, though, working conditions had become unbearable: Mae had permanently flushed cheeks, her speech was frenetic and she was subject to sudden impulses and the craziest of whims.

Several times I tried pleading with her to stop taking the things, and she would say, 'All right, love – to please you' or, 'But I've only had one all day'. Once, she handed me the bottle and told me that she would take no more. All that came of this gesture was that, for a while, she took them secretly from another bottle.

Naturally, business hotted up and there was a larger-than-ever quota of men – sometimes two rows deep – using the spyhole in the kitchen or trussed up in the waiting room. The landing and the staircase above us were pressed into service as a waiting place. The dogs, too – either or both – were appearing more often and adding to the general pandemonium.

But it was the change in Mae herself that I found most difficult to adjust to. She altered terribly, taking to changing at least one item of her clothing between each client; scuffing through drawers and cupboards and throwing things around in her search for some particular article. When it was found, I was faced with the job of putting everything away again before she returned with the next man. This she did so rapidly that merely trying to keep the place tidy was a killing job.

All and sundry took advantage of her drugged state: the other girls came to borrow clothes and money from her, knowing that in her unnatural exuberance she would forget who had had what. There was nothing whatever

I could do to stop it and no conceivable way of reasoning with her.

She had odd dietary fancies, too. 'Do you know,' she would say, 'I don't half fancy a good old-fashioned stew. Let's have one tomorrow.' When tomorrow came and, amongst all the daily turmoil, I had managed to produce one, she didn't feel like eating. Then she would say, 'Don't bring anything tomorrow; we'll eat out for a change.' The next day she would feel too busy to go out for a meal but would claim to be ravenous.

Eventually, as she became more loquacious and erratic, the Purple Hearts had an adverse effect on her earning capacity. Clients would be treated to her reminiscences and would find it difficult to get away from her. She wasted valuable time by trying to talk men into doing it twice for double fees, which was as wearing as three fresh men would be.

As her takings diminished, her borrowing from money-lenders increased. Betty Kelly became a far too regular visitor in our little flat, interest payments mounted, and the vicious circle spun faster. Mae's Persian-lamb coat languished in the pawnshop, soon to be joined by a beautiful sapphire and diamond ring that Tony had given her.

'I'll do better with that out of the way,' she said. 'Diamonds are unlucky for me.'

She searched for ways to raise money. Faithful Fred, the judo expert, came in for a particular trouncing. She took full advantage of his affection and wheedled extra money out of him every time he visited. To start with it was only ten pounds, but her demands grew to twenty, fifty and eventually a hundred pounds. She described these as 'loans', although she knew – and he did too – that she had no intention of paying them back.

Soon after his savings were gone, we received a phone

call from his brother to say that Fred was in hospital. He had been teaching an enthusiastic novice a particular judo hold and the novice, in a fit of exhilaration, had broken Fred's back. The brother told Mae which hospital he was in and how anxious Fred was that she should visit him. Mae made sympathetic-sounding promises, but although Fred lay for months encased in plaster and occasionally sent her pathetic little letters containing oblique requests for a visit, she never did go.

This callousness clouded my feelings towards her. Although I tried to excuse it by the fact that she was in a permanently drugged condition, I knew in my heart that she would have been exactly the same without drugs. I had the cynical feeling that, had Fred not lent her money – which conceivably he might now need back – she would have been willing to visit him.

Nevertheless, I still loved the girl, and although things grew steadily worse, I stuck it out because I felt she needed me. It had always horrified me that apart from Fred and me, everyone else saw her as a glorious, super-deluxe money-making machine. She was such a master of charm that when I felt I couldn't go on a minute longer, she would slip an arm round me and, rubbing her chin in my hair, say, 'Poor old Babs. I don't half give you a time, but you know I love you, don't you?' And of course, I was soft putty once more.

Every night when I got home, I fell asleep as soon as my head touched the pillow – and sometimes before. However, there was nothing I could do but follow the path that Mae was marking out.

Twenty-Eight

~

Tony's time in Malta had persuaded him that he was no longer safe in Rickmansworth, and so, on their return, he and Mae rented another furnished house, this time in Slough. He didn't rush into buying another car; instead, he hired different ones, reckoning that continually changing number plates would make it harder for the police to keep tabs on him.

Mae kept pestering me to go and see their new house. 'You must come and see it,' she said. 'We've got chickens in the garden. You could stay for the night and have a nice, fresh chooky egg for breakfast.'

I could imagine what sort of a break it would be and avoided her repeated invitations for as long as I could, but the day came when I couldn't put her off any longer.

'I'll think you don't want to come, soon,' she complained. 'I'm fed up with going home and Tony going to bed. I've got no one to talk to.'

Obviously, the effects of the Purple Hearts didn't wear off until long after she got home.

'All right,' I said, giving in as cheerfully as I could. 'What about tonight?'

'Done.'

At about one thirty in the morning, we arrived outside

a seedy-looking semi-detached with a *Chez Nous*-type name board hanging from rusty chains in the porch.

Inside, the wallpaper had taken on a uniformly dun glaze and all the furniture had the appearance of worn suffering. Tony, as usual, had dined out at a reasonable time and was ready for bed. He was more morose than ever and had not spoken at all during the whole journey. Yawning loudly, he ambled across to the chipped stone sink and, leaning against it, gazed around moodily as he drank a cup of water. Then, without a word, he took himself upstairs.

Naturally, the place was superbly messy – Mae lived there, so it would be – and the sink was full of washing-up.

'Shall I do that for you?' I asked, gesturing towards it.

'Certainly not,' said Mae, indignantly. 'You're a guest. Sit down and I'll make you a nice cup of tea, and then I'm going to cook you a meal.'

With that, she shot a heap of junk off a cottage-type armchair and pushed me into it. She decided we would have cold chicken with bubble-and-squeak.

'Oh, that's good. A nice quick meal,' I said. I was ravenous.

'Well ... not really,' she replied. 'I haven't cooked the cabbage and potatoes for the bubble-and-squeak. I thought while they're boiling I could bleach my hair and do a bit of washing while I've got someone to talk to.'

My heart sank. After an hour, I was gnawing at a piece of curling bread and butter and a couple of soft biscuits, still waiting for the bubble-and-squeak – Mae had firmly declined all my frantic offers to help speed things up. For one thing, I was a guest, and for another, she wanted to show me she was capable of being domestic. She bleached her hair, washed her undies and when, at four in the morning, we sat down to our meal, I was almost too exhausted to eat.

I fell into a doze in the armchair, only to be woken – it seemed like minutes later – by Mae telling me brightly that it was time to go into the garden and hunt for my nice fresh chooky egg.

After that night's ordeal, I tried desperately to avoid further invitations, but despite all my efforts, every three weeks or so I found myself inwardly groaning whilst being transported Slough-wards.

On top of all the other trials caused by the drugs, Mae was not as careful and watchful with clients as she needed to be. Although I could keep a wary eye on those in the waiting room and kitchen, the ones with her in the bedroom were another matter. I had no illusions that any of those squinting through the two-way mirror would rush to her aid if they saw any violence; they were more likely to beat a hasty retreat. As it turned out, when trouble did strike, I was the one who got struck.

Mae had brought a very large bearded chap back and had got as far as taking his money and handing it to me. She was chattering away to him while she undressed, not noticing that he was making no move to do likewise – then, at the point where she was removing her skirt and was therefore hobbled, he rushed out of the bedroom and into the kitchen, in time to see where I was putting the cash. I spun round in surprise, only to meet with a great fist that landed on my jaw and knocked me out. (Afterwards, I learned that he'd stepped over my slumped body, grabbed all the available notes and bolted.) With amazing clarity of mind, Mae rushed to the window, grabbing one of her china cats on the way, threw it open and hurled the cat out, shouting, 'Stop, thief!'

The man's timing was ill judged: he ran through the front door and straight into the arms of a policeman. A struggle ensued, during which the policeman lost his helmet and got hit as well. A second policeman arrived on the scene and it was all over. They marched the thief up the stairs and presented him to us, demanding to know what had happened. By this time I had recovered and was nursing my swollen jaw. I glowered at their prisoner and told my story while he glowered back. He was a vicious-looking specimen.

As she had her money back, Mae was all for letting the matter rest. The policemen pressed us to lodge a complaint, but in the period before the court case, they changed their minds. We were told that the bearded giant was about to become an art student; he was down on his luck and was already on probation for robbery. Allegedly, his widowed mother had taken to charring to support him. The policeman who related all this to us had apparently fallen for the man's sob story.

'It'll break the old girl's heart if he's sent away for several years,' he said. 'And that's what he's facing if you say he socked you on the jaw. Perhaps you can say in court that you sort of walked into his hand in surprise.'

The bearded monster was a most unlikely art student, and I wasn't persuaded by the idea of his widowed mother, but Mae agreed on my behalf. For people in our position, any suggestion from the police was best taken as an order.

In due course the trial came up at Marylebone Police Court, with Mae looking very fetching, in her Kravetz coat and me trying to look dowdy and – as there was a public gallery – anonymous. As witnesses, we were put in a little room together with the two policemen, who, after a few pleasantries, went into a conference with each other. They could, of course, have done this before and in private, but they needed to make sure that we'd heard their plan and wouldn't say anything in court to contradict their story.

After rehearsing the fiction, the first policeman briskly knocked his sheaf of papers together, then looked at us and grinned. 'Got to get our homework right,' he said.

I did my stint in the witness box. To make things a bit lighter for the accused, it was made pretty clear what sort of business Mae and I were engaged in. I was uncomfortably aware of the public gallery, which appeared enormous and filled with intently watching faces. Fortunately the case was not a long one, and the outcome was that the phoney art student was placed in corrective custody for six months and recommended for psychiatric treatment.

But this incident wasn't enough to scare Mae off the drugs. That summer and autumn is forever tinted in my memory by their shadow.

Twenty-Nine

~

Drugs or no drugs, the aspect of Mae's work that troubled me most was her extensive dealings with masochists. In the beginning, I had found it difficult to believe the proof of my own ears. Even amongst Mae's ordinary clients, one in three would want to be caned. These men were so mild and constant in their regular demands that I didn't consider them to be masochists in the true sense. I found them tolerable and sometimes even funny. On occasion, not wanting to spoil the pleasure of the punishment by actually asking for it, they would bring little notes of instruction – ostensibly written by someone else.

Dear Miss Angela Brown,

Here is Richard's school report for last term.

Position in class: Bottom
Attendance: Very bad
Truancy: High

I am afraid I cannot have him back next term unless he is taught some manners and punished for his bad behaviour. I understand you are a big strong lady and I know that you will be angry with him for this behaviour. I could strongly suggest that when you speak to him about this you might consider the assistance of a hairbrush or a wooden spoon.

Yours truly,

Miss Williams (Form Mistress)

What I found harder to accept were those who experimented with pain to greater and greater degrees. Some of them seemed hell-bent on self-destruction. Talking a deep breath, I dive back into memories that even now I find disturbing to recall.

Perhaps it was my art school training to treasure creativity that made the destructive nature of masochism so acutely unpleasant. It horrified me that such a beautifully made and miraculous thing as the human body should be so wilfully damaged. Every punishment I saw inflicted, every cut, bruise or burn, became almost my own personal pain.

It was impossible for me to hide from these episodes, for they generally took place in my domain – the kitchen or waiting room – to keep the bedroom free for Mae. I was often an unwilling witness to the long build-up necessary to achieve the right degree of degradation and pain.

Even when they arrived, they would be trembling and perspiring at the thought of their coming ordeal. They wore an expression that I learned to know at a glance: a look that spoke of the terrifying, exquisite possibilities before them. Soon these men would be in agony again, and though they could avert it, they knew that they would not. After a long period of such obsession, that look became habitual, and I am not able to forget it. I have often met it since, in all sorts of unlikely places. I can recognise it across a crowded room and I wish that I couldn't, for I feel as guilty as an eavesdropper.

Up to a point – but only up to a point – the man Mae and I nicknamed Houdini was amusing. He arrived regularly, once a week, bringing a holdall with him. He visited of his own volition, but he might as well have just been forced through Traitors' Gate in a barge. He was a young man with prominent eyes and the ruddy, open-air face of a farmer's son. On arrival, his character switched for a few minutes to that of a brisker, more businesslike person as he explained any new items in his bag and how they were to be employed. Then he would hand over ten pounds and immediately revert to the prospective martyr.

After he had stripped off, he would be trussed up tightly and gagged. This done, Mae would batter him about the head and then leave him, while she got on with other clients. He would immediately begin to writhe and contort in efforts to free himself from his bonds. After about half an hour of superhuman struggle, he always succeeded in doing so. When he was at last standing up, panting and exhausted from his exertions, it was my duty to inform Mae of the fact. She would then come and retie him, beat him again – harder this time, as a punishment for escaping – and leave him once more.

This would go on for the whole evening, with the beatings growing more brutal and the young man weaker and more abject, until Mae, getting fed up with the procedure, would drag him by his increasingly purple ear into the bedroom, where even worse would happen.

This, for him, was what the whole evening had been slowly building up to. He would then wash, dress, pack his gear and depart, with Mae shrieking after him – all part of his original instructions – that she would kill him next time. She would then collapse into a chair and say, 'Thank God that's over. Give us a cup of tea, love.'

This performance was carried out week after week, with a few variations invented by Houdini. One day, well into the Purple Heart era, Mae, on being told that he had broken free once more, gave a gusty sigh and exclaimed, 'Oh, sod it!' Then, pleadingly, 'Could you throw a few ropes round him, Babs, and I'll come in later?'

She had disappeared down the stairs to get another client before I had a chance to say, 'But . . .'

I slowly returned to the waiting room and found him standing as I had left him – wide-eyed and trembling. He had obviously heard what Mae had said, and was highly nervous about this unexpected change in his programme.

On reflection, I suppose the fact that I didn't just leave him standing there until Mae returned speaks volumes for the force of her personality. As I approached him, my legs were like jelly and I felt sick. His ropes were strewn all over the place and bits of adhesive tape were everywhere, some trodden underfoot and others hanging and flapping from various parts of his anatomy.

While I was unravelling some of the ropes, Mae came back with another client. I went and took the money from her, then pottered about, procrastinating, waiting for her to emerge, but whether out of devilment or from a desire to make sure that I became broken in to yet one more task, she was taking ages, and so, reluctantly, I began applying the first rope.

Thereafter, of course, tying up Houdini became my job and his beating up Mae's. I found myself lying awake at nights trying to think up methods of knotting. Whichever way I tied him, he still managed to squirm free in about his usual time.

Once, I very nearly took a couple of swipes at him myself. It had been a bad evening, commencing with a strenuous half-hour trying to prevent our drunken stockbroker, Mr Tucker, from falling off his chair whilst at the same time endeavouring to avoid his groping hands. This had been followed by a solid procession of men wanting to use the spyhole – which meant that I hadn't been able to get into the kitchen for a couple of hours. On top of that, Vera had been ineffectually flicking around me all evening with a particularly frivolous and stupid-looking feather duster. When Houdini shed his tethers for about the fourth time, I drew in my breath with a sharp hiss and bounded across the room, arm raised.

Simultaneously I heard a little giggle from Vera and spun round. 'Oh, temper, temper!' she said, grinning from ear to ear and wagging her feather duster at me. Houdini had the light of anticipation in his eyes and I let my hand drop. I made a mental note to watch my character, for I could sense that it was changing.

Mae told me that on one occasion a punter had persuaded her to leave him overnight, locked in a cupboard, sitting on a bottle with his hands and feet tied.

'He gave me fifty pounds for that,' she said, 'but I'd never do it again, although he keeps asking. He was unconscious when I came in the next day and it took Rabbits and me about half an hour to bring him round. Think what it would be like for his family if he pegged out like that.'

She laughed suddenly and her tone changed. 'Did I ever tell you what happened to my friend Coral?' she said. 'She had this geezer one night – great big chap and eighty if he was a day – and he kicked the bucket while he was on the job. Smashing way to go, I suppose. She had to get her maid to help get him off her and then she came tearing round to me in a panic. "What shall I do? What shall I do?" she kept saying. "I don't want the law nosing around – and what about the poor old boy's family? They're not gonna like it, knowing he pegged out stuffing me." I said, "Hold your horses and I'll pop round when it gets a bit quieter and we'll do something about it." So later on, I went round to her gaff. Me, Coral and her maid carted this bloke downstairs and round the corner of the street. We dumped him in a phone box and put tuppence in his hand. Then we went to another phone box and dialled 999. We scarpered back to Coral's flat but we left her maid with him, to see that no one picked his pockets. No one was any the wiser. Poor old boy! Still, that's life.'

If there is any lesson in all this, it's the infinite variety of the male appetite. Once that autumn, for example, Mae had gone out to look for a client, leaving the previous one – a kink, presumably – in the bedroom. This wasn't unusual, and I went in to tidy up. I had expected that he was probably roped up in the wardrobe, but as I straightened the bedspread, my toe hit against something soft under the bed and a masculine voice said, 'Watch where you're stepping!'

When Mae returned with the next man, she hung back and whispered to me: 'Seeing is believing. Look through the hole.'

I did what she told me, and when the man on the bed had finished his mission and collapsed, I saw Mae quickly remove the rubber and dangle it over the side of the bed.

The head of the man below emerged, with mouth wide open like a fledgling bird, and Mae dropped the rubber in. There was a gulp, the rubber went down like an oyster and the head withdrew into concealment again. This transaction was accomplished so swiftly and dextrously that the donor was completely unaware of it – which was just as well. The lurker under the bed repeated this audacious performance throughout the evening, and when he finally left, Mae said to me, 'He's already had one operation when one swelled up inside him and caused a blockage.'

I wondered what the surgeon who had removed it had thought; but then, with my growing knowledge of the peculiarities of men, I reflected that he probably had habits of his own that were just as funny.

Thirty

~

Mae invited me to Slough for Christmas. The thought of spending the festive season in Tony's company was not a happy one, and I wriggled out of it as gracefully as possible with the quite truthful excuse that I needed a rest.

'Resting? At Christmas? Can't take it, eh?' said Mae, bright-eyed and full of Purple Hearts. 'Well, if you get fed up, give us a ring and we'll come over and fetch you.'

Several other invitations had come my way – including one from Rita – but as they were all from members of the sisterhood, I couldn't accept without Mae hearing of it and feeling hurt. I spent that Christmas on my own and was happy to do so, because although I was only twenty-two, I felt as old as Methuselah. On Christmas Eve, I rushed home laden with exciting boxes of provender from Lyon's Corner House. I swiftly undressed and threw on the dressing gown that I'd decided to remain in for the whole of my two days' holiday.

It was a wonderful Christmas. I listened to endless 'Noels' and 'Wenceslases' on my little radio. With loving fingers I re-examined the drum-tight surface of my year-old, still virginal canvas and weighed the small, heavy tubes of paint. I revelled in a large book on Michelangelo that I'd bought as a present for myself. Then, with two old and comforting favourites, *The Herries Chronicles* and *Cranford*, I would fall into contented dozes.

That solitary Christmas was a minor paradise, a little oasis. I even nourished hopes that the new year might bring with it some ease-up in Mae's love affair with Purple Hearts. But by halfway through January, I realised there was no chance of that. Even the less ambitious hope – that things would at least get no worse – had proved in vain, for amongst Tony's New Year resolutions had been one that Mae should work harder and earn more.

In his greed, he was disappointed that Mae was no longer continually breaking her own record, as she had earlier in their association. In fact, she was taking home less and less. The tough new regime he insisted on involved a seven-day week, with Mae staying at the flat most nights so as not to waste time and energy in travelling.

I had been gradually jettisoning my other Sunday jobs in order to recharge my batteries, so, albeit reluctantly, I was able to accommodate the extra day. Mae did not like being at the flat alone, and my days with her began to stretch like elastic, starting ever earlier and ending ever later. It didn't surprise me that all the extra working hours didn't result in an increase in takings. It wasn't that Mae didn't *try* to earn more; it was more as though she was semi-paralysed by Tony's high expectations of her and her now chronic debts. She seemed to be jinxed by a desire to slack off whenever she began doing well. Once Tony had swallowed this bitter pill, he sought a sleeping partnership in another 'business venture'.

Thoughts of money were beginning to worry Mae constantly, and there was an edginess about her and a sense of falsity in her gaiety. I felt pretty sure that Tony knew all about her dealings with the moneylenders and her trips to the pawn shop – there wasn't much privacy in Soho – but it suited him to say nothing. Her forays even extended into my savings. That was on the day she talked me into buying her pawn ticket from her.

'There's a nice mink stole, as well as the coat and ring; I hocked it while Rabbits was here – never been worn. Might as well keep them in the family. I'll let you have them cheap.'

There was almost six months' worth of interest to pay, but in all fairness, it wasn't a bad bargain. Even so, the last things I wanted or needed were a Persian-lamb coat, a sapphire and diamond ring and a mink stole. In fact the mink stole has still never been worn.

And then, of course, Mae was Mae. She was too restless a soul to allow anything to remain as it was for too long, so she began augmenting the Purple Hearts with anything else that came her way. Having run the gamut of everything obtainable, she settled on two drugs in particular. One was known as a Bomb: a large, clear capsule filled with green and white hundreds-and-thousands that exploded inside you at intervals. The other was a Black Bomber, a form of speed made from a combination of amphetamines and dextroamphetamines. She must have had the constitution of an elephant.

Unable to work off her surplus energy on Tony, she began to use her clients. The masochists started to get a lot more value for money – almost more than they wanted. Then she began taking on all-nighters, which shrivelled me up with fear for her safety, and she began to play irresponsible, kinky games with her straight clients. It was these that caused the first real drop of poison to be injected into my affections for Mae.

There was one client who said that he was a bit bored with straight sex and wondered if Mae could suggest anything new. He couldn't have consulted a better person. Mae came out and whispered salaciously into my ear, 'Keep your eye glued to that hole in the wall, or you'll miss the sight of a lifetime.' Then, aloud, grabbing the man from the kitchen chair, she said, 'You want something different; well, I've got it.' And she pulled him into the bedroom after her.

I saw the thrill-seeker strip naked and bend over to touch his toes and another client, equally naked, approach him. The evident relish on his face showed that he too had paid for something different, and he was all for it. Client No. 1 was not so happy; after several attempts, during which he let out sharp yelps, he eventually retreated into a neutral corner. Not to be outdone, Mae talked them into changing drivers – but with similar results. She enjoyed every minute of all this and had goaded them on throughout.

Though it's not to my credit, I watched right through to the bitter end, hardly believing it. It was not until I saw the two men leave, separately and shamefacedly, that I began to have misgivings. They had been coaxed into performing acts that they would never otherwise have dreamed of. I was uneasy about what effect this episode might have on their self-esteem and was disappointed in Mae for having engineered it. I decided that although it was within the rules to give men all the things they might have thought of themselves, it was quite wrong to persuade them to act against their instincts.

From then on, my feelings for Mae subtly altered. I had seen my idol's feet of clay, and although I still loved her and remained loyal, my love and loyalty were no longer absolute and unquestioning. The unthinking, light-hearted frivolity had completely gone; now, beneath the smiles and bonhomie, her eyes took on the calculating watchfulness of the professional entertainer. I notched this up as one more black mark against Tony, and my hatred of him grew so strong that I could barely speak to him.

Thirty-One

~

Towards the end of January, Mae erupted into some of her old, spontaneous gaiety.

We'd just had a severe spell of icy weather and for several days our phone number was being dialled by people who had got hold of Mae's 'F. Martin, Plumber' business cards at second hand. One of these was a woman who'd found the card in her husband's wallet and had kept it for an emergency. Mae relished the opportunity for double entendre.

'Sorry, love, we're up to our eyes with bursting pipes just now. We're on the job day and night with leaks.'

Later, a man called – he'd no doubt been given the card as a joke. In a cooing and seductive voice, Mae said, 'Frozen, you say? Oh, you poor dear. Why don't you come up here and I'll thaw it out for you.'

This was a brief respite. Dark clouds continued to gather around Mae. Because she was so much away from Tony, she began to suspect him of being unfaithful. He was allegedly spending most of his time at a Maltese club in Greek Street that was run by a man known as Big Frank. Mae began sending me to check on him.

It was a very large room, about as inspiring as a church hall. In the far corner was a bar, and near it, a cluster of card tables. The only lights were behind the bar and the ones that illuminated several billiard tables. A dozen or so pallid, dark-haired men whiled away their days there. The air was permanently thick and blue from their cigars. Big Frank spent his time strolling amongst them, looking imposing and placid.

The ponces found this place highly convenient. It was handily placed for checking up on the girls every so often and was a good centre for news. Most of the time they simply lounged about listlessly and the place reeked of boredom. On my first visit, it occurred to me that this boredom was the natural payback for their determination to fill their days without doing a stroke of work. Whenever I opened the door, all heads swung round in unison.

Mae sent me there with such transparently unnecessary messages that I was embarrassed. As her mistrust of Tony grew, my excursions to Greek Street became more and more frequent. It was absurd, especially as Tony always *was* at the club anyway.

'Mae,' I said. 'How can you get so worked up about Tony going around with another woman – or even sleeping with one – when you're doing all this?' I waved my hand to indicate the bed, the box of Durex and the canes strewn about.

She gave me a long, thoughtful look.

'A bloke's got to feel like it before he can perform,' she said. 'I haven't.'

With that truly wonderful piece of homespun wisdom, she packed me off to Big Frank's place once more.

Tony was indeed messing, but he was too careful to fall into Mae's traps. He'd been doing it for some time and everyone knew it except Mae. No one dared tell her, least of all me. Eventually, though, the storm burst with unexpected suddenness, and all hell broke loose.

Mae had spent one of her rare nights at Slough. Whilst sleeplessly prowling about the house, she'd come across Tony's latest bank statement. Her calculations were never wrong where money was concerned, and she knew the statement should have shown five thousand pounds or so; instead it read four pounds fifteen shillings and twopence.

Whilst still enraged by this discovery, she also came across two brunette hairclips. She nearly went berserk. In a boiling frenzy, she phoned for a taxi and returned to the West End, leaving Tony snoring in bed. She spent the rest of the night rushing from one all-night café to another, questioning everybody. Tactful ignorance disappeared when challenged by this screaming virago: at last, she ferreted out the truth.

She then went and woke the girl in question from a tranquil sleep. She removed a few handfuls of hair, beat her up and left her sobbing on the floor. It was about seven in the morning, and so she went on to the flat and phoned me to join her. When I arrived, she was lying flat on the bed, puffing hard on a cigarette and staring grimly at the ceiling. It was obvious that something cataclysmic had happened. In silence, I made us a cup of tea and, after a few sips, she poured out the story of her night's adventures.

No repercussions occurred all morning: Tony was a great sleeper. Mae and I sat – as women from time immemorial have sat – drinking tea, me uttering condolences and both of us mulling over the iniquities of men. After midday, when clients began to arrive, she took them, from force of habit, but her heart wasn't in it.

Then, at about three o'clock, we heard thunderous footsteps on the staircase and Tony burst in on us in a murderous fury. He made as though to attack Mae, but thought better of it and just stood there, breathing hard and glaring with blazing eyes. She glared back, breathing just as hard.

'Don't you dare lay a finger on me, you fucking bastard,' she hissed.

'Lay a finger on you, you filth! It makes me sick every time I have to touch you. I have to force myself to touch you.'

He said this in a low, vicious voice, and I thought to myself, This is the truth she's hearing at last; this is the good Catholic boy talking.

'This is what I think of you,' he said, and he spat full in her face.

There was a poignant silence. Then Mae brought her hands up to her face and began to cry with the most racking sobs I ever want to hear: as though she were disintegrating into her hands. As he remained glaring at her with an air of satisfaction, I stepped towards him.

'You're a guttersnipe,' I said. 'And in five years you'll be a fat, ugly guttersnipe. She gave you everything you have. How dare you!' I was beside myself with rage and gave him a push. 'Get out, before I make you ugly, now!'

My fingernails were right up to his face like the claws of a cat. If he'd made the slightest move towards the pocket where he kept his flick knife, I would have had my excuse, and the way I felt, I could have killed him. He glared at me for a moment longer, then he muttered something and flung himself out of the room.

I turned to Mae, who was still racked by heartbroken sobs. I put my arms round her and cuddled her.

'What he said! What he said!' she cried over and over again.

'You're worth ten of him,' I said. 'Other men pay to touch you.'

This notion seemed to have some cheering effect on her, and the sobs gradually turned into sniffs. I brought her a cup of tea and locked the door.

'It's no good, Babs, is it? Can I come and sleep with you tonight? You're the only friend I've got,' she said, giving me a watery smile.

We went home to my place by taxi and warmed our toes in front of the gas fire, drinking endless cups of tea. We were calming down by degrees, when the front doorbell went. We looked at one another nervously, but I knew I had to answer it. Tony was on the doorstep, and two other men were waiting in his car.

'I want to speak to Mae,' he said, in a voice that brooked no opposition.

'I'll see if she wants to come,' I replied, trying to grasp back some of my earlier bravado.

'Get her,' he demanded ominously.

My heart thumping, I shut the front door on him and went back upstairs. 'It's Tony,' I said. 'He wants to speak to you.'

She looked scared. 'I thought it would be,' she said. 'He'll make a scene if I don't go. Come with me, will you?'

I didn't relish facing him again but I had to cover my fear and be Mae's strength. Together we went to the front door and opened it. To my evident disbelief, there stood a completely transformed Tony. His face had creased into a relieved and humble smile, and freshly applied fake tears glistened on his cheeks.

He flung his arms wide open and said, 'Oh Mae, my darling. I thought I'd really lost you. Don't ever leave me like that again, or I'll kill myself; I swear it. I can't live without you.'

With a little sob, she rushed into his arms. With the

mock tears already drying on his face, Tony smiled at me triumphantly over her shoulder.

Nothing was ever quite the same from then on. There was constraint – a sense of embarrassment – between Mae and me. She wanted to forget Tony's insults, but she couldn't because I'd heard them too. More than that, she'd heard me tell Tony what I really thought of him; my long-term concealed dislike had become apparent. I had made a classic mistake: I had taken sides in a fight between partners; the rift was no longer between them, but between them and me.

Left alone, Mae and I would have forgotten this unpleasant episode and, in time, returned to our old, easy relationship. But we were not left alone. In Tony's book, my days were numbered.

I knew that I had always been a thorn in his side; moreover, I had stood toe-to-toe with him in open conflict. I knew enough of him to realise that he wouldn't be happy until I was out of the way. This fact should have made me nervous, but I felt nothing but cold anger. He knew that resorting to the customary threats of violence wasn't going to work with me. He recognised my principled nature and so hit on a more subtle and cunning plan.

Guido's Lulu – already responsible for Mae's drug addiction – began visiting us every evening, ostensibly to make up her face before going to work. At first she performed this task in the waiting room so that Mae could carry on working if she wanted to. One evening she began to complain that the lighting in there was bad and asked if she could use the bedroom. Not being able to do anything whilst Lulu was in there, Mae sat on the bed and chatted with her. The following evening, Lulu went straight into the bedroom as a matter of course, 'absent-mindedly' closing the door after her to exclude me.

From then on, there was a noticeable decline in Mae's manner towards me. It started as a slight decrease in her warmth and cheerfulness. It was nothing much: as though she weren't feeling too bright. It was strange enough to arouse my suspicions but not enough for me to be direct. I asked if she was worried about something, but she said no, everything was fine.

Gradually, after two or three evenings of being closeted with Lulu, the change became so marked that she wouldn't look at me when I spoke to her and wouldn't speak at all unless I did first. I wasn't able to suffer in silence for long.

'Mae, what is the matter? Have I done something wrong?'

She wouldn't look at me, and said nothing.

'What is it?' I said. 'It's not fair to be like this without telling me why.'

Slowly, still without looking at me, she said, 'I've heard that you're going around telling everyone that I take it in the mouth and go without rubbers and do all sorts.'

It was a relief not to be guessing what was wrong any more, but at the same time I suddenly felt weary and sick of everything. It was a stock insult from one prostitute to another – a real old chestnut – and Tony had dusted it off and succeeded in ascribing it to me. I was shocked that after so much time spent together, Mae had so little understanding of my nature. Our friendship had been so important to me that I would have fought a horde of dragons for it, but she had let a few calculatedly spiteful words destroy it.

Memories of the past flooded into my mind; amongst them were the words of the kind policewomen who had tried to prise me away from Mae: 'Promise me you won't waste your loyalty. Don't throw it away on something worthless . . . Just wait and see; you'll learn in time.' That time had arrived. My idol's feet of clay had finally crumbled and pitched my first, passionate friendship into the dust.

At last I made myself say something. 'You believe that? You really think that's my style? Is this what Lulu's been saying?'

'Several people say you've said it,' she answered, still avoiding my gaze.

'So it was Lulu,' I corrected her, firmly.

At last she turned to me. 'Did you?' she said.

I didn't grace the question with an answer. I had a vision of Lulu's doll-like face and her large, innocent blue eyes turned on Mae while she watched the effect that her slow poisoning was having; then I thought of Tony's satisfied grin as he received her daily progress reports.

Even now, I thought cynically, all will not be lost if I start to shout and scream – if I threaten to go and carve up Lulu. Mae would understand that: it was the accepted defence strategy. But I was so hurt that Mae didn't understand quiet, unostentatious loyalty – didn't recognise true friendship – and I wasn't about to demean myself.

'Just tell me you didn't say it,' she insisted, now eyeing me quite hard.

My pride shot up to the roof of my head. I looked at her coldly and turned away.

'Maybe, one day, you'll learn who you can trust,' I told her over my shoulder. Then, 'Can you get someone to take my place by tomorrow?'

Thankfully, there wasn't much of the evening left; the atmosphere was too strained to be endured much longer.

Several times Mae looked as though she wanted to say something, but she didn't. After locking up, we said good night and parted company. In the taxi going home, I burst into tears.

Thirty-Two

~

A few evenings later, the telephone rang about four times in one hour, and I finally took a deep breath and picked up the receiver. It was not Mae, but Rita. Her raucous voice came bellowing through to me with all the comforting reassurance of a Wagnerian overture.

'You poor bloody sod,' she said. 'I've heard all about it. What surprises me is how you put up with it all for as long as you did.'

My gratitude bubbled up and I told her that she was like a tonic to me. She brushed my words aside and continued:

'I told Mae straight, she must be potty believing anything that bleeding Lulu says. One day that girl's going to end up with her throat cut, you mark my words. If it wasn't for all them pills Mae takes, she'd never have been took in. Hasn't she bleeding changed? I'd never have believed it.'

Her tone deepened confidentially. 'But here, what do you think? That bastard Tony has taken her out of the flat and put her in one that's got a maid that goes with it. That's so she won't get no ideas about having you back. But listen . . .' Here, her voice gathered all the gusto and dramatic effect of someone who has left the best bit until last. 'She's going to marry him next week – special licence, she says. It would have to be a *very* special bleeding licence before I'd marry that sod. She must want her fucking brains tested.'

She paused while I voiced my surprise at the news, then she burst into full spate again. I was listening merely to the cadences of her voice as it crashed like breakers against my eardrums, when something she said caught my attention once more:

'So look, I've had a smashing idea. I don't like the flat I've got now and I don't like the bleeding maid that goes with it. If I was to take another flat – I've got one lined up – would you come and maid for me?'

I was taken off balance for a moment and didn't know what to say. I had got on well with Rita during the month when Mae was in hospital and had enjoyed that first Christmas with her, but as she considered sentiment a weakness, I hadn't realised she was so fond of me. I was surprised and touched that she had taken up cudgels on my behalf and was now prepared to uproot herself to accommodate me.

'Do you really want us to do that?' I asked. I realised I was close to tears.

'Course, mate,' she answered gruffly.

'When do we start?' I asked, breaking into a grin.

I powdered my nose, put on some lipstick and went to meet her, feeling happier than I had for a long while.

Our inspection of the new flat was cursory and routine. Naturally, it was in a state of utter filth, so we decided to give it a good clean before Rita attempted to do any work there. We thought we could get it presentable during the afternoons of the following week, leaving enough time for a quick meal before Rita went on to her old flat for the evening's hustling.

'Bleeding nice, isn't it?' she remarked. 'Charring all fucking afternoon and whoring all sodding night. Talk about being a lady of easy virtue – I haven't seen nuffing easy about it yet.'

The flat was situated at the bottom end of a long, narrow mews that was approached through an archway from a northern Soho street. Nowadays the term 'mews flat' conjures up visions of elegance and grace. Our mews was not like that: it was an original murky, Dickensian mews, a Jack the Ripper alley, unlit even by gaslight. It was monopolised by barrow boys, who at night-time used the old stables to house their portable stalls, along with their unsold fruit and veg. In the morning, before first light, these street traders brought fresh produce from nearby Covent Garden and reorganised their displays. They threw wrappings, wooden boxes and yesterday's bad fruit on to the cobbles, where they awaited the midnight gangs of refuse men. By the time we arrived each day, there was a mash of slowly putrefying vegetation amongst the debris, overlaid by that pungent, winey smell of rotting oranges. Even now, the faintest whiff of fermenting oranges takes me back once more to that place. It makes me think of picking my way through the puddles and filth, between the blackened and decaying buildings, up to Rita's flat.

After dark, when we were pretty much its only inhabitants, the mews had a sinister quality. Lit only by the feeble light from the street beyond the distant archway, the puddles took on a baleful gleam and the unhoused barrows and piles of boxes had the appearance of crouching, furtive monsters. Rita bought herself a powerful and heavy flashlight to serve her during her repeated excursions to the world beyond the archway.

There was a bright new lock on the door of our flat, gleaming like a jewel on the leprous surface. Immediately inside, there was a steep, narrow flight of bare wooden stairs. These gave out on to a large room carpeted in red and furnished with heavy Victorian furniture – well abused, but polishable – and a double bed with brass knobs and a deep sag in the middle. Rita later claimed it had done her back in for life.

Reluctantly she forwent a repeat of the operating-theatre sterility of her previous flats. With a few pretty shaded lamps – bought under pressure from me – and a judicious plant here and there, the place looked quite nice. Through a curtained doorway at the other side of the bedroom you entered the kitchen, which justified that title only inasmuch as it held an old stone sink – an everlasting attraction for cockroaches – and an ancient black iron gas stove. The floor here was just plain boards, and a much-splintered tea chest served as a table. At the side of this was an old Windsor chair with part of its back rest missing and the remaining spokes waiting their turn to do someone damage. Best of all, through a door at the end of the kitchen was a real toilet. Almost the first thing we did was to buy a pretty toilet roll holder, some coloured paper and a lavatory brush. With this priceless luxury in our midst, the future had to be all right, we reckoned.

We draped a chequered tablecloth over the tea chest and, during the first tea break of our actual residency, debated whether we might prepare a roast in the antiquated oven. Everything seemed very rosy, and as we sat eating our meal after Rita's first day's trial run, we were filled with a sense of well-being and of bright new vistas opening before us. Rita even bought a couple of canes and hung them on a nail in the bedroom.

'They're to make you feel more at home,' she announced sheepishly.

Apparently she was determined that this time she was going to make a bomb and set herself up in a proper business. It was a nice thought and we both let ourselves believe it.

Rita and I had always got on pretty well together, but the fact that we were now a permanent team improved on that and created a closer rapport between us. Our days were spent in the relaxed and easy intimacy of established friendship. I even dared to criticise her treatment of the clients.

'Think I can't be nice to 'em, eh? You just wait and see, mate,' she declared.

Knowing that I could hear every word through the curtained kitchen doorway, she became treacly sweet to the men for my benefit, loudly admiring their suits, their physiques and their looks, no matter how ghastly their appearance. Amazingly, no one ever seemed to have the slightest idea that she was lying.

She certainly could have made a bomb if she had really applied herself but that was not Rita's way. She was quite content to earn the rent, fund her leisure activities and buy small luxuries. On days that were running with liquid gold, days when any other girl would have kept going, Rita would say, 'Come on, mate, let's sling our hook and go and have a nice salt beef sandwich.'

She was mad keen on Jewish food and taught me to like it too. In fact, it is Rita, Cindy and Tina who I have to thank for my now cosmopolitan tastes in food. Rita introduced me to Chinese and Jewish cuisine, Cindy to the delights of Indian cooking and Tina to all the Latin specialities. It's strange to think, that Mae, who as a person was the most individualistic of the lot, stuck doggedly to sausage and mash or chicken and chips.

So it was that, on busy Saturday evenings, when all the other girls were working like robots, Rita and I would be sitting in the Nosh Bar in Great Windmill Street, shovelling

265

down delicious slabs of hot salt beef and latkas, gazing out at the scandalous Windmill Theatre with its constant queue of slightly furtive men.

She was very proud of her home and happy to invite me round to admire it. We often sat in front of her new lighted-coals-effect electric fire, drinking gin, whilst everyone else in the West End was grafting.

Since I had first met her, Rita had been married and divorced again, but she still went under the name of her notorious first husband, who was now doing time – as, indeed, was her second ex-husband. They both happened to land up in the same prison and, having her in common, had become friends.

'Oh well,' she said. 'At least I know where they both are now, and that's more than I could ever do before they was nicked.'

Rita's love life was always careless during the periods between husbands, and she invariably chose men younger than herself. She ruled them with a rod of iron and treated them more like sons than lovers. There was something of the deadly siren about her, and all her husbands and lovers gravitated irresistibly towards prison. The clang of the great doors marked the end of each romance, but the current young man, Eddy, appeared to have a charmed life. Consequently, he was outstaying his welcome.

Arriving at Rita's house in the early hours, while we were still talking and sipping gin after a day's work, he would dump all his swag on the carpet at Rita's feet. Then, fastidiously and imperiously, like a dowager at a jumble sale, she would pick everything over, admiring some items and condemning others. Mostly, she condemned:

'What a load of rubbish! Where's all the bleeding Georgian teapots and carriage clocks these days?'

Her bark was worse than her bite, and when all the

'junk' was stowed away, fabulous things were produced from her new fridge. We munched our way through chicken and smoked salmon while Eddy told us of hair-raising hazards encountered during his nocturnal endeavours, before swaggering off to bed.

'Silly little bastard,' she said sourly, almost to his retreating back. 'Gets on my bleeding wick. He don't know Ming from Minge. Why can't he get nicked like all the others did?'

Though I was becoming settled at Rita's, I still missed Mae. I felt angry with her. I hated Tony and the vicious effect that he, along with the avenging angels of Drugs and Debt, had had on her. At the same time, I was too proud to seek a reconciliation. I knew that if I had gone round and made some of the noises expected of me, Mae and I would instantly have embraced, accompanied by tears, laughter, promises and tea. Yet Tony and I had fought over her, and Tony had won. A friendship carried out under his gloating eyes would have been no friendship at all. So although I missed her, I let her go. My life was moving on.

Thirty-Three

∾

After working with Mae for so long, my life with Rita was delightfully peaceful, with not even the swish of a cane to break the tranquillity. She was terribly strait-laced in some ways. According to her, if a man wanted 'six of the best', she would scornfully condemn him as 'kinked up to the eyebrows'. The props she had bought to make me feel at home remained merely decorative and were unused. I was thankful.

Eyeing the stove one day, Rita remembered that as a child, she'd loved bread pudding, and she suddenly developed a craving for it. Until we both got sick of it, she prepared a bread pudding at home each day, bringing it for me to cook at work. For several weeks, the clients' nostrils were assailed with the homely smell of hot spice and currants.

For quite some time, the new flat and the bread pudding kept her mind off the irritating boyfriend. But as the novelty faded, her boredom with her love life increased and she started speculating hopefully on Eddy's lack of fidelity. One evening she got a really hot tip. She had been told in roughly what area he might be found, and after reaching it and instructing the driver to keep circling until she told him to stop, she saw Eddy walking along the street with his arm round the shoulders of a young redhead.

'That's it! I got you!' she said jubilantly. 'Look hard, Babs. Remember you've seen them too, just so we don't got no fucking arguments from him.'

With that, she called to the driver, 'Home, James, and don't spare the horses.' We hadn't gone far when Rita decided on a change of tactics. She said she wanted to find out the girl's address; I demurred.

'Oh, do leave off!' she said. 'I'm not going to bleeding bash the poor little madam. I'm glad she's taken him off my hands.'

It wasn't difficult to find out where she lived; Rita had the information in no time at all. Still in the same taxi, we sped back to Rita's house, where she went rushing round collecting all her newly appointed ex-boyfriend's belongings and stuffing them into boxes. I helped her to stow them in the waiting taxi, and we then drove to the 'fancy piece's' address, dumped them outside her door and got back in the cab.

'Right, mate,' chortled Rita, hugging herself with glee. 'Let them put that in their pipes and smoke it – and I hope it don't choke 'em.' Then she turned and slapped me on the knee. 'And now,' she said, 'we're going to celebrate.'

From then on, Rita thoroughly enjoyed the freedom of her manless state, but also took great pleasure in choosing her next mate.

Wherever she went, there was much flirting, ogling and innuendo between her and any unattached males present. Rita loved every minute of it, but conveyed the impression that she barely tolerated these vulgar advances. Surprisingly enough, her indifferent responses seemed to have no chastening effects whatsoever. After every snub, the competitors for her favour bobbed up again and again like cheerful cherries in a bowl of water. After all, Rita was a beautiful, wealthy woman. The magic of her first husband's name still invested her with a kind of glamour in the eyes of lesser crooks, and her little girl was a distinct asset: to be stepfather to the great man's daughter was tantamount to wearing a lifebelt in these turbulent Soho seas. Remorselessly, destiny was jostling Rita towards husband number three.

One day, after one of our grand 'blow-outs' at our favourite Chinese restaurant, she suggested a bottle of Beaujolais. We had finished our meal and the bottle, and had an amusing time getting back to the flat, where we flung ourselves on to the sagging double bed. We must have fallen asleep; the next thing I knew, Rita, obviously still drunk, was leaning up on one elbow, prodding me awake with a bony forefinger.

'Fine fuckin' maid you've turned out to be, letting me sleep half the night! Come on, I've decided I'm gonna get myself a bloke today.'

Still slightly tipsy with wine, we sallied forth to a place called Leo's – the most favoured thieves' kitchen of them all. On the ground floor, ordinary mortals sat amidst tropical plants with concealed lighting, but the in-crowd used the basement. It smelt like a damp air-raid shelter, there were no plants and the electric lighting was harsh and crude. It was open all night, and for many who went there, it was the nearest thing they had to a home.

There were thieves and crooks there of every denomination. The girls with them were mostly clip-joint hostesses and mysteries. Prostitutes seldom went there, as they considered themselves to be a cut above this rabble. Rita's arrival caused something of a stir.

She had been gradually sieving through the candidates for her affections and had ended up with a shortlist of three; it was pot luck which one of them got to her first.

There was not long to wait: no sooner had we sat than one of the chosen arrived at our table.

'Wotcher,' he said. 'How's tricks?'

And with that, the romance commenced.

His name was Tom, and he wasn't quite so young as Rita's previous lovers. He was large and cheerful, with that honest, candid gaze that is the successful rogue's most valuable stock-in-trade. His eyes were a warm brown, and he had neat, well-oiled chestnut hair; his clothes were smart and his tie bore a discreet monogram. His speech was heavily larded with rhyming slang and his gestures were virile, with lots of muscle-flexing. It was clear that he was out to impress.

Rita reacted to this mating display with demure coquetry and fluttering eyelashes. After about a quarter of an hour, I couldn't stand any more of it and went home to sleep off the residual effects of the Beaujolais. The following day Rita was all smiles; Tom had thawed the snow maiden to a greater degree than I would have thought possible.

At the beginning of May, she married him. Although this was her third stab at matrimony, she made as much of it as if it had been her first. No expense was spared to make it a great and memorable occasion. Rita was opulently lovely in velvet and fur, and with her little girl in a smart dark suit, the couple appeared to be the epitome of hard-working honesty. After the registry office, we moved to a hall adjoining an East End pub, where a band played until the early hours of the morning and the booze flowed non-stop. A good time was had by all, and Rita, flushed with happiness and with sparkling eyes, confided to me that this time she was sure it was for keeps.

Afterwards, she found it difficult to settle down to hustling again and the clients began to suffer once more. She took a lot of time off to be with Tom, so when rent nights came round, there was never enough in the kitty to pay.

'Your heart isn't in it any more,' I said. 'Why don't you retire? Then you could have a proper married life with Tom.'

She was scandalised. 'What? Me chuck the game? I wouldn't know what to do with myself. I'd go spare!' Then she looked at me with genuine affection and added, 'Anyway, what would you do if I went straight?'

'Me?' I thought for a bit. 'Well, I suppose I might go straight too.'

'Cor, strewth! You must be mad!'

She was so outraged by my suggestion that she pulled herself together and, as if to absolutely refute it, made enough for the rent in two hours flat. The vision she'd glimpsed of herself as a happy housewife had shaken her. After that, things returned almost to normal.

My twenty-third birthday came, and Rita and Tom gave me a slap-up supper. They also gave me a lovely coffee-set, whose cups, when held to the light, revealed a Japanese lady's face hidden in the porcelain at the bottom.

'Don't worry, they're new: they're not nicked,' Rita assured me.

Not long after that, after much conjecture, consulting of calendars and, finally, the onset of actual symptoms, Rita came to the conclusion that she was pregnant.

'I'd have an abortion if it wasn't Tom's baby, but I suppose it's time my kid had a brother or sister. I'll go on working for another couple of months and then stop until after the nipper's born. What are you going to do? Myrtle round the corner would have you like a shot – but I'd want you back after, mind.'

'I don't really know what I want to do yet,' I told her.

'There's plenty of time to think about I. Anyway, I might take a holiday too.'

Life, in its perplexing and unpredictable way, was sweeping me inexorably forwards, towards new horizons and new choices. If Rita left the game for a few months, would I really start work again for a girl I cared little for? Or take a holiday? In which case, how to use it?

I didn't think much about the situation, just took things day by day. Sooner or later the decisions would come, and I was content not to hurry them.

Thirty-Four

~

The following Monday, after only a couple of minutes in the street, Rita came hurrying back looking agitated. She'd seen a policeman laid out by a drunk with a beam of wood and didn't want it known that she had witnessed it, 'or there'll be all the argy-bargy of making statements and attending court'.

It was the following day – as though the spirit of violence was hovering in the air – that we heard that Mae had been stabbed. At first, rumour had it that she was dead; then that she had nearly died but was hanging on by the skin of her teeth. We were shocked and shaken and couldn't work for thinking about it.

'Cor. Makes you bleeding think, don't it?' said Rita. 'You going to see her?'

'Well, you know how things are between us,' I answered. 'She may not want to see me. I'll wait a bit, I think.'

A few mornings later, Mae's maid phoned to say she'd been asking about me and wanted to know whether I would go to visit her. She was at the Middlesex Hospital.

I went immediately and found her propped into a half-sitting position with masses of pillows. She looked very white and immobile. I laid my bunch of flowers on her lap and, to break the ice of our estrangement, said, 'I'm glad it didn't have to be a wreath: they're so bloody expensive.'

She was obviously pleased to see me. Putting out a hand to take mine, she said in a feeble voice, 'I didn't think you'd come. I was rotten to you. Give me a kiss and say you forgive me. Nothing's been right since you went – and I have found out all about that bitch Lulu.'

I kissed her on her forehead – carefully, for she seemed so fragile – and told her that I'd long since forgiven her. She squeezed my hand in answer; there were bright tears in her eyes. Wanting to give her time to collect herself, I went off to find a chair.

'Now, tell me what happened,' I said, when I was finally seated. I pointed to her torso, which was bandaged almost from her neck to her waist. 'Did you prick yourself sewing?'

'Oh, for God's sake, don't make me laugh,' she said, with something like her old giggle. Then she proceeded to tell me about the 'closest shave' she'd ever had.

She, her maid and a couple of the maid's friends were playing cards. Mae went out for cigarettes, leaving her maid to play her hand. On her way out, she noticed a man wandering about in the street. He was still there when she came back.

'You know me: never want to go up the stairs empty-handed. Funny-looking geezer he was: hat turned down, coat collar turned up and his hands stuck in his pockets. Right miserable-looking, too. I said to him, "Come on, love, let's cheer you up."'

They had gone straight into the bedroom. Engrossed in her card game, the maid hadn't even realised Mae had brought someone up.

'I took his money and shoved it in a pot until afterwards. I started to take my skirt off, but I saw he was just standing there with his hat and coat still on. I said to him – joking

275

like – "Come on, love, aren't you even going to take your hat off?" And I went up to him to help him undress. Just as I was unbuttoning his coat, he brought a knife out of his pocket and just stuck it in me. I was too surprised to scream; all I can remember is thinking, This is it, Mae. The knife had gone through my lung and nicked my heart and it really was a bit dicey, they tell me.'

She said this with a faint hint of relish, and then added, with a little twisted grin, 'But they can't get rid of me that easy, can they, love?'

I was appalled by the narrowness of her escape, but with a professional's assessment, I was also critical of the maid. I could not believe she had been unaware of the man's presence, and she should have made herself known to show him Mae was not alone.

Mae broke into my horrified abstraction: 'Anyway, 'nuff of that. How are you getting on with Rita?'

'Oh, fine.' I told her. 'A real rest cure, after you.'

'Why don't you come back to me when I get out of here?' she said suddenly. 'If I could get rid of that sod Rabbits, I'm damn sure I could get rid of this one.'

'I couldn't leave Rita just like that,' I protested. 'She's a good sort and I wouldn't want to let her down.'

I didn't tell her that Rita was going to have a baby and was going to dispense with my services soon.

Mae was looking at me from under her eyelashes, flirting with me.

'You'd come back if I asked you nicely, you know you would. You know you love me.'

Once more – and against my better judgement – I felt myself drawn towards this infuriating creature. There was something magical about her, something fascinating, like quicksilver, and addictive.

'You'll be the death of me!' I laughed. 'I'd better go.'

The place was beginning to sprout impatient-looking nurses wielding bedpans. Before leaving, I asked Mae if there was anything she needed or anything I could do.

'Well, there is one thing that's worrying me a bit,' she said. 'I've got two little kittens at the flat now. They're ever so sweet – I call them Tiger and Blackie – but the maid doesn't know much about animals. Would you have a look at them to see if they're all right? Tony's found a temporary girl for the flat, so it is open.'

Good old Tony – always up to scratch, I thought. I told her I would have a look at the kittens after finishing work that night.

'Give my love to Rita,' she said as I bent down to kiss her goodbye.

'I will,' I told her. 'Oh and by the way, she goes without rubbers, too.'

She grabbed at her side, trying not to laugh. Then her face took on a rueful look.

'I am sorry, love,' she said.

I was determined to be brisk and bright. 'Ta-rah,' I said.

'Ta-rah. Be suing you. Come and see me again, won't you?'

'I will,' I replied. 'You can't get rid of me that easily, either.'

I waved back from the doorway and she returned the wave with a weak flap of her hand on the counterpane. She was grinning widely.

As I had promised, I went straight to Mae's flat to check on the kittens. The elderly maid immediately began talking about the near tragedy.

'Oh, it was terrible,' she said. 'I didn't even know she had a man in there with her until I heard him rushing off down the stairs. Then I shot out of the kitchen to see what was happening and heard her moaning. I tore in and there she was on the floor, with blood all over her. I can't think how she let it happen – with all her experience.'

I agreed, but said that I supposed really it could happen to anyone, at any time. She clutched eagerly at that; she had obviously been wondering how much she was to blame. She offered me a cup of tea, and I accepted.

'How are the kittens?' I asked.

'Oh, they're moping,' she answered. 'I think they miss Mae. They won't eat, and I got them some lovely steak today.' She pointed towards a dinner plate on the floor piled with enormous lumps of raw meat.

'Can I have a look at them?'

'Sure, they're in a box in that cupboard.'

She busied herself with cups and saucers while I knelt to inspect the kittens. They were no more than six or seven weeks old, one tabby, one black, and they were huddled together in a tight little ball. I reached my hand in and found that their ears were icy cold and their noses hot and dry. I peered closer and roused them so that I could see their eyes. The third eyelids were almost halfway across. It was obvious that they were very sick.

I wrapped them up in woollen sweaters and took them to a branch of the PDSA. It was really for people who couldn't afford vets' fees, but I didn't know anywhere else that would be open at that time of night. The vet was staggeringly drunk and had to steady himself against the table whilst he examined the kittens.

'Enteritis,' he said, and tottered off to get a hypodermic syringe.

He injected Blackie without too much trouble, but when he tackled Tiger, he hadn't screwed the needle in properly and it was left sticking in the kitten's leg, while the fluid flooded out over his fur.

'Oops,' he said as he made a more successful attempt on the squealing kitten.

As I left, I put two pound notes in the little wooden collecting box and observed, as tactfully as I knew how, that perhaps he shouldn't drink quite so much when he was on duty.

He flew into a towering rage and, making a wild gesture towards the collecting box, said, 'I could report you to the authorities. If you can afford that much money, you should have gone to a proper vet.' With that, he slammed the door on me.

I got the kittens home, where Tiger immediately went into a fit. Not knowing what else to do, I treated it as hysteria and gave him a sharp little slap. Surprisingly, it did the trick. After giving them both some warm milk, I took them to bed with me. Blackie curled up against my neck inside my hair and, finding the lobe of my ear, began sucking it. Amused, I carefully hoisted little Tiger up and proffered the other ear lobe – with the same results. Drowsing off, my final thought before falling asleep was, 'Yet another pair of earrings from Mae.'

As time passed, Mae's health improved. The kittens were getting better too – rushing around and enjoying themselves by wrecking my bed-sitter. If I kept then any longer, it would be a hard wrench to part with them, so I took them back to Mae's maid. I gave her enough suitable food to last them for a few days and instructions on how to look after them. Then I went to the hospital to see Mae.

She was almost her old self by now, wearing make-up and one of her own pretty nightdresses in place of the hospital gown she'd had on on my first visit. From what I could hear, she was the life and soul of her ward.

'Have you got everything you need?' I asked her.

'Well, I could do with a bit of money,' she said. 'Trying to get any out of Tony is like getting blood out of a stone. I just need enough for a newspaper when the boy comes round or something off the trolley.'

I felt in my handbag and, taking out a five-pound note, gave it to her. She seemed very grateful and slipped it under the bedclothes, but then became jokingly accusatory.

'A little bird told me that Rita's going to have a baby,' she said. 'So now there's nothing to stop you coming back to me, is there?'

I stared at her and burst out laughing. 'You're a terrible woman,' I said. 'What makes you think I could put up with all your shenanigans again?'

'Oh, I'll be ever so, ever so good,' she said in a baby voice.

I found myself really weakening. Then I glanced up the ward and saw Tony swaggering towards us. I just could not stay and be affable.

'I'll leave you alone for a bit, so that you can talk,' I told Mae.

Giving Tony a nod as I passed him, I went outside into the corridor. He was with her for a mere five minutes, and then he left. As he reached me, he paused, smiling, and lifted his hand to flaunt my fiver. Then he tucked it ostentatiously into his breast pocket. His expression was one of malicious pleasure as he stood facing me for a moment before sauntering off.

I was appalled by the way Mae had used me. Whatever powers of persuasion she'd had, I resolved they would have no effect on me any more. I was done with her. I looked through the little glass panel in the door leading to the ward. She was leaning back, her face silhouetted against the white pillows. I gazed for a minute or so at that

Nefertiti profile, committing it to memory. Thinking it likely that I would never see it again, I turned and left the hospital.

I felt bereaved, but also cleansed – ready to move on. In a strange way, I was pleased.

Thirty-Five

~

In the week before Rita's 'maternity leave', Myrtle from round the corner and Betty, her maid, arrived carrying an old brown carrier bag. With some reverence they placed it between them, then both started speaking at once. They had just had an elderly client who'd been recently widowed. Carrying the bag, he had walked backwards and forwards past Myrtle, as though sizing her up.

'When I got him up to the flat, he dumped the carrier bag in front of me and said, "That's for you",' Myrtle said.

She bent down and opened the bag dramatically. It was full of banknotes.

'How much?' Rita whispered.

'Five thousand quid,' said Myrtle and Betty in awed unison.

Myrtle continued, 'When I'd got over the first shock, I said to him, "What's this?" and he said, "I'll tell you what it is: it's twenty-eight years of bloody scrimping and saving, twenty-eight bloody horrible years." Then he asked me to go out for a drink with him, so I locked Betty in the flat with the money and went with him.'

The man had told her that from the beginning, his wife had demanded his wage packet intact and had given him just enough to get him to and from work every day. She'd said that she needed the rest for housekeeping. According to her, he hadn't earned enough for smoking, drinking, holidays or evenings out. He had accepted the frugal meals and the spartan lifestyle, and even believed her when she told him her doctor had forbidden her to have sex. He had lived, as he termed it, 'like a bloody monk'.

Then his wife died, and hidden amongst her belongings, he found nearly fifteen thousand pounds.

He told Myrtle: 'I just sat around feeling sick. I didn't know what to do with the money. Then I decided I'd do the most stupid thing I could: something that would make her go mad. I do hope there's an afterlife and that she knows just what I've done.'

After Myrtle and Betty had gone on their way rejoicing, Rita was morose.

'Makes you sick, don't it? I knew I should have had that abortion. Makes you realise how much money there is sculling around, and we won't be here when it's ready to drop into our laps. I could bleeding spit.'

I couldn't help laughing. 'Well, it'll still be around when we're dead, too – and we won't be able to do much about that either,' I said.

'That don't make me feel no bleeding better,' she replied truculently. She glowered at me. 'I don't know why you can't take your turn on that bleeding rotten bed in there, and let me be bleeding maid.'

I treated what she said flippantly. 'I'm not as mean as you,' I said. 'I'd get myself a new bed.'

She wasn't smiling.

'If I thought you meant that, I'd put a deposit on one tomorrow. If you played your cards right, you could have your arse hung in diamonds.'

She put some more lipstick on, preparing to go out. As a parting shot, she said, 'Now think about it, mate. I'm serious.'

So I was left thinking about it. She was gone for about twenty minutes; that twenty minutes was my Moment of Truth: the little patch of time that shaped my future more than any other.

I had no doubt that Rita was serious. From her point of view, it would be a very convenient arrangement for the duration of her pregnancy. She had accused me of doggedly hanging on to my virginity, but it was not quite like that. I was not primly retaining it for any specific reason; it was merely that I had never got round to losing it.

As for my mental virtue, that had gone long ago. I saw nothing at all wrong with prostitution on moral grounds. For me, it had become a bona fide business, albeit one that continually irritated me with its poor standard of service. I had seen so many girls working in so many different ways that I had it in my power to become the perfect whore. It was a shock to realise it, but it seemed a pity to waste my expertise.

I could save enough money for a really good hustling flat of my own. I would decorate and furnish it to a standard none of the other girls thought they needed. It wouldn't be necessary to go out looking for clients; with the right maid, they would come to me. I would be a wealthy woman before I reached thirty.

During that twenty minutes, I came within the breadth of an eyelash of deciding to take up Rita's offer. I mentally planned my campaign and made my fortune, and then, in a moment, I lost it.

It would be nice to report that it was an innate sense of virtue that won through – or even that I didn't wish to go back on the promise I'd made to the nice policewoman two years earlier. But in fact what made the difference was a strange feeling that life wasn't meant to be that easy. Along with the feeling came memories of things that held far greater potency for me than either righteousness or wealth would ever do: the pungent smell of turpentine and linseed oil, the almost erotic pleasure of dipping a good brush into rich paint, the gently responsive sensuality of a canvas and the magical joy of alchemy – of transmuting the basic and crude colours on the palette into a picture.

I realised that I was now, of my own volition, bringing an important and valuable phase of my life to an end. I knew I had to leave Soho before I weakened and my desire to paint grew weaker and eventually died. I knew that if I allowed that to happen I would have forfeited something immeasurably wonderful.

When Rita next came into the kitchen, I was unpinning my calendar from the wall.

'Chickened out, then, have you?' she observed drily.

'Chickened out,' I affirmed.

But it wasn't true. I was ready to take on my own life, on my own terms. After twenty-one years in my family's loveless care, and two in Soho's riotous embrace, I had finally learned to walk on my own two feet. I had grown up. I knew what I wanted and I was determined to get it.

After our last day's work together, Rita and I stowed all our possessions into holdalls, leaving the canes hanging on the wall for the next occupier. Then we locked the door and, for the last time, picked our way together through the treacherous, malodorous mews. Rita waved to me from her taxi and said she would phone me. I watched until she was out of sight, then turned and walked away, feeling suddenly desolate.

Somehow, I didn't feel like going straight home. I wanted to get one more whiff of this life that I was leaving and what better swansong, I thought, than a visit to Tearaway Tina.

When I got to Tina's, news of Rita's impending 'retirement' had reached her ears. She sent her maid for cigarettes, and the moment the door was shut behind her, spun round to me.

'Now look,' she said, 'I've been thinking. I could easy get shot of that old cow and you could come here to work. How about that? Us would have some lovely fun.'

I thought of the 'old cow' and how she did all Tina's washing, prepared her meals and, in general, clucked over her like an anxious hen.

'It's a very kind thought, Tina,' I answered. 'But I'm going straight.'

'You must be mad,' she said, disbelievingly. 'What you going to do?'

'Paint,' I told her.

She was so astonished that she leapt off her chair. 'You going to what?' she shrieked.

I feasted my eyes on her. There she stood, in fishnet stockings, French corsets and a flimsy short black negligee. Her legs were wide apart, her hands on her hips. She was staring back at me from under multiple layers of eyelashes, her vermilion lips curled in derision. She was corrupt, vicious, evil, rotten to the marrow of her bones – but so magnificent. I found myself sending up a prayer that some day I would be given the insight and the skill to be able to transfer what I now beheld on to canvas.

'And what the bloody hell are you going to paint?' she shrilled, moving into an even more devastatingly primitive pose.

Something like a great smile of excitement and joy welled up from the soles of my feet. I felt it rush through my body and almost explode in my head.

'Why,' I said. 'With any luck, perhaps someone like you.'

Thirty-Six

~

My professional association with that life was over, but it would have needed a much stronger will than mine to make a complete break, and I didn't see any necessity to do so.

At first it was quite impossible to settle down fully to my new regime as a painter. I would down tools at the least provocation and make my way back to the dim little streets and obscure cafés where my old friends hung out.

Rita – whose back really had been done in by the sagging old bed and who had now been advised to sleep on a board – finally had her baby. It was a boy, and he was the image of Tom.

I hoped she would find sufficient contentment and happiness to retire. I was both surprised and relieved when one day she phoned to tell me that she had decided to go straight.

'Rita – that's wonderful,' I said. 'I never thought you'd do it.'

'No, neither did I, mate. And what d'you think I'm going do now? I'll give you three guesses.'

'I give up. Tell me.'

'I'm going to run a clip-joint,' she said. 'I've been told they're bleeding gold mines.'

Sadly for her, Tom was arrested one night with his pockets full of objects that were not rightfully his. He was given nine years 'hard', and later, Rita was herself arrested for receiving and sentenced to three years in Holloway.

I heard snippets of news – that Cindy was still with her ponce, Mario; that aristocratic Anne was still playing the lady in her prim little parlour and Fiona was continuing to have trouble with her epileptic maid; Lulu was still creating distress and havoc in her orbit and Jessie was in debt as always. Candy, a drug addict, died – as did poor Treesa, who slashed her wrists one lonely night. Old Hilda, permanently drunk, was living on handouts from the other girls. Benzy Nell had disappeared – it was rumoured she had forgotten to about-turn at the end of her beat and had gone marching on until she vanished over a cliff at the coast. Tina also disappeared into limbo – although some said it was Manchester.

Gradually I became more engrossed in my painting. I trotted round all the galleries, studying the 'greats', and took further courses at art school. When my savings ran out, I did any old part-time job to tide me over and painted in every spare minute. In short, I became dedicated. Now and again my longing for the bright lights would overwhelm me and I would take a trip to town, but to economise, I'd had my telephone removed. As a result, my links with Soho became more and more tenuous.

I could see enough, however, to know that things there were changing. A Royal Commission was set up to report on prostitution, with recommendations for abating the practice, and the results caused shock waves through the streets I used to know so well. Because of the commission's findings, the government devised a law that would make it virtually impossible for girls to solicit men in the streets any longer. It was, in effect, so tough that even a smile from an upstairs window might be construed as soliciting, and sufficient cause for arrest.

For a while before this law came into force, there was considerable anxiety in the trade, and doubts were voiced everywhere as to whether it would be possible to continue at all; but when the blow finally struck, and zero hour arrived, the ready wits of those involved swiftly found ways and means to carry on. The word 'Model' was scribbled roughly on to pieces of card and pinned to the open street doors of the various gaffs; and any shopkeeper possessing a glass advertisement case became richer by virtue of that asset, as, for rocketing fees they pinned up postcards bearing the telephone numbers of young ladies available for French lessons, corrective therapy, soothing massage and other equally ambiguous services.

During this period of adjustment, there was a fair amount of gloom and hardship, but justice was done too, in that the girls who had been conscientious enough to always please their clients and had acquired plenty of regulars were the least hard hit.

One rather unpleasant side effect caused by the apparent disappearance of the prostitutes was that men desperately hunting round the streets looking for them began accosting any ordinary women who paused to look in shop windows. But gradually the dispirited and aimlessly wandering men learned the new order of things, and began to understand what the word 'Model' meant, and in no time at all they were galloping happily up and down the numerous staircases again.

Soon the furore died down, and everything was very much as it had been before; except that now Soho *looked* clean, for the girls had been, metaphorically speaking, swept under the mat.

Then, as though all this outward purity were anathema to the very fibre of Soho, clip joints began springing up everywhere. Along with these, strip clubs began to burgeon, and gradually everyone settled down to the new lifestyle and eventually forgot the days of walking the streets.

It was only by chance, some while later, that I heard that Mae had married a grocer. At first I couldn't believe the news, but everyone confirmed it. She had left the West End and was serving behind the counter of her husband's shop in the suburbs. Several girls had even taken taxi rides out there to verify this phenomenon. By all accounts, they returned rather speechless and a trifle sorry for her.

My own life, away from my old habits and friends, gradually became ever busier, crammed with personal events and endeavours. Time was at a premium and not to be wasted on luxuries. All superfluous activities had to be pared back. Sadly, Soho and my friends there fell victim to this economy.

The antipathy I had always felt for men had increased enormously during my time as a maid, and I had become totally sickened by what I saw as universal sweaty sexual eagerness. When at last I met a man who was able to approach the subject of sex with light-hearted bonhomie, I was so impressed that I married him. In due course we had a daughter. It was a perfect marriage.

My relations with my own family never became warm, but I did start to resume occasional contact with my mother and half-sisters. Now that I had a family of my own, I felt I had to try. My grandmother, however, I never saw again, nor ever wanted to.

The years passed with frightening rapidity. My daughter grew up and herself had a daughter. I achieved some success and a few distinctions as a painter, and took great pleasure in knowing that reproductions of my paintings hung in thousands of homes. It was what I had always dreamt of when I got that first job, painting silk. Finally all my hard work was bearing fruit. Despite being immersed in a different world, I did what I could to set my Soho life down in paint. Two of my favourite pictures – which I have never sold and never will – are one of Mae and Rabbits, and another of Tearaway Tina, she of the magnificent appearance and the rotten heart. I have never yet painted the perfect picture, but I am only eighty-three, so there's hope for me yet. Perhaps I shall find success in some afterlife.

And then one day: a minor miracle. A small hand-written poster caught my eye outside a Spiritualist church and stirred up poignant old memories. The next visiting psychic medium was, apparently, none other than Rita. It was over twenty years since I'd last set eyes on her.

Nothing could have been more ludicrous than the thought of Rita turning spiritual; I would have thought she was more likely to be running an opium den in Wapping. I laughingly told myself that lots of people bore the same surname and it just had to be a different person. Nevertheless, the nostalgia seeped through, and I made a mental note of the time and date.

The advertised night arrived and I sat in the small hall along with about fifty others. The door near the little platform opened and the leader of the church emerged, followed by the visiting medium – and glory be, it *was* Rita!

I was quite overcome. I leaned back with a sigh as her now bespectacled eyes swept round the hall and inevitably met my astounded gaze. For a moment her expression was just as astonished as my own, but she recovered swiftly and took her place at the rostrum with no further sign of recognition. Her dark hair was slightly streaked with grey; it was cut short and cemented into a prim permanent wave, and her make-up was so pale as to have hardly been worth the trouble of putting on. The voluptuous, mountainous curves of the bosom that had once been the pride of Soho had been mercilessly subdued and then hidden behind the façade of a neat grey woollen dress with a white Peter Pan collar.

She led the congregation in prayers and then proceeded to give them messages from their departed loved ones. She surely can't be sincere, I thought, but everyone was lapping up the things she said. The cockney twang had gone and so had the belligerence. If anything, she was now a little refined.

'Ooh, she's good,' whispered the woman next to me. 'Have you heard her before?'

I nodded.

Just before the meeting ended, Rita pointed to me. 'Will that lady there stay behind afterwards, please? There's something I'd like to say to her in private.'

It was some time before we were alone, for it seemed that *everyone* wanted to have private words with Rita. At last we found ourselves walking away from the church.

'Feel like a bite to eat?' she asked. 'I'm starving. I have to fast before a meeting or else Spirit can't come through.'

We went to a little café nearby, where she ordered a simple omelette. She eyed my chop with distaste.

'You ought to give that up, you know,' she said. 'You'll never get Spirit while you go on eating meat.' She'd given it up years ago, she said, and all intoxicants – even wine – for the same reason. 'That means no more Beaujolais,' she said with a grin. For a moment, the old Rita peeped out from behind her eyes.

I laughed, then said, 'But even Jesus approved of wine.'

'That's as maybe,' she answered grimly, and the old Rita fled.

'What about sex?' I asked.

The word seemed to shock her, and she lowered her eyes to her plate.

'No good at all. Spirit has to have a pure vessel to work through.'

This meeting had a powerfully unsettling effect on me. It evoked memories – never really far below the surface – of old friends and old events. I felt restless, sad and full of nostalgia; I thought about the past incessantly and found it hard to concentrate on my work. After one strenuous but unrewarding day at the easel, I could contain myself no longer. As usual, my poor husband bore the brunt of my outburst.

'All those fabulous characters and the things they did,' I said. 'No record of them – nothing. I can't bear the thought of them eventually having no existence.'

As always when I was upset, he gave me his complete attention. He thought for a while, then said, 'Why not take a sort of sabbatical and write about them?'

The suggestion struck me as unassailable in its rightness. I said yes straight away.

I decided I needed to drink in the atmosphere once more and wander my beloved Soho streets. When at last I made my trip, I was amazed. Coventry Street and Charing Cross Road, where they bordered Soho, had augmented their gaiety with more amusement arcades and ice-cream kiosks, and many small boutiques selling anything from baubles to next year's fashions. A goodly sprinkling of Indian shops were easily spotted by their open-air racks full of fluttering cheesecloth garments and vivid silk scarves, their insides filled with colourful gowns and saris and Afghan coats, and the windows a tumble of glittering bracelets, belts and chains.

I strode past them into the hinterland, only to be even

more surprised. Soho had certainly thrown the covers off. The clip joints and strip clubs were still there – the latter even more profuse – but the discreet façades were gone and the tiny photo displays of strippers had blossomed into huge enlargements covering the outside walls. There were sex shops, massage parlours and sauna baths. Here and there, two or three shops had been knocked into one and the premises converted into cinemas that exhibited lurid photographs advertising films with even more lurid titles. Soho had turned into a great, greedy, grasping hand. I found myself filling with a sense of angry disgust.

Was this garish, pornographic panorama, I asked myself, visually more moral and respectable than the small groups of prostitutes one *used* to see? Was it for *this* that the girls had been pushed out of sight as unseemly? Why, in comparison with this, the whores in their tailored and stylish clothes would have seemed eminently respectable!

Moodily I plodded around until I discovered that habit had led me to the locality of the cut-price shop from which I must have bought at least two hundred gross of Durex. I recalled how once my footsteps had lagged in traversing this street, anxious to delay my embarrassing errand. Now I hastened, eager to see if something remained of the things I had known.

The shop was still there and looked exactly the same. The large and blatant fascia that had once seemed so audacious was almost staid by comparison with the rest of what I had seen. For old times' sake I crossed the threshold, using the need for a lipstick as an excuse to enter.

'Hullo. How are you, then?' demanded a voice from the back of the shop, and the short, dapper, slim man came into sight from a quarter of a century before.

Then a voice from behind me said, 'Back in the fold,

then, are you?' and there was the short, dapper, *stocky* man, returning from an errand.

At first I was almost speechless with surprise and pleasure at seeing them, but we soon fell to sharing our annoyance about the changes around us. Finally I bought my lipstick, and as I reached across the counter for it, I was blasted full in the face – as of old – by a spray of powerful perfume. As I left, I recalled that once upon a time, I had been ashamed of leaving that trail of scent in my wake, but now it didn't seem to matter. Now, it was like a banner billowing triumphantly behind me. I was exultant that something had survived.

My spirits revived, I felt cheerful enough to go hunting for some ginseng, and made my way to where there had once been one or two Chinese shops. The ginseng bought, I had taken no more than a dozen paces when my eye alighted on the name 'Mae' written on a piece of cardboard pinned on the side of a doorpost. Underneath was a small visiting card: 'M. Roberts, Plumber'.

Thirty-Seven

~

Past grievances were forgotten in an instant. I shot in through the door and raced up the stairs two at a time. I arrived, panting, on the second floor, where there was a door bearing a much larger piece of cardboard with Mae's name on it. I rang the bell, and only then did I suddenly feel frightened.

Mae would be in her late fifties now; she might be like old Hilda. I couldn't bear it. I would rather have remembered her bright and vivid as she had been. Why hadn't I stopped to think?

The maid opened the door a few inches as I was beginning to turn away.

'I wanted to see Mae,' I told her. 'But if she's busy, I'll come back some other time.'

'No, she's free. Come in,' she said, opening the door wider and standing aside. 'She's in the bedroom. Just round that corner. Her door's open.'

Bracing myself, I walked along the short corridor and, turning the corner, arrived at the open bedroom door.

Mae was lying on her stomach on the bed, her feet towards me. There was a grey poodle beside her. She was propped up on her elbows as she flicked through a magazine. Her flared miniskirt was dark against a light sweater. I noted with pleasure and enormous relief that her legs and her figure were as lovely as ever. For Mae, time had stood still.

'Hey, you know what, Stella?' she began as she swung round to face me. Her eyes widened with astonishment. 'Babs!' she called out at the top of her voice.

She sprang into a kneeling position on the bed and threw her arms wide open. I rushed to her and, with our arms wrapped round one another, we rolled over and over on the bed, laughing like a couple of lunatics. The poodle began yapping and the maid gazed in bewilderment. Eventually we pulled ourselves together and sat up.

'If you knew where I was, why didn't you come and see me before, you rotter?' Mae said. 'Hey! Put the kettle on, Stella, there's a dear.'

I began explaining that I'd found her accidentally, on the way out of the Chinese shop. She interrupted me.

'What is this ginseng? Why haven't I ever heard of it? Show me.'

I showed her the bottle explaining that I hadn't tried it before and that I'd heard about it on the radio.

'Mind if I try one? I could do with a bit of vitality.'

Obviously still mad keen on anything that might pep her up, she tipped half a dozen into her hand and swallowed them.

'Here,' she said, rounding on me suddenly. 'What happened to that bottle of Purple Hearts I gave you to look after? Have you still got them? I'll have them back.'

I was thunderstruck. 'But Mae, they're over twenty-five years old now. I shouldn't think they'd be safe to take. And anyway, they're in my museum.'

'Well, rake 'em out of your fucking museum; they're hard to come by these days. You know it'd take an atom bomb to finish me off – and that's only if it made a direct hit.'

We laughed. Marge called out from the next room to say the tea was ready. 'Come on,' Mae said. 'Let's have it in the sitting room; it's more comfortable there.'

'Sitting room, eh? My oh my, things *have* improved!'

'That's not all, my dear,' she said in her 'haughty' voice. 'I've got another floor above this that comes in very handy. Come and have a look.'

This upper part of her domain was in the eaves of the building, with sharply sloping ceilings and tiny windows. It was divided into three rooms and minimally furnished. Mae took me from room to room, showing me the assets of the place, like a proud suburban housewife.

In each of two of the rooms a naked man was trussed up on the floor, exhibiting that expression of moroseness and defiance that I remembered so well. Mae went and administered a few vigorous kicks and thumps while she was there, just to keep them happy for a bit longer – and to save her coming up the stairs again. In the third room a figure sat brooding by the window, like the Lady of Shallot.

'Want a cup of tea with us, Trix?' Mae asked.

The figure uncoiled itself and stood up. It was a tall, rather hefty man, wearing a black lace peignoir. He was heavily made up and wore an elaborately coiffured black wig and extremely high-heeled marabou-trimmed mules. His hands and arms were sheathed in elbow-length white doeskin gloves overlaid with numerous bangles and brace-lets.

'Don't mind if I do,' he replied in a very deep and gravelly cockney voice.

Nothing had changed at all. I glowed inwardly.

'Does Vera still come?' I asked.

'No, love. He got married again and his new wife doesn't mind him dressing up,' said Mae, with the satisfaction of a teacher whose pupil has won through to university. 'No need for me any more: he's got it made, hasn't he?'

We descended to the sitting room, which was very comfortably furnished with fitted carpets, easy chairs, a television set, stereo record player and a cocktail cabinet. From this room, a door opened into a nicely appointed kitchen. I congratulated Mae on how pleasant everything was.

'Oh, it's not so bad, I suppose,' she agreed modestly. 'But I like it nice, 'cos I live here most of the time now.'

'No husbands or boyfriends?'

Mae went quiet for a moment. 'Hey, Stella, if anyone comes, tell them to wait.'

In the brighter light in this room, I could now see lines and small sags that time had wrought on Mae's face. Even so, she looked no more than forty. She gulped her tea and went on talking.

'My last old man nearly finished me. That was husband number five. I'd learned my lesson by then and never did bung him all the gelt. We seemed okay together, until he forged my signature on a cheque and got everything out of the bank. He pinched pretty much all my jewellery – I had some nice things then – and then he scarpered. I've never done it before to anybody but I had him nicked for it.' She looked contrite. 'He was a Malt,' she said. 'I know you never liked them, but they've got something I rather go for.'

'What happened to Tony?' I asked.

'Oh, it's pitiful, love! You should see him. He works in a tailor's shop in Shaftesbury Avenue. He's got a tape measure round his neck and he's got all fat and half bald. You *said* he'd get fat. I hear he does all his money in, gambling, just like he did all mine.' She sighed wistfully. 'Oh, but he was smashing once!'

'I heard you'd married a grocer and gone straight,' I said.

'Oh, I did. I did.' She burst into laughter and leaned

forward to beat a tattoo on my knees in an excess of glee. 'And what an error of bleeding judgement that was! I thought it was time I got myself a bit of security, and he wasn't a bad bloke – English. I stuck it out for four years, serving old biddies with lumps of cheese and going to bed with a cup of cocoa at half past ten every night. But then I got so fed up, I thought I'd rather die in the poorhouse than go on like that.' She paused and thought for a bit, 'Makes you feel bad, doesn't it, knowing some people live like that all their lives? Enough to drive you potty.'

Suddenly she jumped up, beaming.

'Hey, I know someone who'd like to see you.'

She rushed to the telephone and dialled.

'Fred? It's Mae. Come on up here straight away. I've got a surprise for you.' And she slammed the receiver down, grinning. 'I'm dying to see his face when he sees you. He often talks about you.'

All this time, Trix had sat demurely sipping her tea, one gloved finger delicately extended. Now Stella joined us.

'There's three of 'em waiting now,' she told Mae.

'Well they'll just have to go on waiting,' said Mae. 'I'm not seeing to them before Fred gets here.'

In addition to the poodle – who was, Mae said, a direct descendant of Mimi – there were two cats and a small kitten viciously attacking some imaginary monster under one of the chairs.

'You still go in for animals quite a bit,' I observed.

'Oh Gawd, yes!' said Stella, with a vehemence I fully appreciated. 'These aren't so bad, but it was murder when she had the monkey.'

'I still reckon you left that window open on purpose,' Mae said darkly.

'As if I would, Mae,' said Stella – rather unconvincingly, I thought.

Presently Fred arrived – walking slowly and painfully with the aid of two sticks – and there was another joyful, poignant reunion. His old back injury had aged him but his expression was just as kind, his manner just as gentle and he was clearly still very much in love with Mae.

'Good heavens!' he kept repeating, grinning at me from ear to ear, 'Good heavens!'

I almost felt like weeping at finding myself back in this environment and amongst the people responsible for so many memories. I was instantly at ease in this place where the restraints, falsities and values of 'sophisticated' civilisation had no real meaning. Here, there was true humanity and uncritical understanding. Where else, I thought, could one find so many unmasked examples of the basic sadness and pathos – the reality – of humanity? Where else could one find such an odd assortment of characters: the two men upstairs, roped and locked in their fantasy worlds; this tall, gruff cockney, quietly contented in his lace and wig; the crippled old man with his steadfast but hopeless devotion; me, spending my life trying to achieve in paint that which I knew to be unachievable; and above all, the great prostitute, growing old with the same splendour with which the planet grows old?

Thirty-Eight

~

On that day, Monday, 14 November 1977, Mae was fifty-nine, still glamorous and still working.

In the early hours of 14 December, I made the final corrections to this manuscript and parcelled it up ready for handing over to a typist. In those same pre-dawn hours, a fire broke out at Mae's working flat in Rupert Street, Soho, and she perished in the blaze. The cosy pink room where she and I had shared our happy reunion had become a raging inferno, and her body was charred almost beyond recognition.

I will not dwell upon the horror I felt that Mae should have suffered this terrible form of death. I was incredulous and shocked that it should have occurred on that day of all days: the day I had so jubilantly completed my story. Mixed with these emotions was a conviction that Mae, with her fantastic aptitude for self-preservation, could not have died in that particular way – at least not by accident.

The following day I heard that her body had been found huddled close to the door of her flat. The door was mortise-locked and there was no key in it. It looked suspiciously as though she had been locked in.

The police called in her maid for questioning. She told them that Mae took sleeping pills every night, and that when she left her, she was usually in bed, drowsing off. It was at Mae's own request that the maid always locked up on leaving and always slipped the key back under the door.

My suspicions grew. There were so many things that didn't add up. Just before Christmas, impatient for answers, I went back to Soho. Beneath the early darkness of the winter sky, I found Rupert Street – age-old home of fruit and vegetable stalls – doing a roaring trade in tangerines, nuts and Christmas trees, as eager shoppers prepared for the big feast of the year. But there, rising out of reach of the festive brightness around it, was the smoke-blackened building. Its window mouldings were like broken sticks of charcoal and the protective sheets of black plastic behind them were snapping and glittering in the icy breeze. It was a sight too stark, too harshly emphatic of the event, and, sickened, I turned away.

I wandered round the market and spoke to several of the street vendors. They had all been fond of Mae and all had different ideas as to what might have happened. There were several, of course, who advanced the 'smoking in bed' theory. One suspected that Mae had taken an overdose and then set fire to the place deliberately. Another told me they'd caught the man who did it – a jailbird, just out of prison. The most terrible information was from a man who'd seen Mae's body brought out wrapped in plastic.

'It was so small,' he said. 'You'd never have thought it was her inside that tiny bundle.'

All the people who knew Mae more intimately and could have answered some of my questions were out of town. Whilst I was casting around for what to do next, Christmas and a ferocious attack of influenza intervened. Once back on my feet, I called at Vine Street police station. They wouldn't answer any of my questions specifically, claiming that it might cause embarrassment to Mae's relatives.

'Just tell me this,' I said. 'Why, if the key had been

pushed back under the door, couldn't Mae find it?'

'Probably got pushed under the lino instead,' the policeman said. He recommended I make any other enquiries at Westminster Coroner's Court, where the inquest had been held. They told me to send a written request to consult the Notes of Evidence. I did so, but the coroner refused my request on the grounds that the inquest had been fully reported in the *Westminster and Pimlico News*.

The 'full reportage' transpired to consist of a small panel at the foot of the back page headed 'Smoking In Bed Caused Death – Inquest Theory'. The column ended with: 'Death was from asphyxia due to inhalation of fire fumes.'

There was nothing to arouse any suspicions and nothing to allay mine. There was nothing to tell me why she had been found on the floor and not in bed, and no mention of that mysterious key. Nobody had asked why she had not hurried up to the safety of the roof, where she could have escaped to a neighbouring building, as she had always said she would if there was a fire.

Mae's funeral had taken place whilst I was ill. It didn't seem right that the woman who was once known as 'the Queen of Soho' should have had a council burial, but I couldn't see who else would have come forward to pay for it. After several enquiries, I was able to contact the undertaker, who told me that Mae had been cremated and that a friend had paid the expenses.

About then, I was heartened to find that several people who had known Mae fairly well were in town again. At last the story of the final few months of Mae's life began to unfold; it was not a happy one.

First I learned that the 'friend' who'd paid the undertaker was Mae's landlord. She'd left him all her money and possessions on condition that he arranged and paid for her funeral. She had been cremated as a Catholic.

'But she wasn't a Catholic,' I said.

'No, but her landlord was,' my informant answered drily. 'I don't suppose there was much in it for him, though – not after that other bastard had been at her.'

I got to hear more about this 'other bastard' from various sources. The most complete account was given by an elderly lady who had known Mae for almost as long as I had. Three months before her death, Mae had fallen in love with what was destined to be her last Maltese ponce, and he was the worst of the lot. Lal was in his thirties, had done time for manslaughter and had been out of prison for about two years when Mae met him. He had casually added her to his string of three other girls. She was not the big earner she had once been, mainly because she hadn't the heart to increase the fees of her old regulars. She did not know she was the least of Lal's considerations, and she doted on him.

'Before he came along,' the old lady told me, 'I'd made her open a bank account and she'd managed to salt away over seven thousand pounds. She wasn't getting any younger, whatever good looks she had. God knows if there's any of that money left. I heard Lal was making her sign cheques all the time she was under sedation in hospital, after her overdose . . . You heard about her overdose, didn't you?'

'No, I didn't,' I answered.

'She found out he was running these other girls and there was a mother of a row. When she calmed down, she said she was going to have a sleep. Well, she just went up to her bedroom and swallowed about sixty Tuinal tablets.

'Her maid felt there was something strange about the way she was sleeping. She found the empty pill bottle and phoned for an ambulance. Thank God she did, because they had to perform an emergency tracheotomy on the way to the hospital, when she stopped breathing.

'I didn't visit her after that. But Lal made her start work again the very day she came out of hospital. I couldn't bear to see what was happening to her. She looked awful.

'He never stayed more than five minutes with her, and that was only when he called for the takings. She even got over him having other girls and just accepted them; she was daft about him. When she asked him why he didn't seem to fancy her any more, he said he couldn't – because of the tracheotomy hole in her neck. She went berserk, and threw him out like she should have done when she first met him.'

The woman told me that only hours before she died, Mae's private little flat in Kentish Town had been ransacked. I also heard that sometime during the night of her death, screams and thumping were heard coming from the Rupert Street flat – the police were not told of this – and three days after her death, Lal was trying to sell pieces of her jewellery in the Venus Rooms.

Then, after a great deal of effort, I managed to track down Mae's last maid, Stella. I had liked Stella on sight. She was an affable person, but was now haunted by the horror of Mae's death and the subsequent ordeal of having to identify the body. She was still having nightmares. It was some comfort to know that at least Mae had had a pleasant and sympathetic maid at the end. Stella and I sat for several hours in The White Horse in Rupert Street, reminiscing about her.

Stella told me that the flat had continued to abound in trussed-up males, and transvestites had been on a fast increase.

'She liked bending straight men, you know,' she said. 'It was her hobby. We'd get a perfectly normal bloke, and before you knew it, she'd have talked him into a bra and briefs and he'd be hooked.'

Fred and many of the old clients had still visited, and most amazing of all, so had the chastity slave, Daisy, who must have been well into his seventies. A couple of weeks before Mae died, Stella had heard Daisy mutter from his agony-racked corner, 'But I don't know what I'm supposed to be. I still don't know what I'm supposed to be!'

For the last few months, Mae had apparently been giving herself daily hormone injections. Stella couldn't bear to jab the needle in, so Mae did it herself, but Stella had to press the plunger because, with the needle in her bottom, Mae couldn't reach it.

'She really couldn't bear the thought of getting old, could she?' Stella said. 'I often think that perhaps I should just have let her go on sleeping when she took that overdose.'

Mae had continued to gamble, right up to the time she fell in love with Lal. One evening, she had been told that the management of her favourite casino had decided that in view of her profession, her patronage was no longer welcome. With her chin thrust proudly in the air in a queenly manner, she had sailed across the road and into the gambling club opposite.

'But she was never the same after that. Developed almost a sort of agoraphobia and didn't seem to want to go out in the evenings – just wanted to watch television. I think that's why Lal meant so much to her. But you know, there's something that keeps puzzling me. That night of the fire, I was the first into the place. I rushed in and up the stairs as soon as I saw the flames, but the heat was so strong I had to come down. The funny thing is, afterwards I realised the street door had been open, and I can't think why. It hadn't been forced, either. Another thing: there's a big gap under the door to the flat, and when I put the key under that night, I heard her come to the door and saw her hand reach down and pick it up. So why couldn't she get out?'

Still looking for answers, I paid a visit to a psychic medium. After switching on my tape-recorder, I gave her an envelope to hold containing an old photograph of Mae. Guardedly, she told me that Mae had been inordinately fond of men and had had many boyfriends. She told me many other things about Mae that were perfectly correct and then began to speak about the accident that had killed her. Suddenly she stopped short, an expression of horror coming to her face, and said:

'Oh, I have such a horrible feeling. This was no accident. This was murder. Oh, I'm sure of it; I'm sure of it; I'm sure of it.'

This was followed by a long pause, after which she said quietly – almost to herself:

'Whatever she was, she didn't deserve that.' Then – although the word 'fire' had not been previously mentioned – she said, 'And the fire was started to hide the evidence.'

She said that Mae had died in terrible fear and that she couldn't get any direct message from her yet, but if I could bring something really personal of hers, she would try again. I said I would try, but that all that was left of Mae was the small amount of distorted and blackened jewellery she was wearing when she died and which the police were still holding.

In February 1978, I heard that the landlord's insurance company had decided that the fire was not an accident. The police had since reopened their investigations.

Sitting here now, writing and thinking, I find myself wondering if, by keeping closer in touch, I could have done anything to avert the final dark tragedy of Mae's life. I sometimes doubt anyone could have done, for she was ever wayward and invariably followed her own inclinations. And now, in fairness to her, I cannot even pray that she rest in peace, for knowing Mae, peace is something she would not want.

The last memory I have of her was about a week after finding her again. She telephoned to ask if I fancied a night out, and I accepted her invitation.

She took me to the casino where, at that time, she was a well-known and frequent visitor. Having no particular faith in my luck, I didn't play but contented myself with sitting and watching Mae as she conscientiously and systematically got through all her money. That was diversion enough, for she was looking particularly spectacular, even for her. She was wearing a floor-length dress: a drifting, pre-Raphaelite affair that seemed to be made of dozens of navy-blue chiffon handkerchiefs edged with white lace. Her blonde hair, tinged with amber by the dim peach lighting, was drawn back from her face and piled high, accentuating the length and slenderness of her neck and revealing perfectly that arrogant and lovely profile, utterly unimpaired by the passage of the years. She was – and to me will always remain – a miracle.

End Note

This manuscript was written some thirty years after the events described. It was initially dictated by Barbara and written out longhand by her beloved husband, who fell about laughing at many of the incidents described in these pages. Barbara edited the document herself, had it typed up and was then puzzled as to what to do next.

On her husband's advice, she bought the *Writers' And Artists' Yearbook*, stuck a pin into its pages, and came up with the name of a literary agency. She sent the manuscript in, in a fever to see what they would say. As fate would have it, a relative of Barbara's, unbeknownst to her, was working there. After strong words on both sides Barbara hurled the manuscript into a bottom drawer, where it might very well have remained to this day.

A few years ago, however, Barbara needed to consult a neuropsychologist (who told her that her memory was in excellent working order). They happened to get talking about Barbara's memories of Soho in the years immediately after the war. Barbara mentioned that she had written an account of her experiences, and the psychologist said that he would very much like to read it. One thing led to another, and before too long, Barbara had been prevailed upon to make a second attempt to get her memoir into print. This book is the happy result. The preceding material has been edited down from Barbara's original document, which was significantly longer. There have been a few adjustments made to ensure a smooth flow and cover joins, but any editorial interventions have been modest in the extreme.

As a schoolchild, Barbara once hesitated between becoming a painter and becoming a writer. At the age of eighty-three, she discovered she was both.

Tragically, however, Barbara lived to see the book deal, but not the book. Not long after securing a publication contract, she passed away early one morning. She had suffered poor health for some time, but had remained engaged, alert and passionate to the end. She was a remarkable woman.

Barbara repeatedly expressed to me her gratitude to everyone involved. As her friend and collaborator, I know she would have liked to acknowledge and thank the people who were touched enough by her story to make this book possible, in particular:

James Tate, her husband, psychological prop, chief whip, and typist during the writing of the original manuscript; Richard Gallagher, for his sympathetic editing of the manuscript, and his entertaining readings; Harry Bingham, from the Writers' Workshop, for his excitement and passion about the manuscript, and for finding a publisher in record time; Genevieve Pegg, from Orion, for her willingness to invest in Barbara's story, and for her sensitive treatment of the material; finally, John Prentice, who started the ball rolling again, giving Barbara new hope and a renewed enthusiasm for life.

A last word about Mae's death. We did what we could to unearth any new facts about her end, including trawling through the British Library's newspaper archive at Colindale and the microfilm collection at the Westminster Archives. The material we uncovered broadly confirmed Barbara's story as it appears here, but it seems that police activity came to an end with the inquest. If anyone can tell us more, we'd love to know.

Hannes Buhrmann, March 2010